"*Live, Love, and Let Go* beautif[...] [...]e
from a Christian perspective. D[...] [...] reflections from his tradi-
tion that could help those who serve the seriously ill."
—*Christina M. Puchalski, MD, FACP*
Director, George Washington Institute for Spirituality and Health
Professor, Dept of Medicine and Health Sciences, George Washington University
School of Medicine; Professor, Health Leadership and Management

"Dr. Abshire's approach to the inevitability of death and dying in his book, *Live, Love and Let Go*, is masterfully done. As a Messianic Jewish rabbi, I have become very familiar with the subject of living and dying, and therefore most heartily recommend Dr. Abshire's sensitive, insightful and practical approach conveyed by his own medical and spiritual experience. This book will help many." —*Rabbi Martin Waldman, Baruch HaShem Messianic Synagogue, Dallas, TX*

"If I had had this book 20 years ago, I wouldn't have been depressed all those years." —*Nancy S. Weber, R.N. Healthcare Consultant, former CEO of Hospice of Howard County, Maryland*

"Most people do not want to talk about illness, especially terminal illness. James Abshire does just that. If you are a Christian and you are going through the struggles of a terminal illness, James Abshire's book, *Live, Love, and Let Go,* is a wonderful guide for Christian patients and their families. It marries the Christian faith and medicine by dealing with the tough and difficult issues that are faced during illness. Abshire uses scripture and medical science to explain both the disease process and spiritual growth process that are instrumental in getting through these very pivotal times." —*Stacey R. Merlin, MS, MA*

"It has eased my anxieties, and I'm still thinking about it a year later. It puts death into perspective." —*Dr. Kathleen Quadro, MD, Family Practice Physician, Sacramento*

"This book will help calm your mind and give you a better grip on life."
—*Spencer Levin, PGA Tour pro golfer*

"Dr. Abshire's insights are very well expressed and personal, which makes for an easy read. As I read each chapter, I could see comfort and help for those whose medical condition leads to thoughts of life and death."
—*Fr. Dino Pappademos, Saint Katherine Greek Orthodox Church, Elk Grove, CA*

"Somewhere, about halfway into the book, it was like an epiphany."
—*Judith Agar, Sacramento*

"In this book, James Abshire shares uniquely with the reader a beautiful marriage between science and faith through his own experiences as a medical doctor and man of faith. Through the lens of optimism, medical expertise, and trust in God, James addresses realities in life and death in a way that is vulnerable, sincere, and encouraging."
—*Andi Linley, Young Life, Area Director*

"Dr. Abshire has done an amazing and wonderful job in tackling a very difficult subject; moreover, by marrying Christianity and his medical expertise, he has successfully managed to provide the reader with a clear perspective on coping with death through the various stages from tragedy or diagnosis, dying and ultimately death. As a Christian woman who witnessed and experienced the tragic murder of my husband, what I appreciated most about this book is Dr. Abshire's strong faith in Jesus Christ, how transparent he is about his own health issues, and his fresh approach to coping with death. I have learned a lot from reading this book and have a different outlook on my own mortality. I have been truly blessed."
—*Karen R. Johnson, author of* Covered & Kept, The Tearing Between Worlds

"*Live, Love and Let Go* is an important book for easing people's fear of the dying process. Dr. Abshire combines good medical expertise with insights from a deep, evangelical Christian faith as he offers both practical assistance and inspiration to people facing terminal illness, as well as to their loved ones. Many will find the book helpful and comforting, if not also transforming." —*William K. Weigand, Catholic Bishop Emeritus, Sacramento*

"In *Live, Love, and Let Go,* James Abshire provides wise and practical guidance for finding our way through a bewildering time of life for which most of us are not prepared. Abshire is uniquely qualified to do so, drawing on the deep knowledge of the physician as well as the life experience of one who has survived cancer and has himself been a bereaved family member. Therefore his handbook can relieve some of the anxiety and instill hope and confidence for individuals and families facing the final phase of life. Having served as a hospice chaplain, I am impressed by his broad knowledge of the subject, yet how clearly and simply he provides an understanding of the process and the resources. More than just handing us medical information and good philosophy, the book causes us to reflect on our attitudes and gives plenty of examples from life. In short, it prepares us. The good doctor has written us a most useful prescription!" —*Rev. George Matranga, B.C.C. Hospice Chaplain*

"The most powerful reconciliatory and therapeutic prescription for end of life issues lies embedded in the 'shalom' of God. Corresponding transformative truth enables us to live with joy and embrace the end of life with peace. Accordingly in this book, James provides the necessary optics that empower us to live, love, and let go." —*Rev. Samuel Rodriguez, President, NHCLC, Hispanic Evangelical Association*

"This book, which is both deeply spiritual and intensely practical, will be enormously helpful to many who are walking through death's dark valley, and James Abshire's insights are all the more cogent because he too is walking in those shoes. Throughout, he seeks common ground with Jesus, whom he clearly loves, with the result that his writing exudes faith, hope and love, refocuses priorities, and brings an eternal perspective that has the power to transform." —*Dr. Jeff Stephenson, Consultant in Palliative Medicine and Medical Director, St Luke's Hospice, Plymouth, UK*

"James Abshire boldly addresses essential areas of concern for those facing their own imminent death or the death of a loved one. Not only does he bring a unique voice as a medical professional who has helped numerous patients with these concerns, but more importantly he has faced his own death and walked through these concerns for himself."
—*Kristina Kays, Psy.D., Associate Professor Department of Psychology, Faculty Development Committee Chair, George Fox University*

"People of faith who are confronting life-threatening illness often seek advice. Advice from a thoughtful person is good. Advice from a thoughtful physician is better. Advice from a thoughtful Christian physician is better yet. Advice from a thoughtful Christian physician who has himself confronted the questions, the issues, and the practical realities is top shelf. Dr. Abshire's book is on the topmost top shelf."
—*Robert D. Orr, MD, CM, is co-chair of the Healthcare Ethics Council and a Senior Fellow with the Center for Bioethics & Human Dignity, Professor of Bioethics at the Graduate College of Union University, Professor of Medical Ethics at Loma Linda University, Professor of Bioethics at Trinity International University, and Professor of Family Medicine at the University of Vermont College of Medicine. In addition, Dr. Orr chairs CBHD's Advisory Board*

"*Live, Love, and Let Go* is a winning game plan for the late innings of life. It hits a home run." —*Greg Vaughn, four time MLB All Star*

"Internist James Abshire has encapsulated almost 30 years of medical experience and his own encounter with cancer into a remarkable and readable exposition on life's final journey. This is not a depressing read! Dr. Abshire peppers his narrative with humor, personal anecdotes, case studies from his medical practice, and practical biblical analysis. Never overly technical, he nonetheless provides practical counsel for anyone who has ever been a patient, anyone who has ever faced loss, anyone who cares for a disabled or dying loved one, or anyone who has or will face death. In other words, he has written this book for all of us."
—*Dennis Sullivan, MD, MA (Ethics)*
Director, Center for Bioethics, Cedarville University

"Few people have James Abshire's expertise as a doctor, patient, and wise Christian. This book is an excellent resource for anyone confronted with a terminal diagnosis or anyone who cares about such a person."
—*Rob Moll,* Christianity Today *editor at large and author of* The Art of Dying

Live, Love, and Let Go:

A Doctor's Insightful Approach to Living and Dying

Live, Love, and Let Go:
A Doctor's Insightful Approach to Living and Dying

James K. Abshire, MD

Evergreen
PRESS

Mobile, Alabama

ISBN   HC 978-1-58169-525-0
ISBN   PB 978-1-58169-526-7
ISBN   E-book 978-1-58169-527-4

For Worldwide Distribution
Printed in the U.S.A.

Evergreen Press
P.O. Box 191540 • Mobile, AL 36619
800-367-8203

Contents

Foreword

On a recent evening I had just finished up participating on a medical panel discussing end-of-life care based on a movie that followed a well known community physician from his diagnosis with cancer to his death. It had been a moving film and the discussion afterwards amongst the panel and with the audience pointed out the many difficulties encountered when a person is facing a terminal illness. As I tried to make my way off the stage I was approached by a vaguely familiar woman* of about my own age. After she introduced herself, I realized that we had trained together during medical residency. Remembering she had left our internal medical program to pursue a career in pathology, I asked about her job and professional life. I could see that she was troubled in some way. She related that she had recently found out that she had breast cancer. She told me that she had signed off on countless pathology reports which diagnosed this deadly illness, but this time her name was at the top of the report, rather than at the bottom. "Each time I signed off on a malignant pathology report I thought 'someday this will be me.'" I could see the fear and struggle that she was experiencing, and it caused me to reflect that as medical professionals we are called upon to make life-altering, life-threatening diagnoses every day, but are we equipped to handle it when our name is at the top of the page instead of at the bottom?

As a medical oncologist I am called upon to give bad news on a weekly, if not a daily basis. "You have cancer" (arguably the three most frightening words in the English lexicon); "Your cancer has progressed"; "The treatment is no longer working"; "You have a terminal illness." As a student of how best to deliver such words and provide comfort and support in the face of such news, I have seen many different responses: fear, panic, denial, anger, hopelessness, defeat. All are natural responses when our human life is threatened. I have seen great courage and the ability to draw on all sorts of supports to face such situations but undoubtedly the most powerful of these is faith: faith that a higher power will support one through the experience of facing cancer and/or chemotherapy, or disease progression or death; faith that will sustain you when you find your name at the top of the pathology report rather than the bottom.

James Abshire is a physician who went in for a routine colonoscopy and found his name at the top of the page. Unexpectedly, the pathology report bearing his name was clear: non-Hodgkin's lymphoma. I first met James when, fresh out of medical residency, he joined our multi-specialty medical group. For several years our offices stood side-by-side in the same hallway. I quickly learned never to call him "Jim" (it's James) and began to admire his quick efficiency, his passion for excellence, and his huge commitment to giving his patients the best care possible. Like me, he has a low tolerance for nonsense or inefficiency in the workplace and has a dry wit which he often uses to combat such nonsense. As I met with James to discuss his disease, its prognosis, and treatment options, I was not surprised that he handled it with his wry sense of humor—that is who James is. However, I was even more struck with the great peace he had in facing an illness for which there is no cure and for which the outcome is very unpredictable. Some patients with this disease do well for years on end. Others have highly aggressive lymphomas and are dead in a year or two. As a man of faith myself, I knew that James was a Christian, but what I saw that day was an intensely practical, powerful sense that God was in control, that his life in Jesus Christ was secure regardless of whether his treatment went well or not. Knowing Jesus allowed Dr. Abshire to face with confidence having his name at the "top of the page."

James has taken this life event, along with the experience that comes from decades of practicing medicine, and has written a wonderful account of how a Christian physician can personalize his faith in real and tangible ways, even in the face of a life-threatening situation. He cuts through the distractions and uncertainties of life and points us to the only important thing, the only eternal thing: finding a relationship with Jesus Christ. That decision has transformed Dr. James Abshire, and I believe it will transform anyone who reads his book.

Robert E. Quadro, MD
Clinical Professor of Medicine, UC Davis School of Medicine
Medical Director, Mercy Hospice
Medical Director of Quality Management, Mercy Medical Group
Chief Division of Medical Oncology, Mercy Medical Group

The details of this story have been altered to protect the privacy of this individual

Acknowledgments

I'd like to thank all those who made this book possible. Thanks to all the proofreaders and contributors including Cindy and Dennis, Stephen and Isabelle, Suzi, Judy, Wendy, Dr. Kathleen Quadro, Bonnie, Sister Marilee Howard, Pastor Ron Mitchell, and Rev. George Matranga. Thank you to Dr. Earl Gear for searching everywhere to find my cancer, and Dr. Bob Quadro and all the medical staff for treating me so well. Thanks to my in-laws, Bert and Gloria, for putting up with me all these years and for forgiving me for the Spanish Inquisition (even though I didn't do it, Bert).

I'd also like to thank all my colleagues and coworkers who assist me with helping patients every day and making my life a little easier. Thank you to all my patients over the years who have taught me so much and inspired this book-it's for you.

Special thanks to my agent, Keith Carroll, whose guidance was invaluable, and to Brian, Jeff, and Kathy Banashak and all the rest of the great people at Evergreen Press that did such a wonderful job.

Thanks to my entire family who made me the person that I am today, and especially for the support of my loving wife, Caryl, and my kids Travis (for technical assistance), Lauren the proofer, Austin the keyboarder, and Chris, his wife, Christina, and their daughter Kayla.

Most of all, thank You to God, the Father, Son, and Holy Spirit for making the concepts and ideas in this book a reality.

Introduction

Martha answered, "I know he will rise again in the resurrection at the last day."

*Jesus said to her, "I am the resurrection and the life. He who believes in me will live, even though he dies; and whoever lives and believes in me will never die." —*John 11: 24–25

"Of all the various religious and non-religious groups of people, Christians are the worst at dealing with death. I would have expected them to be the best at handling death." This came from a conversation I had with a physician colleague of mine, based on years of experience working in the medical field. My friend agreed with this assessment.

Christians seem to be more shocked, overwhelmed, and depressed, and they grieve more than other groups. Christians seem to have a greater tendency to "fall apart" upon hearing of the death of a friend or loved one. Christianity offers the promise of being saved for all eternity, and yet it seems like we are the worst at coping with death. We should shine as being clearly the best.

I asked myself, *Why should this be the case? Do Christians view death as the "last enemy to be destroyed"* (1 Co. 15:26), *rather than as a phase of life to be lived? Do Christians have a lack of knowledge about their faith? Do Christians have more doubts about their faith than followers of other religions? Do Christians develop personal relationships that make it harder for them to lose someone?* These are all likely parts of the whole answer, but I suspect the key answer is **great expectations.**

We learn that with Jesus, all things are possible. We've seen prayers answered and have come to hope and expect prayers to be fulfilled. We believe our bodies will be healed one more time. When death inevitably arrives, we are especially devastated and bewildered. "Given the wonderfulness of our God, how could this have happened?" we ask. At this point, we may lose the focus and perspective of our faith.

I'd like to see Christians excel at being the best at coping with death. People should be saying, "Those Christians have something special," not "They are the worst at dealing with death." This book is meant to open up a conversation on death and dying. I want to develop some thoughts and attitudes for the reader that will provide comfort in this troubling time of life.

People look upon the topic of death with avoidance, as an unpleasant subject not to be mentioned. As a result, what do they do? They either ignore it or change the subject if it comes up in conversation. The discussion of mortality often leads to embarrassment or awkwardness. We are not used to talking about it. Therefore, we avoid talking about mortality because we do not know what to say. However, I would argue that some consideration of your own mortality is not only practical, but also important for your mental and spiritual health, benefitting both yourself and your loved ones.

As a physician, I have seen so many patients come through my office over the years, all struggling with mortality issues. Over those same years, I have been saddened that I haven't been able to provide those patients with as much assistance as I would have liked due to the lack of time, tools, and training needed. I suspect this is true not just for myself but for the medical community as a whole. Many of these issues just can't be adequately addressed in one doctor's visit.

I started working on this book five years ago in an attempt to provide people with the tools, comfort, and confidence needed to manage this most difficult phase of life. It relies on a positive thought process that uses both medical and practical knowledge set upon a strong Christian foundation (which I pray works for all denominations).

I am a board-certified internist with over twenty years of experience in a busy medical practice, having recently passed my recertification exam. I have buried both of my parents due to cancer. They were both hospice patients. I was also executor of my father's will—which was a poorly done, clumsy affair, to say the least.

My experience as a patient has involved being in a propane fire, which not only took the skin off my face, arms, and legs, but required bone graft surgery and fusion of my neck. I have known pain and suffering up close and personal.

The topper came halfway through the writing of this book, when I was given my own terminal cancer diagnosis: non-Hodgkin's lymphoma, which is a non-curable, but slow-growing cancer. Now I do have firsthand experience of being put through multiple tests, scans, and biopsies, as well as being hooked up to an IV for chemotherapy. Despite my diagnosis, I believe that I am one of the most happy and confident cancer patients around. In fact, I honestly believe that I am the *luckiest* person on earth: certainly there are none luckier. This is because of my positive **attitude**, my **focus** on the Lord, and my **perspective** on life.

This book details the spiritual as well as the physical and practical aspects of our mortality. I encourage a positive and proactive attitude toward the issue of death. It's an approach that too few of us take. Considering death in such a way that will lead us to a happier and fuller life. Let's take a look and see.

1

Getting the News

Anyone with only a week to live will not find it in his (best) interest to believe that all this is just a matter of chance. Now, if we were not bound by our passions, a week and a hundred years would come to the same thing.[1] —Pascal

"It looks like you have non-Hodgkin's lymphoma, but we need to do more testing to be absolutely sure." The news hit me like a slap across the face. I was thunderstruck. Woke me up, it did.

I had just received the biopsy results from my screening colonoscopy. I did say *screening* colonoscopy. Screening, meaning I was normal, healthy, and just getting tested to be sure. Going into it, I was thinking that the worst thing that could happen would be for the doctors to find and remove some precancerous colon polyps. The news that they thought I actually had cancer was a shock. Colon cancer would probably have been a better finding than non-Hodgkin's.

Quickly I tried to search my memory. I needed to retrieve the statistics of what I could remember on non-Hodgkin's lymphoma. Let's see, it seemed like the five-year survival rates weren't too bad, probably at least 50/50 anyhow, depending on the stage and aggressiveness. Wait a minute, I was only fifty-one; why was I trying to remember five-year survival rates? I was only fifty-one; I needed to remember *cure* rates. What were the cure rates, anyhow? Why couldn't I remember them? Was I choking under pressure?

I decided to get back to my research and check out *UpToDate*, the computer program, to find out the latest medical information on this subject. There it was, the reason I couldn't remember cure rate statistics—non-Hodgkin's lymphoma is generally considered incurable, depending on the type!

Yes, shock indeed. I felt healthy at age fifty-one and was now being told that I probably had an incurable cancer.

Denial is one of the first phases of the grief process. My denial phase was brief. I think that was due to my medical background. I briefly thought that maybe they had switched specimens and that the diagnosis really belonged to another patient.

No, I was sure it was the correct specimen. It was my biopsy. You see, I know people who work at the endoscopy center. The hospital with the pathology lab was the hospital with which I was associated. I knew the people there. It was one of the top one hundred hospitals in the country. These were all excellent, high-quality people who wouldn't have made a simple mistake like mislabeling a specimen. In addition, I saw the polyp that was taken out. I can recognize a normal, benign-appearing polyp from an abnormal one. Mine was not a typical polyp. When Dr. Earl Gear was done with the colonoscopy, he stepped out and told my wife, Caryl, that it was a good thing he got it out, as it was definitely a bad one—one that would become cancerous. The visual appearance of the specimen, in combination with the specificity of the pathology report showing atypical B-cells, was enough to clear my denial.

Suddenly, I had gone from being a physician and author of a book on death and dying, to being a patient and a subject of the book. What a switch!

I'd have to say that the next emotions and thoughts to hit me were those of fear and sadness. The sadness was caused by the thought of leaving my wife, Caryl, and my family. I had just had my first grandchild, Kayla. I had just seen my son, Austin, graduate from high school. Non-Hodgkin's meant that my odds of seeing Kayla graduate were not good. Yes, I would miss out on plenty.

Because of my past experience and medical knowledge, my fear was different from that of many other patients. Fearing symptoms of pain and suffering would be a common emotion. However, I experienced significant pain when I had been burned in a propane fire. I do have medical knowledge of how symptoms can be handled. People generally fear the unknown. That was not my case.

What I did fear was telling Caryl my diagnosis. I knew she would worry and that it would upset her. Also, I knew she'd kill me if I died early on her.

So there I was with all of these thoughts running through my head. My, how we get caught up in the secular world and forget God! Turning to God was, of course, the answer to my problem. I remembered what Job did when he received bad news. Job was a rich man with many servants, belongings, and ten children. When he got the bad news that he had lost everything, including his children, he fell to the ground in worship and said:

> *Naked I came from my mother's womb, and naked I will depart. The Lord gave and the Lord has taken away; may the name of the Lord be praised.* —Job 1:20

Like Job, I needed to turn to God with my bad news.

Now, doctors can learn a lot from their patients. I try to make a point of learning at least one thing every day. (For instance, today I learned that making this point can sound a bit pretentious to some people.) Anyhow, I have a patient named Rick who is a man of great faith. Rick has end-stage renal disease—his kidneys are failing him. Rick came in one day needing to make a decision on his options in the near future. He has been contemplating getting a kidney transplant, versus going on hemodialysis. His third option is doing neither, in which case he knows he would most likely die in the next six to twelve months. He does not like the thought of surgery, the side effects of transplant medications, or the potential complications from dialysis. Because of his faith, he knows that (with all three scenarios) in the ultimate analysis, he'll eventually go to be with the Lord. He just needs to choose what path is most right for him. As long as we've decided to follow our Judeo-Christian faith, we cannot make bad choices.

I was also reminded of an old story that demonstrates attitude is everything:

Two young boys shared a birthday party. One boy got a shiny new bicycle and was mad that it was the wrong color and wasn't quite the right style. The other boy was given a huge pile of manure. He immediately cried out with joy and started digging in the pile. When asked why he was so happy to get a huge pile of manure, he responded that it was so big that there must be a pony in there somewhere.

Keeping Job and Rick's faith in mind and keeping a positive attitude, I proceeded to tell Caryl about my probable non-Hodgkin's lymphoma. It was even harder to go to her one to two weeks later when the diagnosis was confirmed. Yes, the biopsy showed a type of follicular B-cell non-Hodgkin's lymphoma, which is incurable with today's technology.

A typical response to bad news is sadness and anger at God and the world. People will often wail, gnash their teeth, and ask, "Why is this happening to me?" Caryl was naturally sad when the diagnosis of terminal non-Hodgkin's lymphoma was confirmed, but I would have been worried for our marriage if she hadn't been upset. Fortunately, Caryl's faith precluded the anger response. Instead, she said, "Maybe God gave you this opportunity for a better perspective on the book you are writing."

Yes, I think God did give me a pony. As long as I keep my faith and don't forget Him, I know everything will be all right. The key will be to *focus* on God, maintain a *positive* attitude, and consider a *perspective* that shines a positive light on the situation.

2

Hope: Jesus Is the Model

For as long as you are not perfectly united to Him, put all your hope in Him.[1] —*Saint Augustine*

One great thing about being a Christian is that there is always hope. When Jesus is involved, there is always a chance for a miraculous cure, always a reason for hope. If we can pray for ourselves, then there is hope. If others can pray for us, then there is even more hope.

Hope is good. Hope helps us ward off despair. Despair leads to a defeatist attitude and depression. Symptoms such as pain and fatigue are worsened by depression. When depression occurs, it is harder to live out the Christian attributes that we want to display, such as not losing faith, being slow to anger, showing patience, and performing acts of kindness.

So hope is paramount in maintaining a positive attitude. Christians should be the masters of maintaining a positive attitude. When others see us having a positive attitude in the face of extreme adversity, they will wonder what keeps us so positive. A positive attitude is needed to grow Christianity. Hope is key to that process.

There are plenty of reasons to remain hopeful. Take hospice patients, for example. For patients to be placed in hospice care, we (as medical personnel) have to predict that the patient has six months or less to live. I have personally seen several patients dismissed from hospice because they were doing so well. I love it when patients prove us wrong in this way.

I have also seen many non-hospice patients live far longer than would normally be expected. In just the year of writing this chapter, I have seen several elderly patients of mine die. Many of these had been longtime patients with medical problems such as diabetes, COPD, congestive heart failure, and coronary disease. Based on their medical history, they lived about five years longer than what had been expected. In other words, people can often live years longer than expected. This can be due in part to modern medicine, but it can also be due to the support of family, friends, and hope for survival.

One aspect of hope is that you have to have something to place your hope in. I have seen several patients decline medical care, stating that they trust and hope in God to fix things for them. However, to not take any personal positive action is really testing the Lord, rather than having hope that He will make something work for us. Being a medical doctor, my bias is in favor of modern medicine and technology. God gave us the ability to think and to reason, which has led to great advances in science over the centuries. These advances in tools and science have created longer average life spans. In this way, God has given us hope for a longer life. **Modern medicine was developed by man but arose out of a gift from God.** (You can quote me on that if you want.)

Yes, there is reason to have hope. Modern miracles do happen. Probably every one of us has either personally known, or heard of, someone who has survived against all odds. Stop a minute and think of that person. Moreover, think of Jesus and keep the hope alive—it's that important.

To take hope one big step further: you see, in preparing this book I could not think of one instance when Jesus Himself talked of hope. Yes, it's true. In fact, *the word* hope *is not even mentioned in the four gospels—*the books telling us about the life of Jesus and His teachings. *The word* hope *is mentioned many times in the Bible, but not once in the gospels.* I believe this is because Jesus did not deal in hope; He dealt in certainties.

Look at some modern analogies. First, suppose you went back to grade school and the teacher asked you what 2 + 2 was. You would, of course, answer: 4. But you would answer 4, not *hoping* you got the answer right, but *proclaiming* the answer was 4, because you *knew* it was right.

Let's take another example. In the world of modern technology, we are able to record TV shows and watch them later. Now suppose you record your favorite sports team in the morning and plan to watch the game later that evening. But before you turn the game on, you have already heard the final score. So while you were watching the game, you would not be hoping your team wins. Instead, you would already know the final score and just be watching to see the details of the game. In other words, you do not even think about hope when you are already sure of the answer to the problem, or when you already know the final outcome.

In the same way, I believe Jesus did not talk about hope since He already knows the final score. Jesus spoke in definitive statements, being certain of His knowledge and His power over death. For instance, Jesus gives us the well-known declaration of John 3:16:

For God so loved the world that he gave his one and only Son, that whoever believes in him shall not perish, but have eternal life.

Notice that Jesus is definitive when He says *"shall not perish."* He does not say *"maybe will not perish,"* or *"can hope they will not perish,"* but instead He says, *"shall not perish,"* with the certainty of His knowledge.

We should use Jesus as our model because of our faith in Him. We would be foolish not to emulate Jesus. From this perspective, in the face of illness, we can hope and pray for healing, but we can be also certain of our eternal life. In this we can be confident.

Dream No More

I think a common daydream that we Christians have is to wish we were living back around the year 30 AD[*] and be able to see Jesus' miracles in person. Wouldn't it have been great to see Jesus continuously feeding the crowd fish and bread when He started out with none Himself?

Well, dream no more. We are actually seeing that same miraculous story lived out in our everyday lives. After all, Jesus gives us hope. The Man who has no hope Himself (because He has no need for hope) is unceasingly able to generate all the hope in the world. The story of the hope that we have today is really the same story as the story of the loaves and fishes, only on a much grander scale. Yes, Jesus creates hope when there was none before. In the same way, God created everything when there was nothing there to start with (i.e., God said, "Let there be light," and there was light [Genesis 1:3]). What amazingly beautiful analogies that God and Jesus have given us.

So, if you are still looking for a miracle in your life, all you need to do is realize that the hope that Jesus has fed you from His own empty baskets *is* that miracle. Open your mind to that thought, and you will see it.

Finally, it should be noted that if Jesus had been a false prophet rather than the true Messiah, He would have talked about hope a lot. Only one with the certainty of God would be able to live their entire life preaching to the masses *and* giving the masses hope, without ever even mentioning the word *hope*. Think about that!

---

*Author's Note: I still use the traditional AD nomenclature rather than CE (Common Era) that the secularists teach in the schools today. After all, AD stands for the Latin phrase Anno Domini, which means "the year of our Lord." It serves to remind us to stay focused on God. Focusing on God is a higher level of thought, whereas "common era" is a "common" thought. Common thought keeps us in the doldrums.

3

Conquering Fear

Don't spend your energies on things that generate worry, anxiety, and anguish. Only one thing is necessary: Lift up your spirit, and love God. —Saint Padre Pio

Fear. We fear many things where the topic of death is concerned. We fear pain. We fear suffering. We fear separation from our loved ones. We fear the moment of death. We fear the unknown. We fear loss of control. My intention is that this chapter, and really this whole book, will help allay these fears. Let's look at each of these fears in turn.

First, we should not be ashamed to admit we have a fear of dying. It is pretty much a universal emotion. It helps to know that other people feel the same way. A biblical example is that of the prophet Elijah. (At this point, it may be helpful for you to stop and review 1 Kings 16:29 through 1 Kings 19:17 before reading further.) God gave Elijah the ability to perform miracles. Some of Elijah's miracles included:

1. He predicted drought (1 Kings 17:1–7).
2. He created an unending jar of flour and oil (1 Kings 17:8–16).
3. He brought a widow's dead son back to life (1 Kings 17:17–24).
4. He called down fire from heaven and defeated the prophets of Baal (1 Kings 18:1–40).
5. He predicted a rainstorm when there had been drought (1 Kings 18:41–45).
6. He outran a chariot (1 Kings 18:46).

But even after performing all these miracles, Elijah ran for his life, hiding in fear when Jezebel threatened to kill him. It's puzzling that someone who had performed such incredible miracles would suddenly be in hiding for his life. Possibilities for his actions include:

1. He had forgotten God—at least temporarily.
2. He had lost faith in God.
3. He was no longer directing the situation, but reacting to it—in other words, he had lost control and become fearful.
4. He didn't know what was going to happen next (fear of the unknown).
5. He was fearful of potential physical pain.

It should be noted that Elijah's fear paralyzed him with the inability to save himself in any other way beside hiding. It was not until the Lord stepped in and told Elijah what to do, that Elijah's fear was abated.

We need to use this information from the story of Elijah, along with our current knowledge, to formulate a stepwise attack plan to ease our fear of death.

Step 1: Recognize that the moment of death is pain-free and symptom-free. When we die, our heart stops, and blood flow to the brain ceases. We pass out as if we have fainted, gone to sleep, or been put under general anesthesia. We have all gone to sleep before. Many of us have also either fainted and/or been put under general anesthesia, so we should realize that there is nothing to fear in that actual moment. This means that our fear should reside in either the period before death or concern about what will happen in the period after death.

Step 2: Recognize that there are multiple ways to treat and alleviate any physical symptoms that occur prior to death. In this way, we have a great advantage over our ancestors. Prior to just this past century, our ancestors did not have much more than a bottle of whiskey or perhaps some opium to help with symptoms. Also, if we think about it, we have experienced many if not all of these symptoms and have already dealt with them at some point in our lives.

For instance, we have all had an upset stomach before, along with all that it entails. We have all had severe pain from an injury, surgery, or maybe an infection that might be as bad or even worse than what we may experience prior to death. In fact, I would say many, if not most, of the patients whom I have seen die have had worse physical symptoms at some point *earlier* in their lives. Try to use this knowledge of unpleasant experiences that you've had in your life to your advantage. Your prior experiences should help alleviate your fears, for it makes the unknown become known.

Step 3: Recognize that the other fears (loss of control, separation from loved ones, and fear of the unknown—death and beyond) demand the ultimate faith in the Lord to conquer.

We will all die someday. Pride in our ability to control our lives makes this loss of control even harder. Even the most rich, powerful, and famous of us cannot control death. The only control at that point belongs to God and our faith in Jesus as Savior.

We will all be separated from loved ones through death. We must rely on God's grace and faith in Jesus to reunite us someday. It is natural to have a fear of what awaits us at death and beyond. Again, we must rely on faith in God's grace and the Lord Jesus to make it right.

So the key to conquering these fears lies in strengthening our personal faith. Stronger faith gives us more confidence that the ultimate outcome will be good. The stronger confidence in a good outcome will bring our fear down to zero. When we're absolutely certain of the outcome, our fears will vanish.

When we revisit the story of Elijah in 2 Kings 2:1–11, we learn that Elijah was taken directly up to heaven in a chariot. Undoubtedly, at that point Elijah had no fear of death. At that point he was certain of his life's outcome, and fear was nonexistent. In other words, **when our faith becomes knowledge, there will be no more fear**.

Step 4: Recognize that when your fears are increasing, you need to remember the Lord. Fears increase when you forget the Lord and/or lose faith.

Remembering the Lord gives us reassurance and lessens the fear. Constant reminders of the Lord strengthen our faith. I believe we all forget God from time to time. It seems only logical that Elijah must have forgotten God, the One who gave him the power to perform miracles. If his memory had been completely intact, he would not have become so paralyzed with fear. A strong faith and diligently working at remembering God are the keys to conquering fear. (See also the chapter in this book on memory.)

In addition, share your fears with someone else rather than keeping them bottled up. This helps you work through the fear and improves your attitude, focus, and perspective. Sharing also aids your support team to work through their side of the situation.

Attack Plan

Like everyone else, I have experienced a fear of death, and I have my own personal approach to it. I believe everyone should develop their own attack plan for conquering fear, and you may want to consider modifying my plan to fit your own situation.

First, as a physician, I think it is important for me to recognize my advantages and disadvantages regarding the fear of death. Being a physician was a huge advantage for me in realizing that the actual moment of death is relatively inconsequential. I've seen plenty of patients who have been given CPR and life support. Therefore, I feel I really have firsthand knowledge that the moment of death is very similar to falling asleep or being anesthetized for surgery. I've both fallen asleep and been anesthetized, and I realize that it's no big deal.

The second big advantage to my being a physician is my medical knowledge, and more importantly, the medical experience that accompanies that knowledge. Yes, I have non-Hodgkin's lymphoma, which is an incurable cancer given today's technology. However, as of this writing, I'm receiving a mild chemotherapeutic agent in terms of treatment, and I feel well. I also realize that this will change someday, and I will likely receive much more aggressive chemotherapy, chock-full of side effects and symptoms. Having seen similar symptoms and the accompanying comfort measures alleviates those fears for me.

Going back to my medical school days, the most fearful medical problem I saw was when I did a rotation in the burn ward. Burn patients seemed to feel the most miserable in terms of symptoms. From 1988 until 2004, the medical problem I feared most was burn wounds—that is, until I was in a propane fire myself and had a brief stint as a burn ward patient. Going through that experience gave me the knowledge and confidence that I could do it again, if I had to. I still have a healthy respect for the combination of propane and oxygen—in fact, my wife won't allow me around a gas grill anymore—but my fear of being a burn patient is gone.

Another example of medical experience along with knowledge alleviating fear is the case of my fifteen-year-old daughter, Lauren, who recently underwent foot surgery. After her surgery, when I first took the bandage off, she saw the stitches and became fearful and started to feel sick. I explained it to her and reassured her that it looked normal. After that first experience, subsequent bandage changes went much better.

"Medical student disease" occurs when medical students gain medical knowledge and then think they have a bad disease whenever they get a symptom. It is not until they gain the experience that accompanies that medical knowledge that the fears go away.

Patients without medical experience can develop great fears, which is nothing to be ashamed of; it's only natural. The problem is, they can gain medical knowledge through reading or word of mouth. This creates fears that they do not have the experience to offset. My advice to this problem is twofold:

1. Be careful in seeking out medical knowledge.
2. Do seek medical experience advice/expertise on how to deal with problems from your doctor, allied medical professionals, or a patient's support group.

Going back to my own case, my medical knowledge in terms of experience has been the key to avoiding the fear of symptoms.

Strengthening faith and memory processes has been my greatest struggle in terms of conquering fear of death. I have been a Christian, going back to my childhood years. I have gradually gained knowledge over the years that has strengthened my faith. My fear of death back in those early years was high. Doubt existed. Gaining knowledge has removed doubt and strengthened faith.

Fortunately for me, by the grace of God, my faith was already very strong by the time I was diagnosed with non-Hodgkin's lymphoma. In fact, my faith had become so strong that I had the confidence to start writing this book well before I was ever diagnosed.

Being diagnosed with a terminal cancer was where the big disadvantage to being a physician came into play. You see, being a physician means I have been trained to solve problems. In fact, I would even say that my ability to solve problems is terrific—for a mere human, that is.

But now that I've been diagnosed with a terminal cancer, I've had to swallow my pride in my own abilities and realize that this is a problem I cannot even begin to think I can solve on my own. No! The only way I can attack this problem is to give it over to God through my faith in Jesus. This is definitely the wisest decision I have made. Jesus conquered death, and through my faith in Him, my fear is being conquered as well.

So I make a point each day of doing something to strengthen my faith. I do this by seeking knowledge of God and reinforcing the knowledge I already possess. This can be through prayer, studying the Bible, and looking up other faith-based writings and philosophy. I look for mini-miracles—the beauty in nature and people overcoming tremendous obstacles in order to witness God's existence, help, and comfort.

The other day here in Sacramento, a young mother was accidentally killed while protecting her two-year-old son. It seems there was a gang-related gunfight at a local shopping mall. She was in the parking lot and heard the shots, and she used her body to cover her child. She was subsequently hit by a stray bullet. Some would use this as evidence that there is no God; otherwise such a tragedy striking an innocent person would never have occurred. However, I would bet the loving mother is up in heaven thanking God for giving her the courage and presence of mind to be able to save her child.

So for me, at this point, the biggest struggle in conquering fear is remembering to focus on God and Jesus. Like Elijah, I get caught up in life's events, and to my embarrassment, I forget God and what He has done for me. Whenever I sense fear or whenever uncertainty creeps into my life, I work at reminding myself of God, and I summon my faith in

Jesus. I sometimes even go and reread what I wrote in the chapter on memory (later in this book). *Focus, attitude, and perspective: Remember, remember, always remember!*

4

Let's Look at History

What part of us feels pleasure? Is it our hand, our arm, our flesh or our blood? It must obviously be something immaterial.[1] —*Pascal*

As we saw in the last chapter, the key to conquering the fear of death is to strengthen your belief that you do have a soul and that it can be saved for eternity. Non-believers doubt they have a soul, as it is not something that we can see, hear, touch, or prove its existence. In contrast, some believers feel it's intuitively obvious that they have a soul—how else can we think, reason, love, and hate?

Is there evidence for the soul in history? Is there evidence of life after death, which gives evidence for the existence of the soul? Let's look to see if anything can be learned from the Bible—not through a "just believe everything it says" attitude. Rather, let's look at the Bible from a logical standpoint to see what makes sense.

We know from sources other than the Bible that a man named Jesus Christ existed and was crucified. We know it, not only from scripture, but from the Jewish historian Josephus, who was not Christian, and so we can assume he was not biased in favor of Jesus. We also simply know it from all the followers that came to be. People do not spend their lives following a fictional character—especially when they are persecuted and killed in mass numbers for those beliefs. Although people back then did not have all the tools and technology that we do today, they were intelligent and quite capable of logical thought. Look at the basic writings of Aristotle, Plato, and Pythagoras, for example.

So, why did Peter and the other original apostles spend their lives

16

following Jesus and spreading His message? While Jesus was alive, we can assume that they followed Him because He was a charismatic leader. Plenty of charismatic people in history have had devoted followers while they were alive. But who has had such devoted followers after they have died, especially given that being a disciple of Jesus was an extremely unpopular thing to be at that time?

Indeed, the apostle Peter gave up his normal life to spend his life teaching about Jesus. In fact, he was eventually tortured and killed by being hung upside down on a cross for his beliefs. Why would he willingly do such a thing for a dead man? Let's look and see what information the Bible gives as a potential reason.

Why would Peter spend his life teaching about a dead man? The answer is found in Acts 1:3. This occurs after Jesus is crucified and buried. Acts 1:3 says: "After his suffering, he showed himself to these men and gave many convincing proofs that he was alive." There you have it—Peter was a lifelong follower of Jesus, at least in part because he had personal evidence that Jesus had risen from the grave!

So, why did Christianity spread so quickly when Jesus' followers could be killed for their beliefs? Why did so many people believe Peter's message? The answer is that Peter was not alone! The other apostles had witnessed the same miracles. People were seeing and hearing of miracles from multiple sources that confirmed each other.

Let's look at another biblical figure—Stephen, who was an early disciple of Jesus after His crucifixion. Stephen worked to spread the teachings of Jesus. For this, he was seized and brought before the Sanhedrin (the Jewish leaders and decision-making authority). They did not approve of what Stephen was doing. What happened to Stephen next? The answer can be found in Acts 7:55–56.

> But Stephen, full of the Holy Spirit, looked up to heaven and saw the glory of God, and Jesus standing at the right hand of God. "Look," he said, "I see heaven open and the Son of Man standing at the right hand of God."

This may be one of the first near-death experiences ever recorded. Stephen was then taken out of the city and stoned to death. Logic says that Stephen would not have given up his life unless he truly believed what he had witnessed. In other words, Stephen died because he witnessed that there is more to life than just the physical body.

Moving to another historical figure, let's take the case of the apostle Paul, whose original name was Saul. Saul was a leading early persecutor of Christians. In Galatians 1:13, Paul states, "How intensely I persecuted the church of God and tried to destroy it." In fact, Saul was even present at the death of Stephen (see Acts 8:1).

Saul was converted to Christianity as he was traveling to Damascus. Acts 9:1–19 tells the story:

Meanwhile, Saul was still breathing out murderous threats against the Lord's disciples. He went to the high priest and asked him for letters to the synagogues in Damascus, so that if he found any there who belonged to the Way (followers of Jesus), whether men or women, he might take them as prisoners to Jerusalem. As he neared Damascus on his journey, suddenly a light from heaven flashed around him. He fell to the ground and heard a voice say to him, "Saul, Saul, why do you persecute me?"

"Who are you, Lord?" Saul asked.

"I am Jesus, whom you are persecuting," he replied. "Now get up and go into the city, and you will be told what you must do."

The men traveling with Saul stood there speechless; they heard the sound but did not see anyone. Saul got up from the ground, but when he opened his eyes he could see nothing. So they led him by the hand into Damascus. For three days he was blind, and did not eat or drink anything.

In Damascus there was a disciple named Ananias. The Lord called to him in a vision, "Ananias!"

"Yes, Lord," he answered.

The Lord told him, "Go to the house of Judas on Straight Street and ask for a man from Tarsus named Saul, for he is praying. In a vision he has seen a man named Ananias come and place his hands on him to restore his sight."

"Lord," Ananias answered, "I have heard many reports about this man and all the harm he has done to your holy people in Jerusalem. And he

has come here with authority from the chief priests to arrest all who call on your name."

But the Lord said to Ananias, "Go! This man is my chosen instrument to proclaim my name to the Gentiles and their kings and to the people of Israel. I will show him how much he must suffer for my name."

Then Ananias went to the house and entered it. Placing his hands on Saul, he said, "Brother Saul, the Lord—Jesus, who appeared to you on the road as you were coming here—has sent me so that you may see again and be filled with the Holy Spirit." Immediately, something like scales fell from Saul's eyes, and he could see again. He got up and was baptized, and after taking some food, he regained his strength.

After that, Saul changed his name to Paul, and he spent the rest of his life traveling, creating churches, and growing the numbers of Christians. Only this time he himself was persecuted and jailed. Paul was eventually beheaded because of his beliefs and experience. From a logical standpoint, something major must have truly happened for Paul to change in this way.

To try to grasp the magnitude of Paul's conversion, let's examine a modern-day event:

In 1993, David Koresh was the leader of a religious sect called the Branch Davidians who lived in a secluded compound outside of Waco, Texas. The group was known to have firearms, and there was concern that minors were being molested and abused inside the compound. The compound was assaulted by the bureau of Alcohol, Tobacco, and Firearms (ATF). Federal agents were killed. The Branch Davidian compound subsequently underwent a fifty-one-day siege by the FBI. Finally, the United States Attorney General, Janet Reno, instructed the FBI to assault the compound. In the ensuing confrontation, the compound caught fire, and David Koresh and his followers died.[2]

Now, suppose that after Koresh died, Janet Reno had a conversion. As proof of her conversion, she gave up her government post, spent the rest of her life preaching about "the gospel" of Koresh, was jailed, and was subsequently executed for her newfound beliefs. *That* would have been an historical analogy to Paul's conversion. It would have taken an extraordinary event for Janet Reno, an intelligent and respected member of society, to so radically transform in that way. In fact, it took such an extraordinary event for Saul to fundamentally change.

Some critics have claimed that Saul's conversion must have been caused by a seizure. I have seen plenty of patients have seizures. Seizures do not make a person completely change their life and core beliefs 180 degrees. Seizures are a temporary loss of neurological control. Therefore, Saul's conversion was not a seizure!

Can you argue that Saul's conversion was a psychotic break from reality? Not when you look at it from an historical perspective. He was a leader who suddenly changed his beliefs and actions. He was able to reason and argue with such logic as to be a tireless champion for Christianity. His actions and letters led to thousands, and eventually millions of converts.

Likewise, suppose that after David Koresh's death, Janet Reno had a psychotic break from reality that made her give up her position and status and become a Branch Davidian. Is it possible that she could be believable at that point? Could she proceed to argue with such logic as to convince millions of people to be Branch Davidians? Could she change her name and expect people to listen to her and become ardent followers? No, she could not have had a psychotic break from reality and still be believable. And neither could Saul!

When people have a psychotic break, they see or hear things that aren't really there or don't actually happen. Those around them realize they are acting differently and no longer believe what they are saying. Historical events following Saul's conversion are proof that the explanation of a psychotic event as the cause of his conversion is implausible.

Can you argue that Saul's conversion was the result of a drunken stupor or drug-induced hallucination? No, when people are in a drunken stupor, those around them can tell that they are under the influence. They eventually sober up and don't lead the rest of their lives based on one hallucinatory event. Could Janet Reno have gotten drunk to the point of thinking David Koresh was talking to her from beyond the grave and still be believable? No. In a similar fashion, Saul could not have pulled off a similar stunt in front of his peers.

The only argument that people have to say that Saul's conversion was not a real event is to argue that the whole New Testament is false. Much of the New Testament is made up of Paul's writings. To say Saul's conversion event is not possible is to say Jesus could not do miracles.

History again refutes both arguments that claim the New Testament is false and that Saul's conversion is untenable. Early Christians were severely persecuted. There was no advantage in that society to becoming a Christian. Peter, Paul, and other early disciples gave up their lives because they believed what they had seen and heard. They did not dedicate their lives to Christianity for money, power, or fame. Humanity's ancestors of two thousand years ago were quite capable of logical thought. They were not crazy. *Something must have really happened!* That something requires and even demands the existence of the soul. That something was the resurrection of Christ. His resurrection gave the early Christians confidence in their knowledge of the existence of their souls. They were willing to risk their earthly lives due to their confidence in their eternal souls. They succeeded in spreading Christianity by *focusing* on Jesus with an eternal *perspective*.

Now let's turn to modern-day evidence of the existence of the soul—the near-death experience.

5

Near-Death Experiences

Will he, who has taught us in his writings the right manner of life, allow us to be without a knowledge of the nature of that life?[1] —*Saint Augustine*

What are near-death experiences? The term *near-death experience* was coined in 1975 by Raymond Moody, MD, in his bestselling book entitled *Life After Life*.[2] Near-death experiences are sensory and emotional experiences that happen when a person is at or on the verge of death. In today's era of CPR and life-sustaining measures, they are being reported more frequently. Perhaps the most intriguing near-death experiences are episodes of veridical perception. This is when a person reports seeing or hearing something that they could not have otherwise known because it occurred while they were unconscious.

In 1988, Dr. Pim van Lommel, a Dutch cardiologist, began a prospective study of 344 consecutive survivors of cardiac arrest. In cardiac arrest, the heart stops pumping oxygen to the brain, and the brain ceases to function after about ten seconds. Dr. van Lommel reported his findings in the well-respected British medical journal *The Lancet*.[3] He found that 18 percent of patients had some recollection of the time of clinical death. There was no relationship of exacerbating factors that might provoke the near-death experience. The study could not find any relationship to psychological, physiological, or pharmacological factors. In other words, near-death experiences are not due to schizophrenia, multiple personalities, depression, medications, or any particular underlying disease other than being unconscious with a nonfunctioning brain. The following particularly interesting case was reported by a nurse of a coronary care unit:

> During night shift, an ambulance brings in a forty-four-year-old cyanotic, comatose man into the coronary care unit. He was found in a coma about thirty minutes before in a meadow. When we go to intubate the patient, he turns out to have dentures in his mouth. I remove these upper dentures and put them in the "crash cart." After about an hour and a half, the patient has sufficient heart rhythm and blood pressure, but he is still ventilated and intubated, and he is comatose. He is transferred to the intensive care unit to continue the necessary artificial respiration. Only after more than a week do I meet again with the patient, who is now back on the cardiac ward. The moment he sees me he says: "Oh, that nurse knows where my dentures are!" I am very surprised. Then he elucidates: "You were there when I was brought into the hospital, and you took my dentures out of my mouth, and put them onto that cart, it had all those bottles on it and there was this sliding drawer underneath, and there you put my teeth." I was especially amazed because I remembered this happening while the man was in a deep coma and in the process of CPR. It appeared that the man had seen himself lying in bed, that he had perceived from above how nurses and doctors had been busy with CPR. He was able to describe correctly and in detail, the small room in which he had been resuscitated, as well as the appearance of those present like myself. He is deeply impressed by his experience and says he is no longer afraid of death.

So here we have an independent observer reporting a patient's near-death experience. He had knowledge of his dentures' location when he was unconscious, despite having no logical reason to know this. That is illogical from a purely scientific standpoint, without taking into account the existence of the soul.

Dr. van Lommel later reported another interesting case.[4] An interviewed patient reported:

> During my cardiac arrest, I had an extensive experience … and later I saw apart from my deceased grandmother, a man who had

looked at me lovingly, but whom I did not know. More than ten years later, at my mother's deathbed, she confessed to me that I had been born out of an extramarital relationship, my father being a Jewish man who had been deported and killed during the Second World War, and my mother showed me his picture. The unknown man that I had seen more than ten years before during my near-death experience, turned out to be my biological father.

We have to take the patient's word on this one, but I don't see a reason for him to lie to the doctor about it. Again, this patient had knowledge of something that can't be explained from a purely materialistic viewpoint.

So at least in some near-death experiences, people are capable of seeing things despite being unconscious with their eyes closed. In Dr. Kenneth Ring's book *Mindsight*,[5] he studies the near-death experience of congenitally blind patients (i.e., blind from the moment of birth). What he finds is that many of them report actually being able to see during these episodes. Interestingly, congenitally blind people do not have visual imagery in their dreams.[6] People who lose sight later in life can continue to "see" in their dreams. So here again, we have a case of people being able to do something while unconscious, essentially dead, that they should not be able to do. It's also evidence that near-death experiences are real events and not dreams.

But what about the possibility of near-death experiences being hallucinations? This certainly does not appear to be the case. Multiple studies of near-death experience patients do not show there to be any underlying psychological disorder. In fact, Dr. Pim van Lommel's study suggests that those with a tendency toward dementia are less likely to report a near-death experience. He found that there was a tendency for younger patients to be more likely to report near-death experiences. Older patients with some short-term memory loss were less likely to have a near-death experience. There have even been many instances of children reporting near-death experiences.

Dr. Penny Sartori did a prospective study on near-death experiences.[7] Some of those patients reported hallucinations. The hallucinations were very random and bizarre. People who had hallucinations could realize that it was a hallucination, whereas near-death experiences were consistently reported as being very real.

From my personal experience as an internist, hallucinations do not make sense as the cause for near-death experiences. I have seen plenty of people (I estimate *well over* a hundred), with dementia, illness-induced delirium, and psychiatric disorders who have had hallucinations. However, I have observed some distinct features of hallucinations that do not hold true of near-death experiences:

1. They have all been conscious at the time of the hallucination.
2. People around them can readily tell that they are having an altered state of thinking.
3. There is a tendency to have more than one hallucinatory episode.
4. They will frequently admit that they are seeing and hearing things that are not real.

No, hallucinations are not the cause of near-death experiences.

Let's look at another case of a near-death experience. Perhaps the best-known and well-documented study is that of Pam Reynolds.[8] In 1991, at age thirty-five, she was found to have a large brainstem aneurysm. She saw Dr. Robert Spetzler at the Barrow Neurological Institute in Phoenix, Arizona. She underwent an unusual surgery in which her heart was stopped, and her body temperature was lowered to 60 degrees Fahrenheit. After the heart was stopped, her head was elevated to drain the blood from the head. Her eyes were taped shut. She was also monitored with an EEG and wore ear plugs that emit audible clicks, which were monitored to ensure that there was no brain activity. The operation was successful, and she completely recovered.

During the operation, Pam Reynolds had a near-death experience. She heard a tone that sounded like a natural D (musical note). She then reports floating around the operating room. She felt more aware, and her vision was clearer than normal. She had expected the doctor to use a typical saw, but instead she saw him using what looked like an electric toothbrush that came in what looked like a socket wrench kit. She heard a female voice say, "We have a problem. Her arteries are too small." In fact, the doctors had to switch from accessing arteries on the right leg, which were small, to the left leg.

At some point later in the operation, she noticed herself being pulled toward a light, which became bright. She could see her grandmother, uncle, and other deceased relatives, in addition to some people she did not know. She enjoyed the sensation, but eventually her uncle brought her back to her body. She did not want to go. She saw her body make a jump (when her heart was given an electric shock to restart it). Her uncle gave her a push, and she went back into the body, which was painful as it felt like going into ice water. She later heard the song "Hotel California" being played (they were playing music in the operating room as they were finishing up).

Skeptics will argue that she was not clinically brain dead throughout the operation. She might have somehow overcome the anesthesia, monitors, and earplugs to be able to hear during the surgery. I think this argument is highly unlikely, but even if it is true, it does not explain her ability to describe the saw. The saw is sterilely sealed off in a pouch prior to surgery, and she could not have known what it looked like. No, there is no explanation for these events from a purely materialistic viewpoint, and they point to existence of the soul and a life beyond the present reality.

Now, if you're really a skeptic, you might want to go out on a limb and say Pam Reynolds made up the whole thing for secondary gain. Secondary gain means a person has an ulterior motive to having a medical problem. For instance, they might want to claim a medical problem to seek attention, get out of work, or collect insurance money. In Pam Reynolds's case, she is a singer-songwriter, so her secondary gain might be to gain some fame to help her career. It would have been hard for her to pull off. She would have had to research the operation details in advance and then have an "inside" person, such as an operating room nurse, feed her details of the operation. It would have been like a magician's act.

Why is this scenario completely unbelievable? First of all, it's just not believable that at the time of the surgery, she would be thinking of anything other than surviving. Secondly, and more importantly, the sheer number of people with near-death experiences is too great for secondary gain to be the explanation. What do I mean by this? Let me elaborate.

In 2004, Don Piper wrote a bestselling book about his near-death experience following a car accident entitled *90 minutes in Heaven*.[9] Obviously people were fascinated with his story, or else his book would not have been a bestseller. What I think many people don't realize is that Don Piper and Pam Reynolds are really not that unique. There are a great number of people who have had fascinating near-death experiences (they are all fascinating).

Surveys from the United States, Australia, and Germany have reported the incidence of near-death experiences in the population to be between 4 and 15 percent.[10] More conservatively, a number of studies[11] have estimated that 10 to 20 percent of cardiac arrest survivors have near-death experiences. This corresponds to an estimated one million or more Americans who have had near-death experiences. So roughly one to two people out of every three hundred have had near-death experiences. In other words, there's a pretty good chance that you know or have met someone who's had a near-death experience; they probably just haven't told you. Why wouldn't they tell you? There are three possible reasons:

1. They're probably still baffled by it and trying to make sense of it.

2. These episodes sound bizarre, and they don't want you to think they're crazy (they are not).

3. *They are not seeking secondary gain!*

Let's look at some more examples of ordinary people who have had extraordinary experiences.

Our church has about two hundred members. I know of at least two people in the congregation who have had a near-death experience. The only reason I know their stories is by seeking them out and being fortunate enough to talk to the right people at the right time. I'd be willing to bet that most of the people in the church assembly know nothing of their stories because they haven't gotten up and announced it to the world.

The first of these involves a man named Richard. I met Richard at a small group class on solving conflict. At the start of the first class, the minister asked us to go around, introduce ourselves, and state why we were there. When it was Richard's turn, I saw a man who looked puzzled and confused. He introduced himself and said, "I really don't know why I'm here." He went on and said, "I survived a cardiac arrest—I died on the operating table—and I'm trying to figure out why I'm here." Later, I had a chance to talk with him privately and got the story.

Richard is eighty years old. He's a retired airplane mechanic who was at the top of his field while working, and he is as still sharp as a tack. He had an uneventful coronary bypass surgery about ten years prior. However, he had a second coronary bypass surgery this past year and it was very eventful. In the middle of the operation, his heart went into cardiac arrest (i.e., stopped beating), and they had to perform CPR to revive him. During this time, he found himself floating above the operating table and could see the doctors and nurses working on him. He saw the medical staff doing CPR on him. They shocked him, and he suddenly went back into his body and did not remember any more until he awoke in the recovery room.

The second story involves a man named Gary. My pastor told me about Gary after he heard I was interested in the subject. Gary later moved out of the area, yet I was fortunate enough to track him down and get his story, and this is what he told me:

> I had a heart attack and was being treated in the hospital. They needed to give me medicines to slow my heart rate. A mistake was made. Inadvertently, two nurses gave me two different drugs that combined to stop the heart. I was dead for a total of nine minutes. The moment of death did not hurt, and I was pain-free while I was dead; in fact, it felt good.
>
> As I died, I felt like I was looking through a kaleidoscope, and then everything closed in and went black. My soul floated out of my body, and I was looking down, face-to-face over the top of my body. I felt a strange force pulling me up to the ceiling. I then went through the ceiling and saw the mechanicals between the floors—like the pipes and such. I then kept going up and went through

another hospital floor, seeing nurses there. I kept going through ceilings and floors till I reached the roof, and then I went out into the night sky and saw the city.

While I was going up into the sky, I felt all the pains, tensions, and stress leave my body, as I went higher and higher. At the same time, the tensions were replaced with being happy, overjoyed, and filled with peace and love.

As I looked down on the city, I continued to go up; it felt almost like I was in a hot air balloon. I think I probably went up three thousand feet or more, when a hole in the sky, or a round portal opened up. At this point, I saw a very intense light, as if from an arc welder. It hurt the eyes to look at it.

At this point, I came face-to-face with my deceased sister-in-law, Tammy. We had been very close. She had died one month prior. Tammy had lots of tattoos when she was alive, but all of her tattoos and wrinkles were gone. Her face looked like it was airbrushed with "gold dust" on the skin. She looked like a spiritual form, made of light. She confronted me and said, "You have to go back." I started to argue with her, as I wanted to stay. But she told me that I had to go back and take care of her sister. She then held up her hand with palm outstretched, like giving the stop sign, and she gave me a shove.

At this point, everything went into reverse and I went all the way back down, seeing everything again. I finally was above my body again, and I saw the medical staff working on me and using the paddles, and I went back into my body. Going back into my body, I felt angry and cheated. I told the nurse, "Why did you have to bring me back? I was almost there, almost home!" The nurse just held my hand and sobbed. There was severe pain all over after I went back into my body, which faded away over the next day.

Gary reported that after this experience, he sees his soul as a form of light. He is no longer afraid to die. He was a believer before the incident, but now he has no doubts. Gary stated that after this experience, he told a few people about it, but then he stopped telling others because the looks he received indicated that they did not believe him. He said, "I stopped talking about it, knowing that one day people would find out I was telling the truth."

The concept that near-death experiences are not as rare as we might think, and that people tend not to talk about them, was hammered home to me the day after I heard Gary's story. I was excited about hearing the story, so I proceeded to mention it to one of my coworkers, Joaquin. He is a physician's assistant whom I have known for about fifteen years. He astounded me by telling me the story of his father's near-death experience.

Joaquin's father, Rudecindo, was a doctor who lived in the Philippines. In the 1980s, he underwent surgery to remove a meningioma, which is a brain tumor. After the surgery, he remained in a coma for three days. One day, he suddenly came out of the coma and told his family about his amazing out-of-body experience.

He was accurately able to describe seeing his family praying for him. He described seeing Joaquin's brother, who was five hundred miles away at the time. In fact, Joaquin's brother reported seeing an image of their father visiting him, while his father's body was still back in the hospital bed. Their dad also described his cousin's house in Australia. He had never seen the house, and yet he still described it accurately in detail, even mentioning a wheelchair that was out front. He described going up into an incredibly white light. He saw deceased family members, and eventually saw the Virgin Mary, who told him he needed to go back down and tell his story to his wife who eventually had the story published in the Philippines.

Some of my own patients have shared their stories with me. The first of these stories is not an out-of-body experience but does give some useful insight into the moment of death itself.

Mr. H. had been critically ill in the hospital. In fact, he had actually died and was brought back to life via CPR. After a somewhat lengthy recovery period in the hospital, I saw him as an outpatient back in the clinic. We talked about how ill he had been. He acknowledged that he was told that he had actually been clinically dead until given CPR. He added, "You know, dying is not all that bad." He wanted to let me know that the actual physical process of dying was not the painful, excruciating moment that some of us may think or imagine. Hopefully, Mr. H.'s story will help allay the fears of those of us who are scared of the actual physical moment of death. Rather, let us continue to focus on the crucial mental aspect of dealing with death.

Sharon is another of my patients. As a young woman, she had a tubal ligation. While on the operating table, she found herself above her body looking down on the staff working on her. One thing she remembered was one of the operating room nurses asking the doctor if she could borrow ten dollars for lunch. Sharon then found herself going into a tunnel of light.

Sharon said that the tunnel of light overwhelmed her with a great euphoric feeling. She felt like the light was touching her all over and that she was everywhere. Apparently she had stopped breathing and eventually just woke up with the medical team working on her. She states that the experience was not painful.

After a successful recovery, Sharon returned to work as a store clerk. One afternoon, a lady came through the line whom she recognized. It was the operating room nurse. She didn't know how she recognized her because the nurse had been wearing an operating room mask. Out of curiosity, Sharon asked the nurse if she ever got the ten dollars. The puzzled nurse asked Sharon what she was talking about, and so Sharon told her the story. The nurse was shocked because there was no way that Sharon should have known about the ten dollars. After seeing the nurse's reaction, Sharon had confirmation that her experience was real and not a dream.

In addition to near-death experiences, there are numerous stories of people having phenomenal or spiritual experiences that really cannot be adequately explained with modern science and technology. These experiences point toward the existence of God and the soul as the most plausible explanation. One of these experiences was well documented by Palm Beach, Florida, cardiologist Dr. Chauncey Crandell.[12]

In 2006, Dr. Crandell was working in the emergency room, and he found himself working on a fifty-three-year-old patient, Jeff Markin, who had undergone CPR for forty minutes. At the end of that time, Dr. Crandell noted the patient to be cyanotic (i.e., blue from lack of oxygen). Dr. Crandell pronounced Jeff Markin dead. However, as the doctor was walking out of the room, he sensed the Lord asking him to go back and pray over the lifeless body. Dr. Crandell went back in and prayed for God to restore life. He then asked the emergency room doctor to shock the patient one more time. This time the heart went back into the normal rhythm, and Jeff Markin was revived.

From my experience as a doctor, I find this case to be exceptional for the following reasons:

1. It is quite rare for a patient to survive after forty minutes of CPR.

2. I have never seen, or even heard of, a doctor going back to resume CPR techniques after pronouncing a patient dead.

3. During CPR, there is at least some oxygen and blood being forced into circulation in the body. CPR is stopped when the patient is pronounced dead. That means there was a period of time between the patient being pronounced dead and when the emergency room doctor delivered one more electric shock. During this time, in which Dr. Crandell was praying and deciding to give him one more shock, there was no oxygen being delivered to Jeff Markin's heart or brain. This means that Jeff Markin not only survived forty minutes of CPR, but he also survived some time with no circulation at all after the end of CPR.

This case certainly suggests that more than modern medical technology was helping Jeff Markin.

Another interesting story involves that of a patient of mine, Connie. She volunteered this story to me one day, long before she knew I was working on a book. Connie is an extremely pleasant eighty-year-old lady, who remains mentally sharp. She told of being visited by an image of her deceased mother many years ago. Her mother was wearing a flowing white gown. Her mother told her to tell her cousin to stop her bad activities, or "she'll be getting caught." Her mother then waved and gave the sign of the cross before disappearing through the wall. Connie did not know about any illegal activities. When she relayed the message to her cousin; she found out the cousin was actually involved in smuggling over the United States–Mexico border.

Another patient, Mr. S., also had his faith and beliefs confirmed. Mr. S. is a vigorous gentleman in his eighties. His wife suffered multiple problems, including chronic lung disease, heart failure, stroke, and dementia. She was eventually placed in a hospice program due to her failing health.

One day Mr. S. was sitting alone at his wife's bedside after the hospice nurse had stepped out. He suddenly saw the young Mrs. S. standing on the other side of the bed. He estimates her age was sixteen, which was before he had ever known her. The young Mrs. S. was a real-life image (i.e., not a translucent or "ghost" form). She lifted her leg and climbed onto the bed. She looked off into the corner of the room as if she were going there, and then she suddenly disappeared. His wife passed at that very moment. He noted that his wife a few days prior had told him that she saw animals in the corner of the room, and he had responded by saying, "That's nice, you'll be visiting them soon." This was the same corner of the room that the young Mrs. S. had so intently gazed upon. The episode strengthened his faith with the affirmation that she had gone off peacefully into the afterlife.

Another story comes from my friend Bonnie. She is a mental health therapist. Some years ago, Bonnie had surgery for ovarian cancer. When she came home from the hospital, she lay on her bed and was feeling lonely. She suddenly saw a ball, or orb, of white light floating above her. It was soon accompanied by two smaller orbs. They moved back and forth like butterflies until they suddenly disappeared into the wall. She found this to be a very peaceful, reassuring experience. She suspects these were angels sent to comfort her.

My wife, Caryl, has a friend, Margaret, who volunteered her story to us one day. Margaret is a retired RN who formerly instructed other nurses. Margaret's husband is a retired radiologist. Her fascinating experience happened when she was a young wife and mother.

One day, Margaret and her husband were entertaining some friends at their home. She had worked hard to ensure that every-thing was well planned for the event. Her husband apparently said something that embarrassed her and hurt her feelings. She went upstairs to be alone in her room. Margaret did, indeed, feel all alone, as she was living in a different state from her mother and siblings. She was lying on her bed, crying with her eyes closed. Suddenly, she felt a very serene, calming sensation in the room. Two thoughts came into her head as if someone was saying: *You are not alone* and *Open your eyes.* She opened her eyes and what she saw amazed her. It was a man's face in profile, with a distinctive long nose, blue eyes, and long, white, silvery colored hair. The face was like a real person's face, but from the neck down, the man was just a vapor. The face in profile continued to encircle the room, appearing high on the walls above her, so that she always just saw the profile. There was a radiant white light around the image. The room was filled with a very calming, invigorating peace, the likes of which she had never felt before or since. The whole experience lasted about twenty minutes or so. Finally, her husband came into the room, and the image disappeared. Unaware of what Margaret had just experienced, her husband sat at the foot of the bed near her. After a while, he turned to her and described feeling the same calm sensation in the room.

I later asked Margaret what she thought the image was, and she replied, "I think it might have been the Great Comforter, the Holy Spirit." She had never had any such experience like that before or since. It was the best experience of her life. She uses the memory of this experience to comfort and console herself in hard times.

Once again, I'd like to emphasize that Margaret is a well-respected professional whom no one would accuse of being "crazy" or "psychotic." Note that Margaret volunteered this story to Caryl before she knew I was working on this book. In fact, in writing this book, I didn't advertise a need to hear people's stories. I just found out about them by chance. This underscores the fact that these phenomenal stories are probably much more common than we think; it's just that people tend not to talk about them, fearing that others will think they're crazy. In fact, when I was talking to Gary, he said that he had told a few people his experience, but then he stopped relating it because people were looking at each other in disbelief.

So, what do we learn from these near-death and other spiritual experiences? I think there are several key points to take away:

1. We do have a soul.

2. Our soul, while generally thought of as residing in our bodies, is not absolutely constrained to staying in our bodies. This is why some of the people who had near-death experiences were able to "look down" on their bodies on the operating room tables.

3. Our soul does not die when our body dies. Indeed, patients were able to report on their lifeless bodies. Not one reported that they themselves or their soul was lifeless. If their soul had been lifeless when their body was, then they would have had nothing to report.

4. Our soul is capable of interacting with other souls outside our bodies. For instance, in the case of Pam Reynolds, her uncle pushed her back into her body. In Gary's case, his sister-in-law pushed him back into his body. This tells us two things: 1) The souls of those who have passed on before us have been capable of transcending the physical body, and 2) It is our soul, not our eyes, ears, mouth, or body, that is the key driving force behind our communicating with others.

5. People do not report pain at the moment of death. I think this is important to know, as so many people fear that dying will be painful. So stop worrying—the moment of death doesn't hurt.

6. These experiences confirm the existence of the soul for these people. This gives them an entirely new level of confidence in the spiritual life.

I suspect God gives a few of us these incredible experiences so that the rest of us can renew our faith in Him. This should give us confidence in our soul, so that we can move on and build on that foundation.

6

Immortality of Your Soul?

Here is a thought experiment for you:

Suppose you are trapped in a maze. You've been wandering inside for a long time. You've been down multiple paths, multiple times. Finally, a stranger appears. He tells you that he knows the way out; you just have to choose his way. But the only way you can go down his path is if you truly believe him, have faith in him, and follow him. Otherwise, you can just continue to wander in the maze, seeking your own way out.

Understanding that you, indeed, have a soul is similar to this scenario. At some point, you just have to believe that you have a soul, which is the real you. Believing that you have a soul and accepting Jesus Christ as the Savior of your soul is the only way to conquer death. It's the only way out of the maze.

Now, in this chapter, I'd like to pursue an argument—or line of reasoning—pointing toward the immortality of the soul. It relies on the reasoning of the Christian philosopher, Saint Augustine, in his book *Soliloquies*. But first, who was (or should I say who is) Saint Augustine?

Saint Augustine was born in 354 A.D. in Thagaste, in modern Algeria. He grew up in North Africa, which was at that time part of the Roman Empire. His mother was a Christian, and his father was a pagan. In 386 A.D., at the age of thirty-two, he converted to Christianity. He went on to become the bishop of Hippo, a city in North Africa.

He was an extremely prolific writer, and as such, he became one of the most influential people in Christian history. He was a strong follower of the apostle Paul and quoted him frequently throughout his writings. He wrote extensively on faith, hope, charity, the Holy Trinity, the teachings of Jesus, and God. He was a central figure in the history of the Catholic Church. He was also studied closely by Martin Luther and John Calvin, and has thus influenced all Christian denominations.

So what of Saint Augustine's book *Soliloquies*? A *soliloquy* is a dialogue that one has with oneself. It's often thought of as a series of self-questioning and answers. Perhaps the most famous example of a soliloquy is found in Shakespeare's *Hamlet*, in the "to be or not to be" scene.

Saint Augustine was actually the person who coined the term *soliloquy*. He developed the concept as a technique to inquire into the nature of God and the soul. He carried on a philosophical discussion with his inner self, or conscience, that he calls "Reason." Let's look at a passage from *Soliloquies* that argues that truth must always exist:[1]

Reason: Be on the alert, then, so that you can answer me carefully and with certainty when I question you.

Augustine: I am right here.

Reason: If this world will endure forever, is it TRUE that the world will endure forever?

Augustine: Who would doubt it?

Reason: But if it will not endure, is it not likewise TRUE that it will not endure?

Augustine: I do not gainsay [deny] that.

Reason: When it shall have passed away—supposing that it is to pass away—will it not then be true that the world has passed away? For as long as it is not true that the world has perished, it has not perished. It is, then, absurd that the world should have perished and yet it be not true that the world has perished.

Augustine: That I grant too.

Reason: What about this: Does it seem to you that something true can exist and truth not exist?

Augustine: Not at all.

Reason: Truth, therefore, will exist, even if the world ceases to exist.

Augustine: I cannot deny that.

Reason: Suppose truth itself should perish, will it not be true to say that truth has perished?

Augustine: Who would deny that?

Reason: But something true cannot exist if truth does not exist.

Augustine: I have granted that a while ago.

Reason: Truth therefore in no way will cease to exist.

Augustine: Go on as you have begun, for nothing is more true than this conclusion.

In this passage, Augustine has logically argued that truth must always exist. If you didn't quite follow that, then go back and reread the last six lines of the passage.

Saint Augustine also argues that since truth exists, it must exist somewhere. He states that truth exists in the science of argumentation. By argumentation, he is not referring to quarreling. Rather, he is referring to learning and the process of reasoning. Learning and reasoning reside in the soul. Thus, truth exists in the soul.

So, let's summarize again. Augustine reasons that truth must always exist, and it exists in the soul. Therefore, the soul is immortal, since it always exists. By knowing that the soul is immortal, our lives can be spent in confidence and peace.

Are we completely satisfied with Augustine's logic to prove the immortality of the soul? Hopefully we are. However, in his introduction to *The Soliloquies of Saint Augustine*, Robert Russell points out that Augustine himself felt the work was unfinished. I agree that there's more to add, and so I'd like to humbly suggest the following:

First, I believe that Saint Augustine's logic is correct and not flawed. However, the path of reasoning is torturous and can be hard to follow. Basically, he is saying that the truth always exists and that it exists in what we have learned. Since truth exists in what we have learned, it exists in us, since what we have learned resides in us.

We can simplify this reasoning by remembering what the truth is. What is the truth? Jesus Christ is the truth! Jesus Christ always is, always was, and always will be!

Things really become very simple for Christians of all denominations, and the question is basic: Do you believe that Jesus Christ is the Savior, the Messiah? If yes, then you have accepted Jesus into your life. If Jesus is in your life, then He's in your soul, and your soul will endure forever!

Let me restate: Jesus conquered death on the cross and rose from death on Easter Sunday. Jesus' life is therefore everlasting. He is immortal. Since we, as Christians, have accepted Jesus into our souls, then our souls are everlasting because Jesus can never die!

Why do Christians fear death? We shouldn't. Thanks to Jesus, our souls are immortal, so we don't need to worry about our souls dying. We, as Christians, should take comfort in the fact that we have Jesus in our lives and souls, and we therefore should have no fear.

We need to stop here and differentiate between the death of our bodies and the death of our souls. We've already concluded that thanks to Jesus, our souls don't die, so we only need to discuss the death of our bodies. Our body does die, so should we fear that? I argue that no, we shouldn't. First, we've already established that the actual moment of bodily death is peaceful, not painful. Second, the loss of the body does not change who we really are. Who we really are resides in our soul, not our body.

We have all lost a body part (e.g., baby teeth), and yet the loss has not changed the essence or spirit of who we are. People commonly have surgical removal of tonsils, appendix, and gall bladder without changing who they are. With the advancements in technology, people have had mechanical replacements of joints and even limbs without changing who they are. We now see even heart and lung transplants, and yet the patient is still the same person. But what about those of us who have never had any surgery? Our bodies are always remodeling. You still constantly lose parts of your body. We chronically shed hair and skin without even thinking about it. Old bone is being destroyed and new bone is being made constantly. Every ninety days we have a completely new set of red blood cells from three months before. Our body is constantly changing, and we never think twice about it. Loss of body parts is nothing new. We should not fear.

Yes, our bodies are constantly aging. Joints wear down. New bone marrow is not as vibrant. Blood vessels clog up, which can cause strokes, heart attack, and loss of limbs. New cells are imperfectly made, which can lead to cancer. Our bodies are not perfect, so we should recognize the importance of not relying on them. But we do have something in us that is perfect and reliable. That something is the love of Jesus Christ, which is perfect, everlasting, and can never be destroyed, just as our love for a favorite person is not extinguished even if one dies. Therefore, if we rely on Christ rather than our bodies, there is nothing to fear. The battle for immortality is already won.

One cannot discuss death without also discussing pain. First, and most important, *death and pain are not the same!* I'm afraid many confuse the two. As we established in the last chapter, the moment of death is not painful. However, the moments of life before death can be painful. I think that often when people are afraid of a painful death, they are really afraid of a painful life before death. I will talk much more about how to deal with pain in a later chapter, but for right now let it suffice to say: Stop worrying, it does no good.

So, I believe that when people fear death, they actually fear one of two things: 1) They fear the unknown of exactly what will happen when they die, or 2) They fear potential pain that may occur in the time they're alive just before death. Let's treat these two fears in turn.

The first fear, the fear of the unknown entity of death, should be a non-issue. This is because we've already established what will happen at the time of death, so it is no longer an unknown. The moment of death is a pain-free, peaceful passing, like falling asleep. Thanks to Jesus Christ, the soul lives on. What will happen precisely to the soul at that point, we can't say with certainty. However, we do know that it will be good, very good. There will be no more pain or suffering.

The second fear is the fear of potential pain prior to death. It is not really death that we fear but rather just potential pain. If we stop and think about it, the fear of possible pain does not need to be associated with death. For instance, pain can be associated with the fear of potential trauma, surgery, heart attacks, blood draws, childbirth, sunburns, dental visits, or even a shave with a dull blade. Furthermore, the pain experienced in the period prior to death will not necessarily be any worse than any of the above common experiences. In fact, there may not be any pain at all prior to death.

Let's take a look at some of the common causes of death and their associated pain. Knowledge will help alleviate the fear of pain.

Take a look at heart attacks. Most people know someone who has had a heart attack and survived. A majority of heart attack survivors will tell you that they had chest pain, arm pain, back pain, or jaw pain. Oftentimes, when patients are having a heart attack or angina and I ask them if they are having chest pain, they will correct me and say there is no pain, just discomfort or pressure. Sometimes they will complain of shortness of breath or nausea. Most often, they are in the hospital within one hour or at least within a few hours after the onset of symptoms. They are quickly given medicines that, to a great degree, alleviate the symptoms. I think the large majority of people do not fear or worry about heart attack symptoms. Rather they fear heart attacks, since they can cause death.

Now, what is the difference between the pain that people experience with a heart attack that they survive and a heart attack that causes death? I would say that there is generally no difference. Why is that? People who die of a heart attack usually die from an arrhythmia (i.e., an erratic heartbeat—including when the heart stops beating). What happens when the heart stops beating? You pass out. Does it hurt to pass out? No. Any suffering involved? No. Does it take long? Stop and count to five seconds—it's less than that. So, the discomfort of a heart attack is not something that we should particularly fear or worry about.

What about congestive heart failure? Congestive heart failure is when the heart muscle has weakened to the extent of causing symptoms, such as weakness, shortness of breath, and swelling. Do people with congestive heart failure complain that it causes pain? No. What do people with congestive heart failure die of? It's usually from an arrhythmia. This is a painless scenario, so there is no physical pain to fear.

What about trauma as a source of death? Certainly, we all know someone who has survived major trauma in their lives. Quite likely it could be you yourself. The trauma could be a fall; a motor vehicle accident; burn wounds; an amputation; a back, head, or neck injury—all painful events. Now, what is the difference in the level of pain experienced by someone with major trauma who survives and someone who suffers a similar traumatic incident that they don't survive? I'd argue there is no difference. Why? People die from trauma due to shock, which is a loss of blood pressure. With a severe loss of blood pressure, the person passes out—a painless event.

What about the fairly common event of a pulmonary embolism as a cause of death? A pulmonary embolism is a blood clot that has formed and traveled to the lungs. The symptoms include weakness, shortness of breath, chest pain, and yes, passing out. It is usually quick with minimal suffering.

What about infection as a cause of death? This may commonly be pneumonia, but really any kind of infection can lead to sepsis. Sepsis is when the infection gets into the bloodstream. This can cause shock, which is again a loss of blood pressure, causing one to pass out. Certainly, we've all had infections to one degree or another: earaches, sore throat, respiratory infections, skin infections, urinary infections, and diarrhea. These all make us feel miserable. However, the suffering is usually brief and nothing to fear. In fact, many old-timers refer to pneumonia as the old man's blessing as a cause of death.

The last cause of death as a source of pain that I'll discuss here is cancer. Cancer is an abnormal growth of body tissue. Any organ or structure can be affected, which is why there are so many different types. In the twenty-five years that I have been in the medical field, I've seen innumerable cancer patients. In fact, on a personal note, both of my parents died from cancer; my mother had ovarian cancer, and my father had melanoma. Cancer can certainly cause prolonged pain and suffering. However, I'd like to make a few comments here that will hopefully allay some of those fears of potential pain.

1. More and more people these days are surviving, given improved technology.

2. There are many ways that we can work to help mitigate pain and suffering. Again, I'll talk more about pain treatment in a later chapter.

3. The last tip is a personal observation. I've seen probably hundreds of cancer patients. I've seen even more with pain from non-lethal sources, such as back, neck, arthritis, headaches, shingles, abdominal pain, and neuropathy (nerve pain). More often than not, the person with a non-lethal source of pain will complain longer and louder than the cancer patient.

So in regards to potential pain prior to death, I think it's not something that we should really fear. Quite likely that pain will be no worse than something we've already experienced in our lifetime.

I started this chapter talking about the immortality of your soul. Your soul has immortality; we know this by faith and acceptance of Jesus Christ as the Savior, and by His teachings. I talked about the two big fears associated with death—fear of the moment of death itself and fear of the pain associated with death. Hopefully, I've helped to explain why we should relinquish these fears.

Yet, I suspect that many of us will still have these fears as death draws near for us. Why would God let that happen, if He loves and cares for us, and provided for our salvation? For that answer, I'd like to turn back to Saint Augustine's *Soliloquies*.

In the *Soliloquies*, Saint Augustine's entire focus is on knowledge of the soul and God, nothing more. He wants to know why, when this knowledge is all that he asks for, the answer is not clear to him. I think the answer can be summed up well in the following passage from *Soliloquies*.[2]

Where are the things we asked and continue to ask of God? We did not ask for riches, for the pleasures of the body, or for popular dignity and honor, but only that He might make known the way for those who search for their souls and Himself. Is it thus, that He abandons us or is abandoned by us?

In other words, I think God does give the answer to these questions. However, we fail to recognize Him and His works for us because we forget about Him as we get wrapped up in the details of everyday life. It's a case of we can't see the forest for the trees.

Keeping *focused* on God and the salvation of our soul through our faith in Jesus is the answer to the challenges we face with the death of the body. We'll use this as the basis of our approach to dealing with various aspects of the dying process in the remainder of this book.

7

"Doc, I've Outlived My Money"

You know what you want. He knows what you need.[1] —*Saint Augustine*

Fred is an affable eighty-nine-year-old gentleman whom I've known for more than ten years now. He comes in and sees me a few times a year. He's a likeable guy—the type whom anyone would want for a grandfather. He's had some heart problems, diabetes, and some muscle and joint aches and pains, but he still gets out and walks and gardens regularly.

He came in and saw me again the other day—just a routine checkup. In contrast to the last few visits, he wasn't having any back pain. It had been gone for a while. In fact, he said he'd been feeling pretty good. Then he added, "But you know what, Doc? I've outlived my money!" He then proceeded to ask me how much longer he was going to live (as if I knew). Of course, my response was, "I'm not God, and *only He* can answer that question." But then I added that he might have a few more years, maybe five, as long as he drove safely and wore his seat belt.

So, clearly, as Fred ages, a major concern for him is dealing with the financial aspects of aging and dying. He's not alone. Most of us are concerned with how to pay for retirement, and if we take that to its logical conclusion—our funeral expenses. Finances can be a major stressor and can affect both our mental as well as our physical health.

Now, I'm not an accountant, a financial planner, or an attorney. I don't pretend to have the best advice for you to earn, invest, and make

45

estate and tax planning to your best advantage. I leave you to seek that advice from those other experts. However, as a physician, I can tell you that financial stress can affect your mental and physical health, but there are coping mechanisms available for maintaining a healthy attitude.

The first step is awareness. What should we be aware of? We need to be aware of how long we expect to live, what our projected living expenses will be, where we'll be living, and what the cost of funeral expenses will be. Do we expect to leave an inheritance or life insurance policy for our children, and if so, how much and how important is that?

Make preparations for handling your financial affairs, which may include putting together a will or a living trust. You should also consider buying life insurance and/or providing for your loved ones.

As part of putting together a will or a trust, you should also appoint a power of attorney and executor to handle your financial affairs. This could be a spouse, a friend, or a family member. You could also appoint a secondary choice in case the primary choice is unavailable. The power of attorney for financial affairs is needed to take care of your affairs if you become mentally incapacitated or physically infirmed to the point of not being able to handle things yourself. The executor of the will or trust handles affairs upon your death. Certainly a person should always seek legal advice in these matters.

In order to plan retirement expenses, you have to have an estimate of how much longer you can expect to live. One fairly good source is to use actuarial tables. For instance, the current average life expectancy for a U.S. citizen is seventy-seven years—a little more than that for the average woman and a little less for men. There are also life expectancy calculators available on the Internet that are probably a little more accurate as they take into account your personal health and lifestyle.

For example, I am currently fifty-one years old, and based on the actuarial table, my average life expectancy would be age seventy-eight. However, based on one of the life expectancy calculators, I have a fairly healthy lifestyle and would be expected to live to age eighty-eight.[2] Since I'm financially conservative, I plan for five to ten years beyond that, which would be about age ninety-five.

In order to plan, you also need to be aware of projected living expenses. You may need a financial planner to help you with this.

Certainly, you would need to know your rent, mortgage, taxes, utility, food, and clothes costs. You need to have an idea of what sort of lifestyle you plan to have—e.g., do you plan to travel, do you have expensive hobbies, or do you plan to have either lavish or modest belongings?

The above living expenses are all fairly predictable. One can get a pretty good estimate of living expenses based on today's dollars. However, don't forget to also consider future costs based on what you believe the rate of inflation will be.

What can be totally unpredictable is how a sudden change in health can affect your living expenses and lifestyle. Heart attacks, strokes, cancer, diabetic complications (e.g., renal failure requiring dialysis), and accidents can suddenly change all the best-laid plans…

Mr. K. is a seventy-six-year-old patient of mine. He is a very bright, engaging world traveler with plenty of stories to tell. Mr. K. did not believe in preventive medical care. He had high blood pressure and high cholesterol, but he did not want to take any medicines unless he absolutely had to. His attitude was if a major catastrophe happened that killed him, then so be it. I certainly think not fearing a major cata-strophe is healthy; however, unfortunately what Mr. K. did not count on was having a major catastrophe that he would survive. In fact, he had a stroke that left him half-paralyzed and required prolonged therapy and long-term care.

Eileen is another patient of mine. She is a delightful eighty-five-year-old lady who looks and feels like sixty-five. I saw Eileen in my office one day for a routine check and noticed her arthritis was causing her gait to be a little off balance. I advised her to get a cane as I was worried she might fall.

"Oh no," she said. "I could never use a cane as it would make me look much too old. Besides, I'm always extremely careful and I've never fallen. *I know not to fall*." Three months later, I saw Eileen in the hospital. She had fallen and broken her hip. She had a complicated post-op course and spent the next six months either in the hospital or in the nursing facility before finally making it home again.

The next time I saw her back in the clinic, she greeted me with a smile. "Look," she said, "I've finally taken your advice and gotten a cane." Unfortunately, I can't tell you how many "Eileens" I've seen since, whom I tell this story to, and they still refuse to use a cane due to pride and denial.

What can we learn from the stories of Mr. K. and Eileen? First, we need to learn to be more realistic. Both Eileen and Mr. K. were previously quite healthy and felt much younger than their actual age. When you feel so young and good, it's easy to fall into denial—thinking that nothing could actually happen to you. Moreover, there's nothing like a major health event (such as stroke, fall, heart attack, or even major surgery) that can change the picture overnight.

Next, Mr. K. and Eileen should remind us of the old adage: *an ounce of prevention is worth a pound of cure.* In Mr. K.'s case, some blood pressure and cholesterol medicine might have kept him traveling the world. In Eileen's case, a cane might have kept her feeling much younger than her actual age of eighty-five. For instance, she was feeling like sixty-five before the fall. A cane might have made her feel like she was seventy or even seventy-five, but that is still better than feeling ninety (which is how she felt after the hip fracture).

An ounce of prevention is worth a pound of cure can also be very true from a financial perspective. Saving and investing wisely prior to retirement can make getting through your retirement years much easier and more enjoyable, especially if you've given yourself enough financial cushions to cover you for potential health and financial setbacks (such as an investment that suffered losses).

Poor health can affect your finances. Both Mr. K. and Eileen would have been better off financially if they had heeded my medical advice. Strokes, fractures, and other *medical disasters* can turn into *financial disasters.* Medical equipment, rehabilitation therapists, caregivers, and assisted living/nursing home facilities can all cost a fortune.

One major area of financial planning and prevention of financial disaster is long-term care insurance. Long-term care insurance covers you in case you become disabled to the point of needing an in-home caretaker or to move into a nursing or assisted living facility. The odds of needing long-term care naturally increase with age. People age sixty-five and older have a 40 percent lifetime risk of needing a nursing facility. For those aged eighty-five and older, the percentage of people who require long-term care goes up to 55 percent. About 10 percent of those who do need a nursing facility will stay there five years or more.[3] So clearly, long-term care insurance can be very valuable. However, the cost of long-term care insurance can be very high; there can be high deductibles, and not everything may be covered. Therefore, long-term care insurance should be considered, but investigate very carefully before buying a policy; it may mean deciding not to buy one.

Certain health problems, such as diabetes, vascular disease, and severe arthritis, will make the need for long-term care insurance more likely. However, insurance companies will also recognize this and raise premiums.

This brings up an area in which something besides earning money and making investments can contribute to your financial security. What is that? Maintaining a healthy lifestyle. Yes, living a healthier lifestyle can potentially help you with your finances. For instance, people who smoke spend a small fortune on their cigarettes. It also increases the risk of medical complications such as stroke, heart attack, lung disease, osteoporosis, and cancer, which may lead to a long-term disability. Quitting smoking saves the cost of cigarettes, as well as the cost of medicines and medical care necessary to treat the resulting complications.

Exercising regularly also decreases the chance of medical complications. I generally recommend to my patients thirty to sixty minutes of aerobic exercise a day, five days a week. This can be a power walk, swimming, biking, tennis, dance, golf (walking the course), or other aerobic activity. This increases cardiovascular circulation, endurance, and muscle tone, and helps keep the weight down. Perhaps most importantly, it decreases the chance of you falling down and breaking a bone that may land you in a nursing home. I think this is not intuitively obvious. I have several patients who wanted to avoid exercise since they thought that when they would exercise, they would be more likely to fall. In reality, when you exercise you tone muscles and strengthen the bones and balance mechanisms, so your chance of falling actually declines. So, if you exercise regularly, the chances of your needing long-term care (and the associated expense) should go down.

Another lifestyle area that can potentially improve your finances is combating obesity—the great American problem. Obesity increases the risk of diabetes, vascular problems, and disabling osteoarthritis. All of these increase your risk for needing long-term care. We've already talked about how exercise burns off calories and helps to control weight. The real key to keeping the weight down and losing weight is taking in fewer calories. This includes calories that you drink as well as food intake. Many patients tell me that they don't eat much, and then we find out they drink juice, milk (whole or skim), sports drinks, beer, wine, liquor—all of which have lots of calories that they don't think about. The majority of calories that we take in for the most part are in carbohydrates—breads, pasta, potatoes, rice, corn, and beans. We tend to overeat these items and really need to cut the portions way back.

Cutting portions also saves money by making two meals out of one. If you go out to a restaurant, certainly look at getting a "to go" box and taking half home for a second meal. The portions given at restaurants typically exceed what we actually need.

A final lifestyle area is mental activities. People who retire and *stay mentally active and engaged* in society are less likely to need long-term care. Mental activities can include puzzles, games, crafts, hobbies, church, and volunteer work. Make it something where you have to think or work through a problem. It is more than just reading a book.

Here are some examples of successful geriatric patients I've seen:

- A ninety-six-year-old lady who did hospital volunteer work
- A one-hundred-year-old lady who still helps manage her apartment complex
- A ninety-year-old gentleman who still goes to Shriners' meetings
- An eighty-year-old couple who do "senior gleaner" charity work (provide food for the poor and homeless)
- A lady who works on her community water board
- Retired ministers who help out at other churches in transition
- Patients doing crossword and Sudoku puzzles while in my waiting room
- An eighty-five-year-old couple who plays cribbage daily
- Retired people taking up foreign languages

- An eighty-year-old lady taking piano lessons
- A ninety-year-old lady who crochets blankets to give away
- An eighty-year-old gentleman who does woodwork
- An eighty-four-year-old in a bridge group
- A disabled gentleman who builds clocks
- A retiree who plots and tracks the stock market
- An eighty-two-year-old lady who belongs to a travel group

All of these people have kept their minds and bodies more active, which keeps them more functional and less likely to need assisted care.

Sometimes, despite the best possible planning, finances become a major issue. Take, for example, Mr. and Mrs. R. He had a history of diabetes, vascular problems, and cancer, while Mrs. R. had been in good health. They purchased long-term care insurance for her, and not him. The thinking was that she was in good health and would outlive her husband. She planned on being his caretaker so he wouldn't need long-term care insurance. However, she developed an aggressive cancer herself. She died and Mr. R. was left in need of long-term care with no coverage.

So, how should we approach the situation of "outliving our money"? The answer is twofold: recognize practical realities and look at our own attitude.

Recognizing practical realities means realizing that we are truly blessed with where we live and the times that we live in. Food is abundant. There are some social safety nets such as social security, Medicare, Medicaid (which is MediCal in California), and government-sponsored low rent housing. There are multiple charities that help people in their time of need. No hospital will turn away a patient due to lack of funds (in fact, that would be against the law). Moreover, no hospital will just wheel a patient out to the side of the curb when it's time for them to be discharged. Rather, the hospital will make efforts to help find the patient a place to live if needed. By one means or another, a poor patient will have basic food and shelter enough to subside, although maybe not to the degree or standard they desire.

In terms of *examining our own attitude*, let's look at some case scenarios. "Once you have a Mercedes, you can't go back to a Civic" were the words of advice from my twenty-nine-year-old son, Chris. He really enjoys cars and knows a lot about them. The week prior, I had just bought Chris's Honda Civic from him as he had upgraded to a Honda Accord. Five days later the Civic was totaled when I was rear-ended on the freeway. Two days later, I took my neighbor up on his offer to sell me his Mercedes for the same price that I had spent on the Civic. I have to admit, the Mercedes is the most comfortable car that I have ever driven. The seats are leather and just perfectly sized for my six-foot-one frame. The steering is easy and the ride is outstanding.

The Honda Civic was nice, but the Mercedes is definitely more luxurious. So Chris's point is that once you get used to higher luxury, it's hard to go back down to a more modest lifestyle.

This is what happens to many people if they "outlive their money." They lament the loss of worldly possessions and a more luxurious lifestyle. They may brood and carry the attitude of "if only this hadn't happened to me." This can lead to depression, isolation, and low self-esteem. The mental attitude becomes negative, which tends to make any physical suffering worse, as well. This scenario can lead to what I call a "negative amplification of symptoms." Let's look at how this plays out:

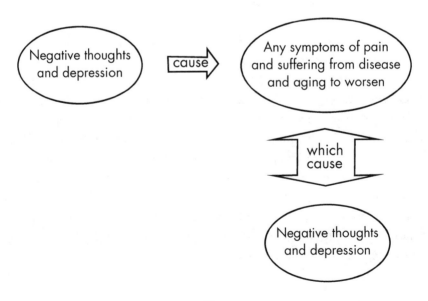

As you can see, the negative thoughts, pain, and suffering will just continue to feed on each other and ramp up. How can we avoid this "negative amplification of symptoms"? We do this by going into the situation with the right attitude. If we already have a negative attitude going in, then we must change our attitude to a positive one. Let's consider some examples of how we can make this happen.

I'll start with a couple of examples from my own life. When we were first married, I was in medical school, and my wife and I were struggling for money. Instead of lamenting the situation, we learned to make an adventure out of it. We would go down to the discount store where they would have big bins of canned foods that had lost their labels and therefore were unmarked. Many of the cans were vegetables, but unfortunately some of the cans were dog food. After some experimentation, we learned how to shake the cans to separate out the dog food from the vegetables before we bought them. It gave us an opportunity to turn a potentially hard time into a fun experience. We had the chance to work together for a common goal—an opportunity that brought us closer together in our young marriage.

More recently, I had another opportunity to change my attitude toward financial affairs. As a medical doctor in the general community, you have to create and build your own retirement funds. For some years, I have been calculating and worrying over my retirement plan. The stock market crash in 2008 changed all that. Basically it put me back to day one, with no signs of being able to retire in sight. My initial reaction was to lament my losses. However, one day somebody reminded me that nobody ever promised I could retire one day. I realized she was right. This was an eye-opener for me. Now, I take the attitude of doing my best to plan financially; and if it works out, then great; but if not, that's okay too. In the big picture, all that matters is knowing that God will ultimately take care of me.

Now let's turn to another example—this time from literature. The Spanish classic *El Cid* is about a Spanish nobleman who was exiled from the kingdom through no fault of his own. He unfortunately got on the wrong side of the king's friends. The exile dispossessed him of his riches and influence in the kingdom. Many people in similar circumstances would have grieved over their losses. However, El Cid looked upon the exile as almost a gift from God. It was an opportunity for him to prove himself. By persevering through difficult times with a positive attitude, El Cid served as a positive witness for God through his own faith in God.[4]

Do not forget to turn to the Bible for help and refuge in troubled times—whether physical, emotional, or financial stresses. Writing this, I'm reminded of the story of Jim, a member of the local church I attend. At our church, there is one Sunday a year that is designated for "stones of remembrance." On that Sunday, various members of the congregation will get up and tell their story or anecdote, accompanied by a stone inscribed with a biblical quote or saying containing a special meaning to them.

Jim had been going through some hard financial times at his business. These were times that he wasn't sure he was going to get through. Instead of just giving up, he turned to the Lord and the Bible for assistance. He used Psalm 46:1–3 for strength in getting through these hard times:

God is our refuge and strength, an ever-present help in trouble. Therefore we will not fear, though the earth give way and the mountains fall into the heart of the sea, though its waters roar and foam and the mountains quake with their surging.

Repeating this psalm reminded him he could get through these hard times by relying on God.

Saint Francis of Assisi also teaches us something about money. Francis grew up as the son of a wealthy merchant in Assisi, Italy, around the year 1200 A.D. Francis began using some of his money (actually his father's money) to help build churches. He found more joy in doing this than in working as a businessman. His father was not happy with his actions.

One day, Francis went to the town square, renounced his father's money, took off all his clothes, and gave them back to his father (not something I would recommend in modern times unless you want to spend the night in jail). At any rate, Francis's joy was in becoming more Christlike and serving the Lord. He went on to found the Franciscan order and became one of the greatest evangelists of all time.[5]

Giving up monetary concerns can be very mentally liberating. I can offer a few examples from my own personal experience.

The year was 2008. I would drive the same route to my office every day. Along the route, I would pass the office of someone who owed me almost $2000. This was not a sum that I needed, but it was enough to irk me that I wasn't getting paid.

Days, weeks, months, and over a year had gone by without the money being repaid. As time went by, I found myself getting just a little angrier each time I passed that section of the road.

One day I was coming up on that section of road, already starting to think about it and becoming angry. I had to turn my head away from the offending office building to try and keep my anger level down.

And there it was hitting me just like a two-finger eye poke from the Three Stooges, and it came so quick I didn't have time to block. It was a giant billboard advertising "Freedom from Religion." *What's this? The atheists are allowed to recruit now? Who let them do that?* (I guess Washington, Jefferson, and our other Founding Fathers did when they created the Bill of Rights, but that's beside the point.) *I was furious!*

The days continued to go by, and I found myself showing up to work so mad that I wanted to hurt the first person I saw. Fortunately, I was able to pull back into my doctor mode and not do that. This could not go on; I had to do something.

So I turned to God. I prayed to God that if He would just fix everything, I would gladly give all that money to the church. The next day we got a call that the check was in the mail. The following week, the atheist billboard was gone, and a Christian billboard had gone up. I want to reiterate that this is a true story.

Some readers might just think that this was an extraordinary coincidence. The rest of you may agree with me that I was rewarded by God. (He heard my prayer.)

And what a reward it was. Yes, I did gladly give up all the money. Talk about mentally liberating. The thought of the unpaid debt was twisting my mind, getting me angry, and raising my blood pressure. Once the situation was resolved, my mind was free. I could show up to work in a good mood. God's show had been well worth the price of admission. Not only did it free my mind, but it served to confirm my faith. And here now, two years later, it's still paying dividends—it gave me a good example to share.

My second example comes directly from this book. As of the writing of this sentence, I had been working on this book for almost two years. I've been busy with work and other things. The task has been slow and sometimes arduous. I've been searching literature and talking to patients for ideas.

At times my mind wanders. I pray that this book will be successful, but fear that it won't be. What keeps me going is the thought that I borrowed from Saint Augustine that if this book helps just one person, then it will have been worth the effort.

At times, I have found myself wondering, *What will I do with the money if this book is successful? I could use it to put my kids through college and maybe help plan for my retirement.* The more I think this way, however, the slower the writing has been.

Once again, I've finally decided to free my mind. I've told God that whatever money comes from the sale of this book will all go to the church to serve His purpose. Now God has a vested interest in this book being successful. I feel good as I surely feel this book will help at least one person. My mind is free from thinking about money. I've given the burden over to God of trying to make this book successful. God can do what He wants with this book. And the ideas are starting to come...

8

Dealing with Physical Pain

Here on earth, we must thirst; in heaven we shall be satisfied.[1]
—*Saint Augustine*

I chose this Saint Augustine quote to begin this chapter because I think it helps us put things into perspective. In dealing with pain, getting the proper perspective is of paramount importance. The proper perspective makes the intolerable, tolerable.

Let me offer a brief example from my own experience. When I was in junior high, my parents took me in to the orthodontist to get braces. I wound up wearing them for the next four years. That was four years of my gums and lips getting sore and periodically cut by the braces. Every month or two, I would have to go in for tightening, which made my teeth ache for the next few days. Although this is a minor medical problem, it was a big deal to me at the time. What made it all tolerable was knowing that one day the braces would come off and that better days were ahead. By looking at the problem with a positive mindset, it made dealing with the braces much more bearable.

Positive Attitude

When we look at pain and discomfort from a negative standpoint, it is much harder to endure. Focusing on the suffering makes us think about it more, which makes us more aware of the pain. When we are more aware of the problem, it becomes more acute; it hurts more. Also, focusing on pain tends to make one depressed. Depression makes pain worse, at which point it all becomes a vicious cycle. The pain increases the depression, and the depression increases the pain and lessens our ability to deal with the pain. This is why it's important to maintain a positive outlook.

I think a great example of dealing with suffering from a positive outlook comes from the 1997 Italian film *La vita è bella*, by Roberto Benigni translated into the English, *Life Is Beautiful*.[2] The movie is about a Jewish man who helps his young son survive a Nazi concentration camp by turning it into a game. Putting a positive spin on a negative event helped him to endure it and increase his son's chance of survival.

Psychologically, how can we overcome a time of suffering? I believe one way is to look at the time aspect of it. We humans measure time in minutes, hours, days, months, and years. God's measuring stick is eternity. So what's a few minutes, hours, days, months, or even years of suffering here on earth compared to an eternity of happiness in heaven with the Lord? Our problems become short and minuscule by comparison. Remember the *concept of time*, to help keep a positive outlook. For instance, any time in pain on earth is short; on the other side of this life, eternity in heaven is a really, really long time.

Another method of keeping a positive attitude is to keep telling yourself that things are not so bad. I'm reminded of a scene from the hilarious movie *Monty Python and the Holy Grail*.[3] In one scene, the king had to fight the black knight in order to pass through the forest. The king didn't want to fight, but the black knight insisted. The sword fight began and the king quickly chopped off the black knight's arm. The black knight claimed it was "just a flesh wound" and continued to fight. The king continued to chop off limbs while the knight maintained that they were just flesh wounds, and he still had the advantage. It was a silly scene but still a prime example of maintaining a positive attitude.

Doctors, nurses, and other medical personnel will often ask patients, "How bad is your pain on a scale of 1 to 10, with 10 being the very worst pain you can imagine?" I've frequently gotten responses of "10" and "11," and even got a "14" when the patient was looking pretty comfortable. I certainly don't deny that my patients had pain, but I think a more positive view would have been beneficial to them.

Let me offer another example from my own personal experience. A few years ago, I was in a propane fire. Basically, the propane tank on the barbeque grill had a leak. While I was squatting next to it in a baseball catcher's position, the tank erupted in a giant flame. The ensuing fire lit me up like a human candle. I had burns to my face, hands, arms, and knees. My hair caught fire, and in the process of putting out the fire on my body, I ruptured a disc in my neck. This caused nerve damage, requiring a subsequent bone graft and surgery to put a plate and screws in my neck. Needless to say, significant pain ensued.

When I arrived in the emergency room, I was asked, "How's the pain on a scale of 1 to 10?" My answer was a solid "8." Caryl, my wife, later mentioned that the pain must have been a "10," so she wondered why I didn't say it was a "10." Well, I called it an "8" because I could always imagine things being worse. For instance, I could have had burns over a more extensive portion of my body or lose an eye or a limb. So, if "10" is the worst pain I could imagine, I would argue that a "10" does not truly exist. Things could always be worse.

I believe that when you tell yourself that things are bad, then that makes them seem worse. However, when you tell yourself that the situation is not as awful as it could be, then that makes it more tolerable.

What would be the worst-case scenario? Clearly, this would be when one is going through an awful ordeal without the knowledge of the existence of God and Jesus Christ, and the comprehension of one's soul. God gives us the ability to know that whatever misery we may currently be suffering will ultimately be healed. Jesus gives us the knowledge, faith, and confidence that one day we will be saved from our current woes. Whatever pain we may have, no matter how bad, will one day seem trivial when we are in the presence of the glory and joy of the Lord.

I've known people who are having an extremely busy or difficult period at their work. They'll often say it's not so bad because they know they have a vacation or even retirement coming up in the future. A bad day at work can be quickly forgotten in the midst of a nice vacation. What we need to do is apply this same psychology to dealing with terminal pain, only on a much grander scale.

In the same way, we can know that whatever pain we have will seem insignificant when we are in the presence of the Lord. The time of pain, no matter how long, is like a fraction of a second when compared to eternal happiness with God. An awful pain cannot be a "10" when we are given the knowledge of the saving grace of Jesus. Without His saving grace, an awful pain could be a "10" or worse.

When dealing with pain, we are much better off trying to shine a positive light on the situation. And what more positive light could we shine other than the saving grace of Jesus? It helps to know and trust that one day all wounds, pain, suffering, and even death will be conquered. This knowledge should help us to maintain a positive outlook no matter what the situation. The problem is that in day-to-day living, we get distracted from focusing on God, so we need to keep reminding ourselves to think about the Lord and keep a positive attitude. We can help ourselves stay focused on God and our faith by going to church, praying, reading the Bible and other religious oriented texts, fellowshiping with other believers, as well as other reminders such as artwork, jewelry, and just enjoying the beauty of nature.

Another example of looking at the benefits of a positive outlook is the placebo effect. The placebo effect is the positive effect of an inert substance on a medical problem. For instance, if you inject someone with normal saline (i.e., salt water) that should have no effect and tell them it's a powerful pain medicine, then many (about 30 percent of people) will get some relief of symptoms. Conversely, there also exists a nocebo effect. The nocebo effect is the opposite of the placebo effect. With the nocebo effect, if you tell a patient that what you give them is bad for them, they will often experience negative or worsening symptoms.

Anecdotally, I've noticed that patients who read all about the potential harmful side effects of a medicine will be more likely to have problems with the medicine than those who just take the medicine and trust it to work. Interestingly, if you look up the side effects of placebo, the same side effects are listed, often in the same frequency as the real medicine. It appears that the nocebo effect is at work here; in other words, those patients who dwell on negative side effects have more problems tolerating the medicine, which keeps them from benefiting from the medicine.

Now that we've talked a little about the philosophy of maintaining a positive attitude toward dealing with pain, let's get down to some nuts and bolts of the action to take.

Make a Plan

First, have a plan. The best plan will be multidisciplinary. In other words, you attack the problem on a variety of different fronts, both mentally and physically.

Let's take an analogy from the world of sports. A good football coach will start formulating a game plan well in advance of game time. There will be a plan of what to do offensively, defensively, and even on special teams. The attitude will be positive to pep up the team. The proper equipment will be ready to go. Players will be well hydrated and fed. Also, they need to keep their mind focused on the ultimate goal. Is the ultimate goal to win by thirty points at all costs, even if it risks your best players getting hurt? Or is it good enough to just barely win or even tie as long as it gets you into the playoffs without injuries?

Likewise, when dealing with pain you need to have a game plan. First and foremost, always remember to maintain a positive attitude. Be your own cheerleader. Constantly remind yourself several times a day to stay positive. Try to post a positive reminder, something to try to pick yourself up with when you find yourself slipping into the negative. Take comfort and pride in what may seem like even the smallest of victories.

Second, set your goals and stay focused on them. Is your goal to be pain-free or is it to just keep the pain level down enough to be relatively comfortable and maintain some quality of life? In other words, is the pain level low enough to let you enjoy some books, movies, games, hobbies, and visits from friends and loved ones? Oftentimes, being pain-free is not a realistic goal; however, keeping the pain level down is a reasonable goal. For instance, being pain-free may well require such a high dose of pain medication as to keep you sedated or basically sleeping twenty-four hours a day.

Have a Good Support System

Third, develop and maintain a "fan base" and use them. Having a good support system is huge. If you don't already have a support system in place, then there's no time like the present to start building one! This can be family, friends, social groups (such as Elks, Kiwanis, Rotary Club, alumni organizations, or Veterans), a hired caregiver, or hospice. Other areas to look include senior centers and illness support groups (such as the cancer society, Alzheimer's, and Parkinson support groups; AA; etc.). Almost all churches will have members willing to pitch in and support in some way. If not, it may be time to look for a new church. Having a personal history of stepping in and helping others in their time of need will usually mean others will be available to step in and reciprocate when you're in need.

A good pet, such as a dog or cat, can be a nice addition to your support system. Studies have shown that people with pets tend to do better than those without. A good pet will give you a companion, unconditional love, and a source of distraction from your pain.

A good support system can help in many ways. They can give you emotional support to help you maintain a positive outlook. They can also provide an outlet to help you vent frustration. More direct practical examples include some chore work, running errands, cooking meals, and providing transportation for you when necessary. A good support system will also distract you from the pain. Any opportunity to distract yourself from the pain is an opportunity that should be relished. Pain tends to be worse at night. During the day you have more mental and physical stimulation that distracts you and lessens pain. If you are a support person, encourage conversation, games, puzzles, books, movies, hobbies, music—anything that will distract from the pain. It's okay to talk some about the pain, and let the patient vent about it. However, most of the conversation should be distracting the patient from it.

Use Prayer and Meditation

Fourth, remember that God gave you a mind to think, so take advantage of that fact. Use your thoughts to distract yourself from the pain. This can be done through *prayer and meditation*. I'd suggest praying at least every morning and evening. Start your day with a prayer. This will provide strength to make it through the day. It also starts the day off on a positive, optimistic note.

It's especially important to pray at the end of the day. Remember, pain tends to be worse in the evening and at night when you're more tired and there are fewer distractions. Use prayer at this time to receive assistance in making it through what may be a painful night. Use the prayer to give yourself comfort and renewed self-confidence. Concentrate on God, not your pain.

When you pray, give thanks, praise, and glory to God. If you are having a particularly bad day mentally and physically, then feel free to complain to God. Tell Him your woes. He can take it. Ask Jesus for help in lessening your pain. Keep in mind that Jesus is your Friend and that you have no greater friend. Don't forget that Jesus knows and understands pain. You can have no pain greater than what Jesus went through with His beating, torture, and crucifixion. So ask your Friend for help with the pain. He's been there, done that, and has the power to heal. Keep the faith; prayers do get answered.

I have a patient, Maryanne, who uses prayer to diminish her pain. She always tries to remember that the cross looks like a plus (+) sign to remind herself to keep a positive attitude.

When you pray, remember to recite the Lord's Prayer (see Matthew 6:9–13). Jesus gave us that prayer to use, so it's good to use it. I'd also suggest turning to the Psalms for assistance in giving praise and seeking comfort. Repeat your prayers. Repetition helps to reinforce your thoughts and focus more on God. The value of repetitive prayer can be seen in early Christianity. Early Christian monks who went out into the deserts of Egypt would "pray the entire 150 psalms each day."[4] The prayer rope, and later rosaries, were developed to help keep track of prayers. These early Christians were following Paul's teaching in 1 Thessalonians 5:16–17 to "be joyful always; pray continually." Repetitive prayer helped these early Christians stay focused on God. Certainly, staying focused on God was key to persevering through the incredible brutality of persecution that they experienced. I doubt many of us could stay as strong if we were similarly persecuted. We should learn from this and use repetitive prayer to stay strong, despite whatever pain you're going through.

Let others pray on your behalf and for you. This is called intercessory prayer. It requires you to inform them of your situation, your pain or discomfort. It can be family and friends. Hopefully, your church will have a group that prays for those in need. Jesus interceded for us. Let others intercede for you too. In this way you are not alone. It gives you a "fan base." In sports parlance, you get the home field advantage. When others are rooting for you, you do better. First Timothy 2:1 states: "I urge, then, first of all, that requests, prayers, intercession, and thanksgiving be made for everyone." Prayer works. Take full advantage of that fact. Before you use any other pain management tool, technique, or medicine, I suggest you say a little prayer to God asking for the method to provide relief and gratefully thank God once you receive some relief.

The next subject I'd like to touch on is *meditation*. Prayer is a form of meditation, where you focus on God. But with meditation, you can also use the power of your thoughts to focus on other things that distract you from the pain and subsequently bring the pain level down.

God created you with a powerful mind that can use thoughts that have some control over your body. Let's look at some examples. If you are ever hooked up to an automatic heart rate monitor or blood pressure monitor, then you can see this in action for yourself. While watching the monitor, concentrate on relaxing and bringing your heart rate or your blood pressure down. You should be able to see the numbers come down, giving you some positive biofeedback that you are moving things in the right direction. Through the numbers, you can actually see yourself relax. The more you can relax, the better off your pain level will be. Another way of doing this is to concentrate on listening to relaxing music such as classical, Gregorian chant, soft jazz, nature sounds, etc. The emphasis here is *really* concentrating on it to the point of trying to anticipate the next musical note.

You can actually meditate on anything to distract your mind from the pain or to actually bring down the level of pain. I've used this technique to my own personal advantage. I mentioned earlier in this chapter that when I was in the propane fire, I knocked a disc in my neck out of place, which caused subsequent nerve damage. The pain from the burn wounds was subsiding. However, my left arm was continuing to have significant pain, and the arm was becoming progressively weak to the point of not being able to open a shampoo bottle or to get out of the bathtub since I could not use the hand to grip or the arm to push off.

An MRI of my neck was eventually ordered. For the MRI, I had to lie still for twenty-plus minutes while they took the pictures. I had not taken any pain medicine prior to the MRI. Unfortunately for me, the position they had my neck in for the MRI really exacerbated the pinched nerve. It felt like an eight-hundred-pound gorilla was squeezing my arm as hard as it could. The pain was excruciating! The really hard part was that I knew I needed to stay still in order for the doctor to get useful pictures.

Now anyone who has had an MRI knows the machine is very noisy with loud clanking. I used this to my advantage by concentrating on the clanks, counting the number of clanks, and monitoring their rhythm. This distracted my mind from the pain enough that I was able to get through the procedure without moving, and the MRI pictures came out successfully.

I have a patient, Dudley P., who uses his mind to control pain. Dudley is well into his eighties and has had a variety of life experiences that included pain. Let me give you the steps of his method:

1. Close your eyes.
2. Take a deep breath and relax.
3. Concentrate on the pain.
4. Tell the pain to go away.
5. Continue steps 2 through 4 until the pain eases.

Dudley frequently uses this method to control arthritis pain. On one occasion, he had a severe burn on his arm from car radiator steam and was successful at bringing that pain level down. In fact, he actually had a police officer see the wounds and rush him to the hospital. He told the officer to slow down as he was able to control the pain and was more worried about the officer's high-speed driving skills. The only pain Dudley has been unsuccessful at relieving with his mind technique is dental pain.

Another example of successfully seeking help for pain relief is Saint Francis of Assisi. Saint Francis saw the whole world, along with himself, as God's creation. He used this thought when he was getting treatment for an eye problem. The treatment in those days was to touch a burning hot iron to the side of the face (and you thought *your* doctor lacked bedside manners!). Anyhow, Saint Francis asked "brother fire" to be gentle to him. He managed to get through the treatment without screaming out in pain and horror.[5] Accepting the situation, rather than fighting the situation, lessened the pain.

Aristotle and Hippocrates used a form of meditation to help their patients. They would have their patients think pleasant thoughts, such as pleasant sights, sounds, tastes, or other experiences to alleviate their pain.[6]

Keep practicing prayer and meditation and your skill at bring down pain, and anxiety levels will only improve.

Alternative Medicine

Now that we've talked about working on the mind to relieve pain, let's talk about treating the body. Although I practice traditional Western medicine, I am not averse to patients trying alternative medicine. In fact, I believe it's often a good idea to try other modalities, as long as they are safe and don't keep you from continuing to seek and receive traditional care, and it doesn't conflict with traditional care.

Chiropractic or osteopathic manipulations can be quite helpful if the pain is coming from the musculoskeletal system—i.e., from joints, muscles, tendons, and ligaments. I do not recommend neck manipulations, due to safety issues. In addition, spinal manipulation, when there is cancer involved in that area, can be dangerous. Also, if the pain is associated with fever, swelling, or neurologic deficit (such as weakness, numbness, or bowel or bladder dysfunction), then you should see your doctor immediately. In general, though, chiropractic care is safe and often worth a try.

Acupuncture and acupressure can also be a useful technique to try. Safety concerns and cost again would be the only reason not to try acupuncture. The safety concern is to make sure the equipment being used is sterile (new). Also, acupuncture should not be done in immune-compromised patients, for fear of introducing a source of infection. These would be patients with diminished immune capacity, such as those with low white blood counts, AIDS patients, transplant patients, and those receiving chemotherapy.

Massage therapy is usually of assistance. I believe it helps in several ways:

1. It helps to stretch and relax tight, sore, and aching muscles.
2. The sensory impact of touch distracts from whatever pain the patient is experiencing.
3. It brings down general anxiety levels.
4. The human touch is comforting; it reassures you that you are not alone.

The massage does not necessarily need to be the area that is hurting. For instance, a back massage may help with a headache.

Massage may also help the family and friends of a dying patient. How might this play out? Sometimes with a dying patient you may be at a loss for words. This can be seen in the book of Job who was stricken with illness and his friends came out to give comfort. They were at a loss for words and maintained a quiet vigil for one week. Massage at a time like this could provide human touch to show you care. There may be times when you don't know what else to offer. Certainly a massage could help the patient feel a little better. At the same time, it would give the friends, family, and caregivers some satisfaction in knowing they did something to help.

Anybody who has had a massage should have some sense of how to give a massage. Basically, if the stroke or light touch felt good to you, then it will probably also feel good to the patient, unless there's a specific contraindication (for instance, you would not massage someone where they have a skin infection, burn, ulcer, etc.).

Stretching, strengthening, and aerobic exercise is usually an important adjunct to any plan. This can be done either informally on your own or through a formal supervised program with a physical therapist or personal trainer. Aerobic exercise can cause endorphin release, which is your body's own natural pain reliever. Exercise also increases circulation, helps digestion, facilitates relaxation, and distracts from the pain. Obviously, an ill patient may be quite limited in terms of exercise ability. Be creative. There is usually something that can be done, such as light calisthenics or even just gripping a squeeze ball.

I highly encourage patients to try most, if not all, of the above non-medicinal techniques to help with pain control. Continue them even if they only help to relieve pain by 5 to 10 percent. Even a little help should be viewed as a positive thing.

I've purposely left a discussion of medications to the end of this chapter. This is because much too often I have seen patients want to just talk about and rely on medications and ignore all the above mentioned modalities to assist with pain management. *Medication doses will need to be higher, and side effects will be increased when the medications are overemphasized and other techniques ignored.*

Medications

The remainder of this chapter is a somewhat dry discussion of potential medications that can be used to achieve pain control. Notice that there are several categories of pain medications, and generally, many drugs in each category that can be used. Even if one drug in a category has been tried and failed, there may be another drug in the same category that may work great.

Keep in mind that your ancestors had to go through the same painful experiences without the help of any medications, except for maybe getting drunk on bad whiskey or wine. I suspect they were grateful for any help they got, even if it was just a cool compress. In contrast, modern technology has often raised our expectations so high that we are displeased if we do not get complete relief of symptoms. **The greatest potential for physical and mental happiness will be reaped if we can put ourselves in our ancestors' shoes in terms of expectations, while still taking full advantage of modern medicine.**

There are several different classes of medications that your doctor may want to use to achieve pain control. Opioids (narcotics) are the mainstay of treatment for terminal pain. However, other medicines will likely be recommended in addition to opioids. There are advantages to using more than one medicine for pain control. Using additional medications will likely decrease the dose of opioid needed and enable pain relief with fewer side effects. Going up on medication dose will often increase side effects more than the medicinal benefit. For this reason, opioids are often combined with other analgesics such as acetaminophen (Tylenol) or nonsteroidal anti-inflammatories, which include aspirin and ibuprofen. Other classes of medicine used for pain include various types of antidepressants, antiepileptic (i.e., anti-seizure) medications, muscle relaxers, benzodiazepines, and steroids. I'll talk a little bit about each of these in turn, in our discussion of pain treatment.

Acetaminophen is generally a very safe medicine, with minimal side effects. The maximum total dose is 4 grams in a twenty-four-hour period, but I often tell patients to keep it around 3 grams per day. It should be avoided as much as possible in a patient with cirrhosis (i.e., liver disease) and monitored in patients taking the blood thinner warfarin (Coumadin). Keep in mind that acetaminophen is often already contained in a combination pill with narcotics, so that needs to be included in calculating the total daily dose.

Nonsteroidal anti-inflammatory drugs (NSAIDs) are a class of medications over twenty in number, of which aspirin and ibuprofen are probably the most well known. They can be used in conjunction with acetaminophen to allow a lower dose of narcotic to be used. The major concern with using NSAIDs is potential to cause gastrointestinal bleeding, such as a stomach ulcer. Stomach acid blockers might be given to try to prevent this complication. Signs of bleeding to watch for besides seeing obvious blood includes: throwing up coffee ground–like material, or having black, tarry bowel movements. If that happens, the medicine should be stopped and your doctor contacted immediately.

Antidepressant medications are often an important adjunct in attaining pain control. Patients with chronic pain are frequently depressed, but antidepressants commonly help patients who are also not clearly depressed. There are many different antidepressant medications that work through various mechanisms. The antidepressants are not addictive medications, so they can be stopped if there is a problem with adverse side effects, or if they are found to not be working. They can take a while, often weeks, to work. They all have potential side effects, but often the side effect can be used to help with other problems, such as insomnia or loss of appetite. Sometimes many different antidepressants have to be tried before finding the right one that works for you. Overall, antidepressants are frequently beneficial, and I encourage you to keep an open mind to using them.

Anticonvulsant medications were developed to help treat patients with seizures. However, they are also used to treat patients with pain that is difficult to treat, such as neuropathic (nerve) pain. These medications are also non-addictive. They are generally well tolerated if started at a low dose and titrated up (i.e., the dose is gradually increased). Examples include Neurontin, Lyrica, Dilantin, and Tegretol. These medications are generally good in terms of lack of interaction with other medications.

Muscle relaxers, such as baclofen, can be useful, if at least part of the pain is from muscle spasm. For this reason, they are probably most used after an injury or a nerve-damaging process that triggers a muscle spasm. In these cases, they can be a good adjunct for pain control.

Benzodiazepines are a class of antianxiety medication that include Ativan, Valium, and Xanax. They work well for anxiety, insomnia, and can also help with muscle spasms and nausea. They may help alleviate pain symptoms by decreasing anxiety and aiding sleep. These medications are generally well tolerated in terms of lack of side effects and drug interactions, but they are addictive. In addition, your body can build up tolerance so that you need a higher dose to achieve the same effect each subsequent time. However, keep in mind that addiction is usually not an issue in terminal patients.

Topical medications that are applied to the skin are usually free of side effects and can reduce the pain. A lidoderm patch put on the skin provides topical anesthesia that keeps you from feeling the pain. Capsaicin cream, derived from chili peppers, can provide relief. Topical anti-inflammatories, including Aspercreme and Voltaren gel, can also reduce the pain. As long as you are not putting it on open wounds, feel free to try any of the over-the-counter balms that are available. Cold compresses are good for acute injuries. I advise using just cold for the first forty-eight hours after an injury, and after that, heat or ice is okay. Warm compresses are good for more chronically sore joints and muscles.

Corticosteroids, such as prednisone, can be given orally to help pain associated with inflammation or nerve entrapment. Steroids also help with cancer, bone pain, spinal cord compression, or increased intracranial pressure, such as seen with a brain tumor. They are also frequently injected into the sore joint, tendon, or pinched nerve. Side effects of steroids include weight gain, insomnia, mood swings, and elevated blood sugar. Atrophy, or thinning of the tissue, can occur at the site of injections. In general, patients feel much better when steroids are used, and steroid use is only limited due to potential side effects.

Opioids (i.e., narcotics) are the mainstay of treatment for moderate to severe pain in terminal patients. The opioid class includes: morphine, codeine, hydrocodone, oxycodone, hydromorphone, fentanyl, and methadone. Methadone is frequently thought of as just a drug to help heroin abusers with withdrawal symptoms. However, it is actually a good pain reliever and should be thought of as such.

Narcotics can be made into both a short-acting formulation, as well as into a longer-acting form. For severe pain, patients should expect to get both a long-acting narcotic to keep the overall pain level down, as well as a shorter-acting narcotic to use for flare-ups. Frequently, patients want to minimize medications, so they don't take the long-acting narcotic on a regular basis. This is a mistake because it's easier to control pain if you keep a constant level of pain control going, rather than wait until the pain is very severe and then try to get it back under control.

Opioids do cause side effects and should be expected and dealt with if they arise. Constipation, nausea, itching, and sedation are all very common. This is the main reason to consider using all the other pain relief techniques and medicines previously mentioned, so as to reduce the needed dose of narcotic. Fluids, fiber in the diet, exercise, stool softeners, and laxatives may all need to be used to control constipation. Additional medications may be needed to help control nausea. Many patients report having an allergy to a narcotic that they have been given in the past. Fortunately, this is typically not a true allergy, but rather a side effect that can be avoided by switching to a different narcotic.

Narcotics are given at a low dose to start and gradually increased as needed until adequate pain control is achieved. If the medication does not seem to be working, then it just may be a matter of needing a higher dose. Narcotic doses can be increased to very high levels in order to keep the terminal patient comfortable.

Medication delivery systems are an important consideration in obtaining pain control. Basically, this refers to how you get the medication into your body. Many of the above medications are available not only in pill form but also as liquids for patients who have trouble swallowing or absorbing pills. Some medications can be dissolved and absorbed just in the mouth. There are also rectal suppositories. Patches and creams can be applied to the skin. Medications can be injected into the muscle or intravenously (IV). Some patients have had pain pumps and also injections around the spinal column.

The bottom line is that an amazing array of medications from different classes can be given in different combinations, in different doses, and via multiple delivery systems. Given this armamentarium, adequate pain control is typically achieved, and fears of intractable pain should be allayed. **We should feel truly blessed, not just because people have developed this technology, but because God has given us the brains and enlightenment to come up with these accomplishments.**

When facing pain, always remember to keep a positive *attitude, focus* on the Lord, and try to put things into the proper *perspective.* Keep these concepts in mind as you work through the following steps:

1. Develop a game plan. Be flexible and adjust as the situation changes. Stay positive and downplay the negative.

2. Create realistic goals.

3. Have a support system, which can include family, friends, care-givers, and pets, as well as activities that distract you from the pain.

4. Use your mind to lessen the pain through techniques such as prayer and meditation.

5. Use physical techniques such as exercise, stretching, massage, acupuncture, manipulation, icing, heating, and medical equipment.

6. Consult your doctor for use of medications.

7. Repeat the above steps.

Find a perspective that gives you something to be thankful for. With modern technology, you are far better off than your ancestors; and by the grace of God, it may seem like you're losing the battle, but **you will win the war.**

9

Time Is on Your Side

There is a time for everything, and a season for every activity under heaven. —Ecclesiastes 3:1

Time can be our worst enemy or our greatest ally—it all depends on your point of view. It's your choice. I have seen many people have a negative attitude, in which case, time works against them. I would certainly say that a majority of people do not take advantage of the time that God gives us. Time is a tool that can be used to make life easier. However, if time is used incorrectly, it will make life harder.

You can think of using time just as one uses a shovel to plant a tree. If the shovel is used correctly, then it's much easier to successfully plant the tree. The shovel helps you scoop dirt out of the hole and then is used to back-fill in and around the tree after the tree is set into the ground.

Now let's suppose someone came along to plant a tree and did not know how to properly use a shovel. Imagine that they had the shovel turned upside down and were trying to dig down in the dirt with the handle. They would quickly get frustrated with how hard the job had become. Similar to the shovel, the concept of time can be used to your advantage or as a source of frustration. I'd like to first explore some examples of how the concept of time can create frustration, depression, and despair.

Time Used Negatively

Beatrice is a sixty-year-old lady who has just retired. She has worked hard her whole life with the goal of enjoying retirement. She has earned a nice government pension that will certainly keep her comfortable in the years to come. She considers herself an outdoors person and enjoys biking, gardening, and playing tennis. She tells me that she is just not the type of person who can sit around.

Unfortunately for Beatrice, she has suffered from systemic lupus erythematosus, which is a life-shortening form of crippling arthritis. She has become limited in what she can do. She has had a series of falls and has developed balance problems. She really needs to start using a cane, but she refuses and states she doesn't want to give in to it as she believes a cane will just lead to a walker and then a wheelchair. She states she will be careful and knows not to fall, as she is fearful of breaking a hip and winding up in a nursing home.

I hear this a lot, but I'm not sure how it helps anyone to know not to fall. The only people I know who set out to fall are clowns, divers, and professional wrestlers. The rest of us only fall by accident. We know not to fall, but it happens to us anyhow. (Tip: If your doctor advises a cane, then get a cane and use it!)

Anyhow, Beatrice has become bitter about spending so many years working hard and now being cheated out of the retirement she had looked forward to for so long. She spends many of her days researching lupus. She has become angry at her rheumatologist for letting this happen to her (even though he provided good standard-of-care medicine). She wants to be referred to an out-of-the-area medical group where "they may know something."

Beatrice has used time to reinforce her negative thoughts. She looks upon her pre-retirement years as a long time wasted in not doing all the things she enjoys. She looks upon her post-retirement years as too short a period for enjoyment, due to her medical condition. She feels cheated and has become bitter and angry at the world. So how can she completely turn her attitude and emotional state of well-being around? Let's consider another case.

Nicolai is a sixty-eight-year-old gentleman with severe vascular disease due to years of diabetes, high cholesterol, and smoking. Last year he had to have an above-the-knee leg amputation due to an infection and poor circulation. He has been left with chronic (phantom) limb pain from the amputation and consequently requires multiple pain medications to try and control the symptoms. He feels victimized. He laments his condition and complains of how long he has had to suffer, and that the pain will never go away.

In a nutshell, Nicolai is miserable. His thoughts on time—how long he has suffered and feeling like it is never ending—have contributed to his misery. He has used his concept of time (a long period of suffering) to his disadvantage, and it makes him feel worse. The worse the pain is, the more negative his thoughts become; and he continues to spiral downward.

Next, let us meet John and Laura. Their daughter, Angie, has been their pride and joy. Angie has just turned twenty. She is bright, beautiful, and is attending a prestigious university on a softball scholarship. Everything seemed to be going just right for them. One day, John and Laura got a phone call from Angie's roommate saying that Angie had just had a seizure and they should meet her at the hospital.

The tests came back revealing malignant melanoma, an aggressive form of skin cancer. By the time they found it, the cancer had already spread to the brain, liver, and bone. It was beyond curable. The doctors recommended hospice as they felt Angie had less than six months to live.

Naturally, John and Laura were devastated. When Angie died two months later, John in particular became angry at the world and angry at God. To John, this made no sense. John reasoned: for this to occur, there could be no plan to life, and there could be no God. If there was a God, He never would have let this happen. John saw life as an eternity without Angie. He turned away from God. Looking at an eternity without Angie and no God, John became bitter and cynical.

Angie had been the glue that held John and Laura together. Needless to say, they drifted apart. A negative outlook and attitude toward life's circumstances was the culprit.

The outcomes in these three scenarios could have been turned for the better. In all three cases, the dimension of time was looked at as a negative factor. What we forget is that time can be looked at in a positive light.

I think the factor that tends to constrain us is how we are taught to think of time—in terms of hours, days, months, and years. God does not have such a constraining measuring stick—He has eternity. Eternity gives us limitless possibilities for a positive outcome. If we can focus on God, Jesus, and eternity, we can't go wrong. After all, faith in Jesus Christ gives us the promise of eternity with the Lord—and that is heaven, eternal bliss.

The Positive Side

So now let's revisit Beatrice with a positive spin on time. As you recall, Beatrice was bitter for having worked over thirty years and not getting to enjoy a healthy retirement on her terms. She views her pre-retirement years as being too long, and her healthy post-retirement years as being too short. She forgets the key concept that needs to be remembered—that the ultimate reward is an *eternity* in heaven, thanks to the saving grace of Jesus Christ.

Beatrice's job was as a public servant with the government. Whether she had worked one year, five years, or fifty years, it still would have been a short time to serve others, given the reward on the other side. Remember your math. Divide years worked, whether it be one year or fifty years, by an eternity in heaven, and you realize the amount of work you do is infinitesimally small compared to your reward. The payback is the same either way—*huge!* She would have worked these years cheerfully had she taken this into account. Moreover, she would have been rewarded with happiness rather than bitterness if she had taken the positive road that Jesus opens up for us. **A positive attitude is key to a positive outcome**.

Beatrice looks upon her healthy retirement years as being too short. She feels cheated, robbed, and has become angry and bitter. The answer is to appreciate whatever time she has been given as a gift from God. *It's a gift, not an entitlement.* Furthermore, she needs to remember that God wants us to try to make the most of whatever we are given. This is illustrated by the parable of the talents found in Matthew 25:14–30:

Again, it will be like a man on a journey, who called his servants and entrusted his property to them. To one he gave five talents of money, to another two talents, and to another one talent, each according to his ability. Then he went on his journey. The man who had received the five talents went at once and put his money to work and gained five more. So also, the one with the two talents gained two more. But the man who received one talent went off, dug a hole in the ground and hid his master's money.

After a long time, the master of those servants returned and settled accounts with them. The man who received the five talents brought the other five. "Master," he said, "you entrusted me with five talents. See, I have gained five more."

His master replied, "Well done, good and faithful servant! You have been faithful with a few things. I will put you in charge of many things. Come and share your master's happiness!"

The man with the two talents also came. "Master," he said, "you entrusted me with two talents; see, I have gained two more."

His master replied, "Well done, good and faithful servant! You have been faithful with a few things; I will put you in charge of many things. Come and share your master's happiness!"

Then the man who had received the one talent came. "Master," he said, "I knew that you are a hard man, harvesting where you have not sown and gathering where you have not scattered seed. So I was afraid and went out and hid your talent in the ground. See, here is what belongs to you."

His master replied, "You wicked, lazy servant! So you know that I harvest where I have not sown and gather where I have not gathered seed? Well then you should have put my money on deposit with the bankers, so that when I returned I would have received it back with interest.

"Take the talent from him and give it to the one who has ten talents. For everyone who has will be given more, and he will have an abundance. Whoever does not have, even what he has will be taken from him. And

throw that worthless servant outside, into the darkness, where there will be weeping and gnashing of teeth."

Not all of us are given the same gifts. However we should try to make the most of whatever gifts we are given. This is what God wants us to do, and we will be rewarded for our actions.

We should not be angry or jealous that others are given "better" gifts than we are. In Beatrice's case, I believe she was angry and felt cheated that some people get years of healthy retirement, whereas she did not. She needs to remember that she has been given some quality retirement years, and she should cheerfully make the most of them. She needs to understand the difference between her *gift* and her *reward*. Her reward, which is hers for the choosing, is an eternity of heavenly bliss through the saving grace of Jesus Christ. Her opportunity for that reward is the same as everyone else's. The reward is so much *greater* than whatever gift we get, the gift just doesn't matter since the reward makes the gift's value insignificant by comparison.

Like Beatrice, Nicolai needs to reevaluate his approach to time, to make it work to his advantage, rather than worsening his situation. As you recall, Nicolai is our gentleman with chronic pain from a leg amputation. He complains of how long he has suffered, which just adds to his symptoms.

Nicolai needs to remember that whatever time he is suffering here on earth is nothing compared to the eternity in heaven that awaits him. This positive approach gives some comfort, which will help alleviate his symptoms and shorten his perceived time of suffering, and thus not make it seem so bad.

I think an analogy here will help to illustrate this. Last year, our family made a fourteen-hour drive to the Grand Canyon. It was a long journey, and the kids would not let me forget that fact. They were anxious to get there, and I kept hearing the following types of comments:

- "When are we ever going to get there?"
- "Are we lost?"
- "This is taking a long time."

- "Shouldn't we have been there by now?"
- "We must be lost."
- "Isn't there a quicker route?"
- "Are you sure we're not lost?"
- "Maybe you should stop and ask for directions." (Like all men, this was not something I was about to give in to!)

Well, thank God we finally did make it to the Grand Canyon, but the drive seemed like it would never end. Then, a mini-miracle happened on the drive home. The anxiousness and anticipation of reaching the end was not there. The "long time" comments were gone. We traveled the same roads at the same speed on the way home, yet the perceived trip was much shorter. The return drive wasn't so bad. The change in attitude mentally shortened the trip.

In the same way, Nicolai needs to remind himself that his pain and suffering is but a short time compared to eternity, and he will perceive it as not being so bad. This will lessen depression, which in turn can ease his actual pain.

In our final scenario, John is devastated over the loss of his daughter, Angie. John sees life as unfair because Angie is gone forever. Instead, John needs to remind himself that through faith in Jesus Christ, he will eventually spend eternity with her in heaven. Looking at the length of time that Angie is gone as temporary rather than permanent completely changes the picture. Though he will still be sad at the loss, it is no longer the devastating blow that drove him away from God.

My own personal approach to my time here on earth has helped me tremendously with my mental attitude and thoughts. Yes, I have been diagnosed with NHL, a terminal cancer, given the current limits of modern technology. However, I feel that I have been blessed with the length of time God has given me. NHL is a slow-growing cancer, so odds are that I have years yet to live. Hopefully, I can use that time to finish writing this book (and I may need every day I can get at the slow rate that I am going!).

Yes, I have been given lots of time. At age fifty-one, I have already outlived a majority of all the people who have ever lived. Up until recent times, life expectancy was much shorter. The NHL diagnosis has also spurred me on to make the most of the time I have, so it has been a blessing in disguise. For instance, I've learned to not let little things bother me. I also have more gratitude for all the little blessings in my life.

As with Beatrice, I think my years of healthy retirement will likely be significantly shortened. In fact, I possibly may not see retirement at all due to my NHL diagnosis and the poor performance of my savings plan in the stock market. I remember back to when somebody said that "no one ever promised you that you would be able to retire one day." This is quite true. People have talked to me about retirement, but no one ever promised it to me.

Fortunately, I have received a much better promise—years of eternal bliss due to the saving grace of faith in Jesus Christ. Eternal bliss is my reward for my acceptance of Jesus Christ. Keep in mind that the reward of heaven is available to all and promised to those who accept Christ.

The gift from God of years of healthy retirement is just that—a gift. It is not promised. Some people may receive years of a happy retirement while others do not. Maybe some people receive years of good retirement who did not deserve it (for instance, maybe they inherited their money, got lucky on the lottery, or even stole to afford retirement). Others may be deprived of retirement due to disease or accidental death. There is no need for jealousy because if your gift is small or even nonexistent, you will still receive your heavenly reward. Keep in mind that disease itself can be a gift in that it can give time to prepare, and the grace to appreciate even more what you have here and now.

Enjoy your retirement gift, if you have it, but never, ever lose focus on your reward. The reward is so much greater that it really makes the gift seem inconsequential.

I think this can be illustrated via the following analogy. Suppose that there are two kings, each of whom is rewarded with infinitely wealthy kingdoms. Now suppose that the first king gets an added gift of $100. Which king is richer? Since both kings have an infinite amount of wealth, they are equally well off. Do the math:

Infinity dollars + $100 = infinity dollars

In the ultimate analysis, the king who gets a little bonus gift is really no better off than the one who received no added bonus. So no better off means there is no reason for jealousy.

In the same way, God can't give me any more time than He already has. I have already been promised an eternity of heavenly rewards, which is an eternal retirement in heaven. How can God give me any more time than He already has (i.e., eternity)? Whatever time He wants me to serve on earth, I should make the most of it, whether it can be measured in days, years, or decades.

When I look at time in terms of my lifespan, I have peace of mind. I do not fret over potential lost days or years. God has already given me more time than I am ever capable of imagining.

This line of reasoning keeps me from depression and despair. It lets me enjoy my days in happiness without worry. In fact, more days than not, I forget that I even have a terminal diagnosis. I think that is because terminal means limited to time as we know it here on earth. Through Jesus Christ, God has already released me from the "terminal" part of my diagnosis. Yes, my mind has been freed from having a "terminal cancer." Time is on my side. And the best part is—it's all true.

10

Memory: The Chapter That I Nearly Forgot

Memory is necessary for all the operations of reason.[1] —*Pascal*

Like our perception of time, memory is a tool that our mind can and should use to enhance our quality of life and ability to keep a positive outlook on death and the dying process. But also like the perception of time, we all too often use our memory to add to our misery and suffering without even realizing what we are doing. Let's look at how that might be the case.

We use our memory when we examine our lives. Old friends will often get together and remember prior events in their lives and laugh about what happened. This is a natural and positive use of the faculty of memory. In fact, people of all ages may use this aspect of memory to stir up good thoughts and emotions.

However, as people approach middle age and beyond, there is a tendency to use memory to put a negative and depressing spin on aging—whether it be with or without associated disease. In these cases, people will project memories of what they did in the past onto their present and future lives. When they compare their current and future situations to their past, everything turns negative in a hurry. To worsen matters, this negative attitude may turn away friends, acquaintances, and loved ones, leading to more isolation and depression. Just ask yourself if you would rather spend time with a person who has a negative or a positive attitude!

So now let's revisit Beatrice from the last chapter. As you may recall, she had a crippling arthritis (lupus) that left her more and more limited in her activities. She had recently retired and was comparing memories of what she used to be able to easily do with her future limitations. She was becoming angry and depressed at this thought. If she did not dwell on her past capabilities, she would not be depressed over her loss. In some respect, she would be better off if she had not been more capable in the past because she would not look back at what she used to be able to do.

Another example is that of Emily, an eighty-six-year-old lady who lost her vision due to glaucoma. She lives in a nice assisted-living facility with good caretakers, but she has a poor quality of life. She remembers back to when she could do art work, read, and exercise. Now, she just sits all day and laments her loss. Without comparing her past with her present, she would probably be enjoying daily activities. Instead, her memories drag her down. Many people, myself included, have tried to refocus her. We point out that many blind people, such as Stevie Wonder, Ray Charles, and Helen Keller, have led productive lives. Instead, Emily fixates on her past memories. She refuses to embrace her current reality and make the most of it.

Once again, we see that people's life situation boils down to a matter of attitude. Those like Beatrice and Emily choose to remember the past and lament the present and future. Yet, I have patients who are blind and still manage to raise families and hold down jobs. I have deaf patients who use sign language and read lips and still lead normal lifestyles. I've seen cheerful patients paralyzed from the waist down who are productive workers and enjoy life. I have a patient, Lee Hubbard, with MS who has been terribly crippled and confined to a wheelchair, yet he comes in telling me about his craftwork in building wooden clocks. These are people who do not dwell on the past and lament their current situation. These are people who accept their current situation as a challenge and thrive despite their limitations. These people should be admired and emulated. These are people I am proud to know.

We see how memory can be used to have a negative effect on our lives. Yet, God gave us memory, so He must want us to use it. Indeed, He must want us to use it to have a positive influence on our lives. How can we use it for the betterment of our lives? We do this by remembering Him. We do this by remembering Jesus and all He did for us.

We must make a point of remembering God, because we tend to get wrapped up in our daily lives and forget about Him. That's when we get ourselves into trouble.

Think about times in your own life where you have done or said something wrong that you later regretted. I'd be willing to bet that these are all times when you have temporarily forgotten God. Think about times when you have become sad or depressed. These are also times when God was not at the foremost of your thoughts. These bad times can be overcome by remembering God, Jesus, and wisdom from the Bible. This is how we need to use our memory!

In his great book *The City of God*, Saint Augustine tells us about the origin of the word *religion*.[2] He tells us that "religion" comes from *relegere*, which means to reelect. Our relationship with God is the goal of all our striving. So our election of Him is our goal, or actually our "reelection" of Him is our goal, for through neglect we forget about Him. Therefore, religion is all about seeking and remembering God (keeping Him in mind).

This point is crucial in our approach to death and the dying process. Without religion, death and the dying process is nothing but doom and gloom. With religion, with faith, there is hope. In fact, there is much more than hope with the certainty of the saving grace of Jesus Christ. The problem is, we constantly tend to forget God, or as Augustine put it, we neglect God and then need to reelect to seek Him again.

We all tend to forget about or neglect God from time to time. For most of us, this can happen even on a daily basis. I find myself forgetting about God, even while I am in the middle of writing a book about remembering Him.

I suspect it is even harder for us who live in modern times to constantly keep God in mind than it was for our ancestors. With all of today's movies, books, plays, electronic gadgets, the Internet, and other news sources, as well as job and family demands, it's easy to be distracted from focusing on God.

It is human nature to forget God, and when we are distracted from Him, we get ourselves into trouble. Trouble can manifest itself as emotional strife, such as anger, jealousy, sadness, depression, and despair. Such trouble can physically damage ourselves and others (e.g., drunk driving). It can create conflict that destroys personal relationships. It is in the absence of remembering God that we sin.

Just examine history to see that this is true. Throughout history, people have tried to build utopian societies. Given human nature, a utopian society is not possible here on earth. The human nature I refer to is that we forget God and sin against God, and in the process we do wrong to our fellow citizens. In heaven, a utopian society will exist because everyone will be 100 percent focused on God, and there will be no sin.

Now I think many of you reading this are like me, whose first reaction is to say "I never forget God." However, I contemplated this for a minute and realized that I forget about God a lot. Yes, we all forget God. Let's look at some biblical examples:

1. *Adam and Eve:* Adam and Eve obviously forgot about who God is and the will of God, or they would never have eaten the forbidden fruit. They failed to recall who God is—the all-powerful, all-knowing Creator. They had to have forgotten who God is to go along with Satan's reasoning to eat the fruit. They were given an amazing gift from God Himself and still they disregarded His command. Their lack of memory bought them a one-way ticket out of paradise. Talk about flunking the test!

2. *The Israelites in the desert:* You have to wonder how the Israelites could have forgotten God in the short time that Moses was up on Mount Sinai receiving the Ten Commandments from God. These are the same people who were given an amazing series of unbelievable miracles from God. After all, they were rescued from slavery, they were spared from the ten plagues that rained down on Egypt, they walked across a parted Red Sea, and they received water and manna in the desert. Yet when Moses came down from Mount Sinai, he found them worshiping a golden calf. It must have been like a scene from a Mel Brooks movie with the Israelites saying (with a Yiddish accent), "Oy vey, did we ever forget God big time! What were we thinking?" Their

lack of memory bought them forty years of wandering in the desert.

3. *Various kings and leaders of Israel over the centuries:* The pattern is repetitive. When the king or leader remembers God, good things happen to the people. When they forget God, then bad things happen, like Jerusalem getting sacked and the people being exiled to Babylon.

One would think that all these biblical characters could not possibly forget God, who did everything for them, and yet they still forgot God. These biblical stories teach us three important points. The first is we are all human: no one is better than the biblical characters, and we all will forget or neglect God at times. None of us is perfect. The second point is that nothing good happens when we forget God. The third point to learn is we must constantly work at remembering God.

Remember God: seek and find a way to do this. This can be done in a variety of ways, all of which are good, and we should use a multiple of reminders for we need all the help we can get.

There are all sorts of possible reminders. For instance, Jews have mezuzahs—little prayer scrolls that they attach on the door frame, which they see and touch whenever they enter or exit their homes. Some Jews also use *tefillin*—mini prayer boxes that they strap to their arms or foreheads to remind them of God.

Religious symbols such as the cross worn as religious jewelry and artwork will remind us of God. But don't just look at them; contemplate God and Jesus when you see religious items. In a similar fashion, pay attention to nature. Whether you see a gorgeous sunset, a beautiful landscape, or a fresh bunch of flowers, you need to use that wonderful sight to remind yourself of the Creator.

Take advantage of friends, family, and even acquaintances to talk about your faith. This can be done on an individual or group basis, or perhaps through a Bible study class. Listen to music, go to plays, or watch shows or movies that have religious themes. Read and reread books about faith, including this one (I just had to put in a shameless plug here).

Read and reread the Bible. It is packed with so much information that a reevaluation may open up a whole new insight. Contemplating later about what you've read will help you stay focused on God.

Go to church regularly. After years of going to church, I find that much of the sermon may be information I've heard before. However, it gets presented in a new way and serves as a great reminder. I think I'm always able to find a new point to take in or fact to learn, plus I always get to hear a new joke or two. The Communion service is, of course, a great reminder of Jesus and His sacrificial love for us. *This, after all, is the key to our approach to death.*

Make a point of praying at least once and preferably several times a day. Each time you pray, you are refocusing on God. When you pray, think about all the times you've heard of prayers being answered—either yours or someone else's. What a great and healthy way to remind yourself of what God has done and what He can do.

So we have many tools to work with to remind ourselves to refocus on God. The problem is, you have to remind yourself to use the reminders. The best way to do this is to lead a structured life. Plan to do certain things at certain times of the day, such as a prayer time or Bible study time. Plan on attending church regularly. Plan a time to contemplate each day on whatever reminder you used that day, and what reminders you plan to use in the days to come. By adding this type of structure, you have set yourself up for success.

Consider journaling your thoughts and daily activities. A periodic review of your journal entries will help you see how God's shepherding hand has guided you through difficult seasons in your life.

Successful people use structure in their daily lives. For instance, athletes structure their diet and exercise routines, and successful businesspeople structure and plan their workday. As a doctor, I tell people to plan and set aside time for an exercise regimen; otherwise it will not likely happen. Likewise, I encourage patients to use structure in taking their medicine. For instance, I put my blood pressure medicine by my toothbrush, so that I can remember to take it every evening when I brush my teeth. I've made it a habit. Also, the pills are packed by individual days of the week rather than loosely in a bottle, so that I can double-check to know that I've taken it that evening. If your medicine is not packaged like this, you can get some pharmacies to "bubble pack" all of your medicine so that the days of the week and time of day are all laid out. Another method is to get a plastic pill box container that you fill up at the beginning of the week to track your pills each day. Some sort of structure or habit like this is needed to help you maintain your medical health. In the same way, we should plan and set aside time to remind ourselves to focus on God.

There is perhaps one time when it is more important to focus on remembering God, and that is in times of mental or physical stress. This includes times of pain or suffering. It includes times when we have to give or receive bad news. Remembering God is the key to easing the burden of the death and dying process—both for the patient, as well as for friends and loved ones. When times get tough, we should remember to focus on thinking about the Lord Jesus, which can happen in two ways:

1. Use a triggering mechanism that stimulates spiritual thoughts.
2. Train yourself to have spiritual thoughts out of habit.

A triggering mechanism can be any object that makes you recall God. In these days of computer applications, a periodic pop-up quote or statement would work well. Personally, I carry a small engraved stone that serves as a reminder. Every day, when I get home, I empty my pockets and see the stone, which jogs my memory.

I also suggest that you make a point to practice thinking about the Lord whenever something goes wrong. Make a habit out of thinking about Jesus, even when trivial things go wrong, and then you will have a better chance of calling on Him in the worst of times. After all, it's in times of extreme mental or physical pain that we get overwhelmed. When we are overwhelmed, it is much harder to think clearly. We become like a ship in a stormy sea that has become detached from its anchor. By focusing on Jesus during tumultuous times, our ship sails back into safe waters.

At some point in all our lives there will be times of overwhelming hardship. If we've practiced focusing on the Lord, we will be able to find strength and comfort in the toughest of times. We find ourselves getting into trouble when we forget to focus on our faith in the Lord.

This lack of focus can be seen from the story of Peter in the Bible. As you know, Peter was handpicked by none other than Jesus, to lead the disciples. Jesus told Peter this in Matthew 16:17–19:

> *Blessed are you, Simon son of Jonah, for this was not revealed to you by man, but my Father in heaven. And I tell you that you are Peter, and on this rock I will build my church, and the gates of Hades will not overcome it. I will give you the keys of the kingdom of heaven.*

The story of Peter's lack of focus is profound. In Matthew 26:31–35, Peter is warned:

> *Then Jesus told them, "This very night you will all fall away on account of me, for it is written: 'I will strike the shepherd, and the sheep of the flock will be scattered.' But after I have risen, I will go ahead of you into Galilee."*

> *Peter replied, "Even if all fall away on account of you, I never will."*

> *"I tell you the truth," Jesus answered, "this very night, before the rooster crows, you will disown me three times."*

> *But Peter declared, "Even if I have to die with you, I will never disown you."*

Then in Matthew 26:69–75 Peter displays a remarkable loss of focus:

> *Now Peter was sitting out in the courtyard, and a servant girl came to him. "You were with Jesus of Galilee," she said.*

> *But he denied it before them all, "I don't know what you are talking about," he said.*

> *Then he went out to the gateway, where another girl saw him and said to the people there, "This fellow was with Jesus of Nazareth."*

> *He denied it again, with an oath, "I do not know the man!"*

> *After a little while, those standing there went up to Peter and said, "Surely you are one of them, for your accent gives you away."*

Then he began to call down curses on himself and he swore to them, "I don't know the man!"

Immediately a rooster crowed. Then Peter remembered the words Jesus had spoken: "Before the rooster crows, you will disown me three times." And he went outside and wept bitterly.

Imagine that! On the very same night that Peter told Jesus that he would never deny Him, Peter broke his pledge. It seems inconceivable to the modern reader that someone could make a promise to Jesus in person, and then break that vow in just a matter of hours.

And yet, we are no better than Peter. We are human; we get caught up in the stresses of life and forget to focus on the Lord. Remember, Jesus picked Peter because he was the right choice, the right person in the right place and time. Yes, Peter forgot something that's almost inconceivable to forget. He failed because he relied on himself instead of remembering to take his strength from the Lord. Later in life, he remembered his purpose and took strength in his faith, and the ultimate outcome for Peter was great. He became one of the great founders of the early church at the risk of his own life. There can be no doubt of Peter's place in heaven.

From this story, we can know that it's okay if we cannot remember to focus. As long as we've committed to Christ, we will be forgiven in our failings.

Dementia

Another situation to consider is people who just cannot remember—those with dementia. Dementia is a disease state in which memory and thought processes have declined. This is often progressive over time. Other bodily functions, such as the ability to walk, are also affected. There are many causes of dementia, with Alzheimer's disease being the most common and well known. But there is also Parkinson's, Lewy body dementia, hydrocephalus, multi-infarct dementia (stroke), and trauma, just to name a few.

When people notice themselves becoming forgetful, they should certainly seek an evaluation from their physician. However, most people who come to me for forgetfulness do not have dementia. More often then not, they are having problems with mental stress or depression. Interestingly, most people with dementia do not recognize themselves as having a significant problem.

Action can be taken to preserve memory. Again, your physician should be consulted on the cause and possible treatment. For instance, there are medicines that will help slow the decline of Alzheimer's. Any stress or depression should be addressed appropriately, with counseling and possibly medicines if needed.

All of us, with or without dementia, should do active mental exercises to keep our minds sharp. These include games, puzzles, crafts, hobbies, playing a musical instrument, or learning a foreign language. Passive activities such as watching TV or a movie will not be helpful. Even reading would be a relatively passive activity, though I'd like to think reading this book works your mind more than reading an old Superman comic.

The suffering that surrounds people with dementia is often worse for the primary caregiver than for the patient themselves. The suffering of caregivers, friends, and family members of patients will be addressed in the chapters on suffering.

The suffering on the part of patients with dementia revolves around the loss of the ability to remember. When the dementia is still mild, patients can read and enjoy their usual activities. Later, music and art therapy can become more important. In particular, religious music will frequently bring a smile to the patient's face. As the dementia becomes more severe, the concern over this loss on the part of the patient fades away as they lose the ability to recognize their own limitations. In fact, severely demented patients are often some of the happiest patients whom I see, for they are easily amused. Some do suffer hallucinations, which is seeing or hearing things that are not real. These hallucinations can usually be dealt with by either gentle redirecting on the part of the caregiver or medicine, if needed.

Forgetting Our Problems

Sometimes forgetting can be to our advantage. By this I mean that forgetting our own personal problems and conditions can be to our advantage.

I see this in my own personal life. For example, I try to recognize problems and deal with them as they come up, but I try not to dwell on them. Instead, I try to remember and concentrate on God in addition to taking care of patients and enjoying time with family and friends.

This point really came home to me the other day when eating lunch with my friend Glenn. I was about halfway through lunch when all of a sudden Glenn asked me how I was feeling. A rapid sense of dread went through me. Why was he asking me that all of a sudden, out of the blue? He must have noticed something wrong that I had not seen. I inspected my sandwich more closely to see if I could locate the problem. And then it dawned on me that he was asking about my cancer and chemo treatment. I had forgotten all about them.

A sense of accomplishment overcame me. I was leading a normal life as if I had no cancer at all. I had been working on remembering God and not dwelling on my own problems. Remembering God is always an ongoing process, but at least I had succeeded in not being dragged down by dwelling on my own woes.

We get ourselves into trouble when we remember ourselves and forget God. Remembering to *focus on God*, not on ourselves, *that* is the answer.

11

Starting Treatment

Do not be afraid of those who kill the body, but cannot kill the soul.
—Matthew 10:28

Pfft. Julie, my nurse, had just deftly slid the IV needle into my left forearm vein. She got a nice little flashback of blood as expected and then plugged in the IV tubing, and the battle was underway.

Before starting the chemo, she had explained the battle plan to me. This first infusion would be the longest—almost six hours—so that my body could get used to the medicine.

First, I needed to be premedicated. A special "cocktail" had been prepared:

- Ten mg of IV Decadron—a steroid to ward off a rejection reaction
- Twelve mg of IV Zofran—to minimize nausea
- A handful of pills—two Tylenol, two Benadryl, and one Zantac to minimize infusion reactions

Thirty minutes of waiting to let the premedication set in, and then she started the main event—Rituximab—a monoclonal antibody designed to attack the B lymphocytes, which were the bad actors of my non-Hodgkin's lymphoma. The hope is that the Rituximab would win this battle, while knowing full well I would eventually lose the war.

The slow *drip-drip* started, and my mind wandered back to the previous month and how I had gotten to this point.

It all started with a routine screening colonoscopy to look for colon polyps. Forty centimeters into my colon, Dr. Gear discovered and biopsied a small, unusual lump that had been silently growing within me. To his (and my) surprise, it came back suspicious for non-Hodgkin's lymphoma, which is essentially unheard of for starting in the colon. He talked to all his colleagues: i.e., gastroenterologists and oncologists, and they all thought the pathology report was in error—a red herring, they called it. More tests would be needed.

I would have to get another colonoscopy. On the second visit to my colon, everything looked normal, as Dr. Gear had already removed the suspicious mass. He resorted to doing sixteen random biopsies. This second procedure took a lot longer—one and a half hours, during which time I woke up for the second half of it. I started to get some serious abdominal cramps, and I had to resort to using some mind control techniques to mentally turn down the pain level (see chapter on pain control).

The follow-up biopsies confirmed non-Hodgkin's lymphoma. I underwent total body and head CT and PET scans, looking for any spread of the disease. These studies all came back negative, but I was still left with a few non-curable cancer cells in my body, i.e., a terminal diagnosis.

I was referred to Dr. Robert Quadro, the head of the oncology department at the Mercy Medical Group. Dr. Quadro presented my case at the Tumor Board. The Tumor Board is a meeting of doctors from multiple specialties, including hematology, oncology, pathology, radiation oncology, and surgical oncology, to discuss unusual and interesting cases, mine being one of them. They estimated there are *maybe* ten cases in the United States like mine. Since it was so rare, there was no definite study telling them what should be done. Since this is a slow-growing cancer, most of the doctors suggested that no treatment be initiated. They thought we should just let it grow and see how I did. Dr. Quadro thought maybe we should get a little more aggressive and use a mild chemo agent—a monoclonal antibody to slow the growth of the cells down even more. It is generally well tolerated but would leave me immunocompromised—i.e., more prone to infection. My first response was, "Let's go for it!"

Before starting this first infusion, I made the mistake of researching the medical literature to find out potential side effects. Don't try this trick at home, folks—it is very scary. I think it is much better to just trust your doctor, keep a positive outlook, and let the chips fall where they may.

Of course the list of side effects included the usual symptoms that most all medications list: dizziness, fatigue, weakness, nausea, headache, fever, shakes, rash, cough, and a runny nose. It also lists some potentially more interesting side effects, including: anaphylaxis—your throat swells shut and you stop breathing; kidney failure; cardiac arrhythmia, including sudden cardiac death; and severe dermal reactions, such as Stevens-Johnson syndrome (your skin blisters up all over your body, including mouth sores) and toxic epidermal necrolysis (i.e., your skin falls off). As I said, reading medical literature is not for the meek of heart, and I don't recommend it for patients. It is enough to scare even me, and I'm used to seeing these things.

As the *drip-drip* of the IV continued, I noticed the coldness of the room. Roxanne, the infusion nurse, was kind enough to bring me a nicely warmed blanket. The Benadryl cocktail was sinking in and I nodded off. Two hours later I woke up to find myself only halfway through the infusion. I started to think about what my disease meant to me.

Cancer—the *Big C* word—is enough to strike fear into the hearts of many. Lord knows I have seen plenty of patients who lose sleep, worrying that they may get cancer, or worse yet, think that they already have it. Here's where reading medical literature is really scary. When you start reading medical literature, you'll think every little itch, scratch, bump, or bruise is a harbinger of cancer, or a myriad of other diseases. I advise seeing your doctor on a fairly regular basis (i.e., roughly every year after age fifty, and every other year before fifty, depending on your personal medical history). Be sure to get the recommended cancer screening tests. A few of my other rules of thumb are:

- Avoid reading medical literature, especially if you think you're an expert, but you're really not (*look up my father-in-law for this definition*).

- If you notice a major change in your body, then you should report it to your doctor.

- Sleep well at night. Don't worry, be happy.

Fortunately, many cancers nowadays are curable, if detected early. Even if they are not curable, often something can be offered to slow it down. There is always something available to try to help relieve symptoms.

I have a slow-growing, terminal cancer that will hopefully take years before it gets me. Basically, small parts of my body, the B cell lymphocytes, have betrayed me and have sentenced me to death. Somehow, this sounds familiar. Where have I heard it before? Time for my most important rule of thumb: *when scary things are happening, always remember to turn to the Lord for strength.*

Jesus was also betrayed by a small part of His body—His body of disciples—specifically one named Judas Iscariot. Suddenly I felt closer to Jesus. We had something in common—being betrayed by part of our bodies. In a strange way, I felt I could identify a little closer with Him. Kind of walk in His sandals, so to speak.

I tried to think of a modern-day analogy to help me solidify the concept. Suppose your brother is very talented at some activity—maybe sports, music, or some sort of creative hobby. Now let's say you wanted to feel closer to your brother. A good answer would be to seek common ground, such as learning about his activity or taking up a related activity. Have similar experiences. This will help you identify closer with him since you have something in common.

Recalling the previous historical example of Saint Francis of Assisi, Francis spent his life trying to find common ground with Christ, so that he could feel closer to Him:

- When he first started his ministry, he had a group of twelve men, similar to the apostles.
- He lived in poverty.
- He sought simplicity.
- He lived with lepers.

All of these acts made him feel closer to Christ, and he took great joy and pleasure in that. Accounts of his life indicate he may have been one of the most truly happy people of his day.

The ultimate expression of Saint Francis's closeness to Jesus occurred on September 14, 1224, on Mount La Verna, in Italy. On that day, he received the stigmata—the wounds of Christ—in his feet, his hands, and his side, to bring him even nearer to Christ. (*Now that is another trick that I don't recommend you try at home, folks!*) He bore those wounds for the next two years until his death. The point here is that he shared common experiences with Jesus to draw closer to Him, and he took great joy in that.

Now, what does feeling closer to Jesus do for me, the cancer patient? The answer is: *It empowers me.* As one with no hope of a cure, at least with today's technology, I need to not feel helpless. Loss of control is one of the worst fears of the human condition. Jesus gives me back control of the situation. With Jesus' help, I have cancer in a headlock and I'm not letting go. Let's explore further how this empowerment works.

The key concept here is that I have a body and a soul. I need to take advantage of this fact. I need to build on my strengths (my immortal soul and my Friend Jesus) and overcome my weaknesses (my mortal body and its susceptibility to cancer). Time to lay out a new and improved battle plan, one that is designed to definitely win the war. Let me explain.

ACT I

The cancer enters my body and starts growing while I am still unaware. The cancer sets up its home base, from which it will move out and attack. My response: I accept Jesus into my life. He sets up residence in my soul.

ACT II

Despite the doctors' best efforts, the cancer breaks out from its home base and starts attacking my body in multiple ways. My response: I seek common ground with Jesus, and my soul grows stronger.

ACT III

The cancer and the chemo treatments battle back and forth over my body. The cancer eventually gains ground and my body is weakened. My response: I unceasingly remind myself to remember God. I improve communication with family and friends. My soul grows stronger. My soul has been empowered by Jesus, the most powerful person who has ever lived. For every step the cancer takes to weaken my body, I have countered by strengthening my soul through Jesus. My body is weaker, but my soul—the real me—is stronger.

ACT IV

Without a miracle, the cancer eventually succeeds in killing my body. However, my soul lives on, thanks to Jesus. I have won the war. That was never in doubt.

Remember, you have a soul. Part of your body can be destroyed, but your soul remains intact. If you have accepted Jesus into your life, then He resides in you, the real you, i.e., your soul. By strengthening your relationship with Jesus, you have empowered your soul to be even stronger. *Jesus defeats death, and if He is in you, then you cannot be defeated by death.* Instead, you are on your way to heaven, eternal life, and eternal bliss.

I sometimes look back to my high school years. I remember studying Eastern religions, thinking about achieving Nirvana, and seeing rock stars travel to the Far East and meeting with their gurus. It all sounded pretty cool, spiritual, and mystical. But now I contemplate Jesus residing in my soul and providing me with eternal life. What could be more cool, spiritual, mystical, and truer than that?

The last *drip-drip* of my first infusion ended uneventfully. The adventure has begun, but the ultimate outcome will never be in doubt. I have already won.

12

Evangelism: A Chance for Empowerment

The Apostles were either deceived or deceivers. Either supposition is difficult, for it is not possible to imagine that a man has arisen from the dead. While Jesus was with them He could sustain them, but afterwards, if He did not appear to them, who did make them act?[1] —*Pascal*

"You have a terminal illness." Terminal—as in not curable, there is nothing we can do to stop it. Yes, those words have been devastating for millions of patients. It takes away their sense of freedom. It makes them feel powerless. It's an utterly awful, empty feeling.

As medical professionals, we try to put some power back into the hands of patients. We try to provide some power of control over symptoms. Patients are given the power to choose among different approaches to treatment. Sometimes, hopefully much of the time, patients are given the opportunity to improve length of survival. Patients are given medicines to use at their choosing, and as needed, to control symptoms. This provides not only some comfort from the symptoms but also some power over their symptoms. However, medicine is not perfect, and so its power is limited.

However, there is an area in patients' lives in which they can take total control. This is the area of evangelism. Evangelism is the Great Commission. In Matthew 28:18–20, Jesus says:

All authority in heaven and earth has been given to me. Therefore go and make disciples of all nations, baptizing them in the name of the

Father, and of the Son, and of the Holy Spirit, and teaching them to obey everything I have commanded you. And surely I am with you always, to the very end of the age.

So Jesus wants us to go and make more followers.

In his bestselling book *The Purpose Driven Life,*[2] Rick Warren talks about evangelism as giving purpose to our lives. Our lives need to have meaning. This is no more important at any time in our lives than in our death and dying phase. Having meaning to our lives gives us a sense of satisfaction, a sense of purpose, and a reason for being. It provides a drive to keep on living. The need for meaning is well described in Viktor Frankl's book *Man's Search for Meaning.*[3] Frankl was a Jewish psychiatrist who lived in Vienna, Austria. He lived from 1905 to 1997 and survived four death camps, including Auschwitz, during WWII. He was able to observe and describe firsthand what it took to survive the most horrific conditions. What he observed was that those who were the most *physically* strong were not the most likely to survive. The survivors were those who were the most *mentally* strong. Invariably, the survivors were the ones who were able to find meaning in their lives. For Frankl, this meaning was to stay alive in order to see his wife and family again.

As Frankl points out, it's important for us to find meaning in our own lives. As Christians, we can find no greater meaning or purpose to our lives than making disciples—followers of Christ. Jesus Himself has empowered us to spread the Gospel. Christians need to realize that we can and must continue to spread the good news of Christ even through-out the death and dying process. I like to think of evangelism as existing in either of two forms: active or passive.

Active evangelism is when one intentionally seeks out others who may not know of Christ. Certainly, patients can continue to do active evangelism, as long as their health allows. Passive evangelism is when one spreads Christianity by letting others observe our lives and learn by watching our thoughts and behaviors, both in good times and bad. When non-believers see Christians living out the Christian lifestyle, they learn what it means to be a Christian. Thinking non-believers will see that there is something unique and laudable about these people. The non-believers would have to say that these people, these Christians, are doing something right. They will see that the Christian way is something to learn from and want to emulate it. The Christian example creates the "I want to be like them" mentality. That is what I mean by passive evangelism.

Passive evangelism can be witnessed through the following acts:

- Accepting help in a gracious and receptive manner
- Not losing our faith when things go wrong
- Making the most of our situation
- Providing forgiveness when wronged
- Not showing favoritism
- Being slow to anger (James 1:19–20 and Ephesians 4:31)
- Being humble
- Not slandering or speaking poorly of others
- Showing generosity. Now is not the time to be a miser, especially since giving can benefit you, as well. Studies have shown that altruistic giving can improve your own sense of well-being.[4]
- Not worrying (Matthew 6:25–27)
- Exemplifying courage in your struggles (1 Corinthians 16:13)
- Living your life doing acts of kindness (2 Timothy 2:24)

  And the Lord's servant must not quarrel; instead, he must be kind to everyone, able to teach, not resentful.

- Loving others. Remember Jesus' words in John 15:12: "My command is this: Love each other as I have loved you."
- Exemplifying the Lord through patience. Remember, the Lord has been extremely patient with us. Paul tells us in Romans 12:12: "Be joyful in hope, patient in affliction, faithful in prayer." Patience in times of hardship can amaze others and make them say, "What do they have that gives them this ability?"
- Continuing to worship and praise God
- Speaking truthfully (2 Corinthians 4:2)

- Recognizing and showing gratitude for the gifts and acts of kindness we receive

Basically, passive evangelism means living a Christian lifestyle. It means exemplifying Christian principles even in the face of adversity, or should we say, especially in the face of adversity. Living Christian principles results in a display of inner strength, joy, and peace. Remember: *Christ is our inner strength.* That is how we can have and display joy and peace, even while dying.

This display of inner strength will amaze some observers, and be a source of admiration for others. When they ask about your source of strength, you let them know that it's a reflection of your Christian faith. This living display of Christian faith makes a much more powerful evangelical statement than just words. This passive evangelism can be much more profound than active evangelism.

Many Christians have a fear of discussing their faith with non-Christians, due to the unknown response they will receive. Non-Christians may become angry if they feel they are being told what they should believe. The response might be ridicule or just cutting off contact with the Christian.

Caryl has experienced both sides of this equation. She was raised Jewish and, through a miracle of faith and prayer, has become a Messianic Jew, a believer and follower of Christ.

Growing up, Caryl was bombarded by Christians wanting to convert her. The harder they tried, the more firm her negative response became. She even had people tell her she was going to go to hell if she didn't convert, which was not the right way to win her over. Unfortunately, her family was even threatened by the KKK (the Ku Klux Klan); this hardened their anti-Christian sentiments.

Now that she has become a Christian, Caryl is on the opposing side when it comes to discussing religion with her family. Clearly attempts to actively evangelize would not go over well. In fact, she was in fear of telling them that she herself had become a Christian, knowing that they would become angry. However, it seems that passive evangelism is softening their hearts. They can see her doing well mentally and emotionally, and they witness her doing good works. They know deep down that something must be going right in her life. They have moved from anger to acceptance, and hopefully they will be won over completely someday soon.

Persevering with Christian virtues through difficult times, including the dying process, can bring new followers to Christ, who will in turn discover the joys of being Christian.

The second accomplishment that can be achieved is to strengthen your fellow Christians. You have many brothers and sisters in Christ. You can strengthen their faith by letting them view your own inner strength, which comes from Jesus. Strengthening your fellow Christians helps empower them to spread the Word, as well.

Your acts of Christian faith and values do serve a purpose. Even in dying you can still serve a higher purpose. Even when your body is weak, your spirit can remain strong and serve a purpose. This can be done by *focusing* on Christ and maintaining a positive *attitude*. Jesus gave you an amazing job to do, and it can be done despite your bodily functions failing. He empowered you with a job to do. Accept the inner strength that comes with that empowerment. Do the job!

13

Code Status and End-of-Life Decisions

In him and through faith in him, we may approach God with freedom and confidence. —Ephesians 3:12

This chapter will explore the practicalities, as well as the philosophy behind the medical code. Medical code status tells medical staff how aggressive to be in the event of a medical emergency, such as if the heart stops or the lungs fail. A "full code" status would mean that everything would be done in an emergent situation, including CPR and life support. Usually when CPR is performed, the patient will be put on life support at the same time. Life support involves the patient being intubated, meaning a tube is put down the throat into the airway, and a machine takes on the process of breathing for the patient.

A "no code blue" status means that CPR would not be performed and there would be no life support given. A "DNR" (Do Not Resuscitate) status refers to not using CPR or life support at all.

Adding to the options of potential codes is the concept of a "medicine only" code. In this scenario, only medicines are used to try to keep the patient alive. If the heart or lungs stop, there would be no CPR, no chest compressions, no electric shocks, and no intubation or breathing machines.

Another option is that of "comfort care" only. This would mean the status would be DNR, and medicines would not be used to try to prolong life. The medical goal in this scenario is to keep the patient comfortable but not to attempt to prolong their life. For instance, medicine would be given to alleviate symptoms such as pain or nausea, but medicine would not be given to correct an irregular life-threatening heart rhythm.

Before discussing decision-making, we need to establish who the decision-maker will be. If the patient is a competent adult, the decision-maker is the patient, possibly in collaboration with family/friends and with input from the doctor. However, we should all plan for the possible event in which we cannot speak for ourselves, such as if we have a loss of consciousness. This can be done by having appointed a trusted family member or friend to be the durable power of attorney for health care.

The health-care power of attorney can be the same person who is the power of attorney for financial affairs. However, it does not need to be the same person, and it is frequently a different person. For instance, you may decide to have your spouse be the durable power of attorney for health care, while having one of your children be in charge of financial affairs.

By filling out *durable power of attorney* for health-care papers, you have appointed someone to be your spokesperson, in case you cannot speak for yourself. You can also appoint an alternate decision-maker in case the primary contact is unavailable. These papers are generally available at your doctor's office or hospital, or can be pulled off the Internet. You will need to either have two witnesses sign them or have them notarized. Whomever you appoint to be power of attorney for your health care should know your beliefs and wishes and be able to convey those wishes to the medical staff. Someone who has trouble making decisions would probably not be your best choice to appoint.

I often encourage patients to establish in writing a durable power of attorney for health care when they are of sound mind and in good health. This provides them with someone to be their spokesperson if they become unable to make decisions for themselves. For instance, if someone has a stroke or a traumatic accident that leaves him or her unable to communicate, then the power of attorney for health care can speak on their behalf. The power of attorney could give permission to the doctor to perform surgery or other medically necessary procedures. The power of attorney for health care would also be needed to make the decision to withdraw life-sustaining measures. I often find that patients automatically assume that their spouse or next-of-kin would have the legal authority to direct their health care should they become incapacitated. *This is not the case.* They must appoint someone to have the durable power of attorney for health care. Again, you may have an alternate person appointed in the event the primary agent is unavailable. Clearly, whomever you appoint should know your personal wishes and beliefs. Without having a power of attorney for health care, the care of the patient may fall into the hands of an ethical review board or even become a court case.

In addition to appointing a power of attorney for health care, you can tell any medical staff your wishes. In the absence of other information, the medical team will assume the code status is a full code, and they will try to do everything to revive you, the patient. If you do not desire a full code, you should definitely tell your doctor your wishes.

If you do not want to have CPR performed, you should ask your physician for a written request stating your wishes for DNR. This can be accomplished by simply having your physician give written instructions on a prescription form. Without written instructions for DNR, paramedics will perform CPR if they are called out to see a critically ill patient. An order in plain sight, such as taped to the refrigerator, would suffice to give them the information that they need. A more formal approach is the Physician Orders for Life-Sustaining Treatment (POLST) form, which exists for many states. The POLST form gives a written directive of your wishes for emergency treatment. The POLST form needs to be signed by you or your legal decision-maker, and your physician. A POLST form and power of attorney for healthcare papers can be found at www.LiveLoveAndLetGo.com.

So the question is, why would someone *not* want CPR or life support to keep them alive? The answer is when it is not beneficial. Contrary to what TV shows and movies would lead us to believe, CPR is not a simple or easy process to go through. CPR is traumatic. It involves chest compressions that often break the ribs. It involves electric shocks to the heart muscle. People who wake up from CPR will be in pain.

CPR and/or life support is not beneficial when the outcome is not a meaningful life. A meaningful life is one in which we have purpose, such as pleasing God and being pleased by Him. As we saw in the previous chapter on evangelism, one purpose is for us to lead others to Christ, either through "active" evangelism, in which the Word is preached, or through "passive" evangelism, in which we live out the Word through a Christian lifestyle. If one is so ill that they are considering life support questions, then they probably will not be participating in active evangelism. So the question really boils down to whether the patient can be passively evangelistic, or whether they can live their life well enough to display the Christian lifestyle characteristics that are so admirable and inspirational.

This question can be extremely difficult for the non-medical person to answer. In fact, it can be very difficult for even the most experienced medical professional. Even similar cases can have different answers. However, I can offer some guiding thoughts and examples. If someone is considered to have an end-stage non-curable disease or organ failure (and is not a transplant candidate), then they are not necessarily a good candidate for CPR or life support. Here is a list of examples:

- Late-stage terminal (non-curable) cancer, such as cancer that has metastasized (spread to multiple sites)

- End-stage liver disease (cirrhosis) from whatever cause

- End-stage heart disease with congestive heart failure, such as having an ejection fraction below 20 percent (i.e., the heart can only pump out 20 percent of the blood each time it contracts)

- End-stage renal failure (kidney disease) in someone who is not a good dialysis candidate—such as, the very elderly

- End-stage lung disease, such as someone who needs to wear oxygen twenty-four hours a day, needs chronic steroids in pill form, or has a lung capacity of less than one liter

- Severe inoperable vascular disease

- Brain disease (such as from a stroke or dementia) causing severely limited cognitive ability. Can they think and reason, do they recognize friends and family members, do they know who Jesus is?

- The very elderly: the definition of this continues to change. For instance, I have patients in their eighties on dialysis (which is really a form of life support, as they could not live without the dialysis machine). Just a few decades ago, dialysis of an eighty-year-old patient would probably have not been a consideration. In general, though, patients in their nineties will not do well with major surgery or CPR/life support, even if they survive it.

- The very frail, which could be due to aging or crippling disease such as the end stages of AIDS, Parkinson's, or MS
- Those who have a medical problem that leaves them with a poor quality of life. This could be from a crippling form of arthritis, spinal disease, a paralyzing stroke, or those with chronic pain. A poor quality of life would be one with a lack of pleasurable activities. This would be an individual patient decision. However, one should keep in mind that the quality of life after CPR and/or life support would be the same at best, and likely worse, with more debility.

The graceful acceptance of no code blue, no life support at the appropriate time, can be our final act of passive evangelism. Acceptance of bodily death is a display to others of our faith in Jesus as our Savior.

Let me explain through an example. One night I was working in the emergency room admitting patients to the hospital. I was called to see an elderly gentleman, dressed in an orange robe, who was sick and needed to be admitted for intravenous antibiotics. In the process of examining him, I noticed that he had thick callouses on the tops of his feet rather than on the bottoms of his feet. Finding this very unusual, I asked how that came to be. It turned out that he was a Buddhist monk. He had spent so much time in his life kneeling in prayer or meditation, that he had actually developed callouses on the tops of his feet where they rubbed on the ground while he was kneeling. This exemplified to me a man who was truly devout in the practice of his religion.

As is my usual custom, I asked him about code status. My understanding of the Buddhist religion is that they believe death gives them the opportunity to move on to a better life. My expectation, therefore, was that he would desire no code blue, no CPR, and to just keep him comfortable and let him die peacefully. But to my surprise, he wanted everything done for him, including life support and CPR to keep him alive. I could be wrong, but my thought was that he had doubts about the religious tenets of his faith; otherwise he would not want to fight death.

Now, having someone doubt my faith and confidence in Jesus when that critical time comes would be the situation that I would want to avoid. Going back to the last chapter, as long as I can function well enough to display passive evangelism, then I want to remain alive. *But when the time comes, and it looks like I can no longer display those attributes, then it's time to show my ultimate confidence in Jesus and gracefully accept the death of the body.*

Jesus exemplified His ultimate confidence in God the Father when He accepted His death on the cross. He could have fought against death and perhaps lived longer, but He did not. He probably could have run and hid from the Romans, but He did not. Rather, in accepting death, His purpose in life (to save us) was fulfilled. In the same way, our graceful acceptance of bodily death when the time comes should fulfill our purpose in life to evangelize by showing our confidence in Jesus, the Savior, as we look at Him as the model.

To summarize, the patient who is not a good candidate for life support should stipulate that in advance by telling their doctor, family, and health-care power of attorney. If they do get put on life support and are not a good candidate to continue life support, then they should have it withdrawn. This can be done, and the patient can be allowed to die in a peaceful, comfortable, and dignified manner.

Christians should be the model for others on how to die peacefully and comfortably. We should gracefully and confidently accept death because of our faith in Jesus. We should make non-Christians want to ask the question, "What do Christians have that makes accepting death so easy for them?"

We can also display our Christianity by stopping life support when appropriate (i.e., when we can no longer anticipate being able to passively evangelize). Keeping patients alive on life support uses up lots of resources. It is estimated that 40 percent of all Medicare expenditures in the United States are spent in the last two years of life.[1] By choosing to stop life support when appropriate, we free up resources that can be used for others in need—such as other sick patients, child care, feeding the hungry, and housing the poor, etc. Jesus was not selfish when He went to the cross for us. In the same way, we should not be selfish in using up health-care resources that do not advance Christianity or our ability to evangelize.

14

Overcoming Suffering

I consider that our present sufferings are not worth comparing with the glory that will be revealed in us. —Romans 8:18

Suffering associated with death and the dying process can take on many forms. Basically, sufferings can be categorized as either mental or physical. In other words, suffering can affect both the body and the mind. There is lots of interplay since when the body suffers, the mind can be negatively impacted and vice versa. Conversely, in this chapter, I'll focus on how easing either mental or physical suffering can have a positive impact on the other. We must accept the fact that there will always be suffering associated with death. It cannot be completely eliminated. However, we can do a lot to help ease both mental and physical suffering and make it more tolerable.

Yes, we have many potential treatments to help ease suffering. Now the question is: Can we do anything to enhance the effects of those treatments? Yes. We can help ourselves by maintaining a positive attitude. A positive attitude can enhance the placebo effect. As we discussed, the placebo effect is where we think a treatment will help us, and therefore it does help us, even if the treatment has no true medicinal benefit.

Just because we think something will help us means that there is a 30 percent chance that it actually does help us. Why not maintain a positive attitude and take advantage of the placebo effect in addition to actual medicinal benefits? Not only do we need a positive attitude, but we need a great attitude. When we combine *great* and *attitude*, we get *gratitude*. Expressing gratitude can multiply the benefits of all treatments.

I believe that living in modern times has had a negative impact on our ability to cope with suffering. Modern technology has been miraculous. People travel all over the world, man has walked on the moon, and all the information in the world is at the touch of our fingertips via the Internet. In the field of medicine, people are living much longer, and there are constantly new amazing medicines and surgical procedures. Expectations have become great. As a result, the attitude has often become, *If they can put a man on the moon, why can't they cure_____ (fill in the disease)?* This negative attitude can have a negative impact on our sense of treatment benefits and thus on our sense of well-being. Conversely, a positive boost would occur with an expression of gratitude for whatever benefit has been achieved.

The benefit of gratitude has been studied in recent times. Studies have shown that grateful people have a greater sense of well-being, cope better, sleep better, are happier, are less stressed, and have better social relationships. Would you rather be around a grateful person or a negative one?

Let's look at a simple example of how gratitude might work. On New Year's Eve, my wife, Caryl, went into a local bank to do some business. Inside, she found the bank employees grumbling that they had to work on a day when many others have the day off. I am thankful that Caryl had the courage to point out to them that they should be grateful that they have a good, steady job, when many people nowadays are unemployed. On top of that, they still have weekends off, whereas our farming ancestors would typically work seven days a week. The grumbling at the bank quickly stopped. Their initial response was probably to think, *Get this woman out of here* (probably with a few vulgarities added in for good effect!). But if they thought about it, they probably went home that day happy and grateful that they had a job, instead of angry that they had to work that day. An additional benefit is that truly grateful employees and their positive attitudes attract more customers than grumbling employees. This would put their manager in a better mood, as well—a true win-win situation.

The benefits generated by a sense of gratitude can improve one's situation, when remembering that no matter how bad things are, there is always something for which we can be grateful. Two big constants come to mind: being thankful for the Bible and for Jesus Christ. But there will always be a myriad of other small things for which to be grateful. Examples include: a warm blanket, a visit from a friend, the farmers who grew the food you enjoy, a medical treatment that helped, or even a clean cup of water. I suggest the following exercise:

1. Pray at least once a day. Find something to thank God for in the prayer.
2. Read the Bible. Contemplate or meditate on the psalms. (In particular, see Psalms 18, 30, 50, 75, 79, 92, 96, 100, 106, 107, 118, 136, 140, and 147.)
3. Make a point of thanking someone each day.
4. Spend a few minutes each morning and evening thinking of the little things for which you can be grateful. Write them down.

These activities are useful for both the patient as well as the caregiver/family/friends.

I was given a lesson in gratitude by a patient named Eddie. Eddie is an elderly gentleman with severe arthritis, atrial fibrillation (a heart rhythm problem), and congestive heart failure. It was in early January that Eddie came in to see me. I asked him how his Christmas was. His response startled me. He said he doesn't do anything different on Christmas, that to him every day is Christmas. He felt every day is a gift from God—even Mondays! He would pray every morning and evening and various other times throughout the day, giving thanks to God. That's gratitude. Eddie is eighty-eight years old and looks like he is sixty-eight. I've no doubt that his gratitude is keeping him young.

Combining Gratitude With Medicine

Let us now look at how we can combine the benefits of gratitude with medical treatment of physical ailments to help alleviate suffering. The treatment of physical symptoms will always begin with the treatment of the underlying diseases. For instance, the symptom of shortness of breath can be due to the underlying disease of pneumonia. The treatment of that disease begins with antibiotics. However, we also treat the symptom of shortness of breath with oxygen and bronchodilators (these are inhaled medicines that help open the airways).

In discussing the treatment of physical suffering, I will concentrate on the treatment of the symptoms rather than the underlying disease. There are two reasons for this approach:

1. Most of us relate much more to the symptoms that we actually feel.

2. There are far too many diseases to discuss here.

Fortunately, there are a multitude of treatments that are available to help with physical symptoms. Table I lists a variety of symptoms along with potential treatments to ease the symptoms. These treatments do not "cure" the symptom. However, there should be something that can at least help alleviate the symptom to some degree. Our job then is to look for and recognize that benefit, however small or large it may be, and be grateful. It may take some work to find some good when all looks bleak, but it will be worth the effort. Remember that most of these treatments were not available to your ancestors. Therefore, give thanks that your suffering is less than your ancestors.

Yes, give thanks for any help you get. Write it down. Give thanks to God in prayer. Your heartfelt gratitude will lift you mentally and spiritually from the depths of despair, even if only for a moment. In this way, you will make yourself a little happier or at least a little less unhappy. Give gratitude to God, and God will give back to you with lessening of your suffering. Decreased suffering could come in the form of decreased pain and symptoms, improved response to medications or treatment, improved relationships with friends and caregivers, and physical or spiritual healing.

Table I

Shortness of Breath	Oxygen, breathing treatments, morphine, steroids, diuretics (i.e., water pills in cases of fluid retention), thoracentesis (a procedure using a needle to draw fluid off the lung), benzodiazpine medicines for anxiety, breathing machines in severe cases
Fatigue	Blood transfusion and/or erythropoietin (medicine to stimulate the bone marrow to treat anemic patients), oxygen, sleep aids, chore workers and caretakers to help do what you cannot, vitamin B12, exercise strengthening programs, yoga, naps, wheelchairs, hospital beds, comfortable beds, pillows, blankets, fluids, food
Dry mouth	Frequent sips of water, artificial saliva, sugarless gum, tart foods (e.g., lemons), pilocarpine, cevimeline (evoxac), acupuncture
Pain	See chapter on pain
Nausea/Vomiting	IV fluids, avoidance of triggers (stuffy rooms, odors, flickering lights, motion), ginger, antihistamines such as: meclizine or diphenhydramine; dopamine antagonists such as: promethazine, prochlorperazine, and metoclopramide; benzodiazepines such as: ativan; serotonin antagonists such as: ondansetron; corticosteroids, nasogastric tubes
Diarrhea	Activated charcoal, bismuth, loperamide, cholestyramine, fiber, dairy (lactose) avoidance, fluids
Constipation	Foods such as: apples, peaches, peas, prunes, raisins, cherries, nuts, wheat bran; psylliums, stool softeners such as docusate; laxatives such as: sorbitol, lactulose, polyethylene glycol, bisacodyl, senna; enemas

Urinary Incontinence	Kegel exercises, bladder training, pads/protective undergarments, bladder catheters, bedside commodes, anticholinergic medicines such as: oxybutynin
Anorexia/Weight loss	Frequent small meals, protein shakes, corticosteroids, megestrol, IV fluids
Visual Loss	Glasses, large print books, improved lighting, Braille, audio books
Hearing Loss	Hearing aids, amplification (volume control) on electronic equipment such as: TVs and phones, sign language, written language
Loss of Strength	Canes, walkers, wheelchairs, strengthening exercises, physical therapists, caregivers/chore workers
Itching	Moisturizing creams and soaps, antihistamines such as: hydroxyzine, diphenhydramine, and doxepin, avoidance of scratching, camphor and menthol lotions, oatmeal, baths, corticosteroids, gabapentin
Hair loss	Wigs, hats, medicated shampoos, medicines
Decubitus ulcers (bed sores)	Pressure relief (take weight off site), pressure relief mattresses, antibiotics as needed for infections, debridement (cleansing of wound), dressings
Dysphagia (difficulty swallowing)	Soft foods, ground foods, medicines that are crushed or in liquid form, pills coated in applesauce, stomach-acid-blocking medicines such as omeprazole or ranitidine, protein shakes, tube feeding, parenteral (intravenous) nutrition

Mental suffering can be eased by treating physical suffering. Mental suffering can come in many forms. Mental suffering can include depression, anxiety, irritability, anger, fear, sadness, low self-esteem, confusion, and concern over separation issues and life regrets. Let's look at each of these in turn and see how we can improve the situation.

At first glance, one might wonder, *How could any Christian become depressed?* But really there is no shame in becoming depressed. In fact, probably most patients with a terminal illness will experience some depression. The most important first step is to recognize it and be willing to admit it to family, friends, and caretakers who can help. In other words, when you are sinking, don't hesitate to ask someone for a lifeline. It only makes sense.

Depression can manifest itself with several signs and symptoms. These include:

- Depressed mood—this can include sadness, crying, emotional distress, emotional numbness, and being anxious or irritable
- Loss of interest or pleasure in activities
- Sleep disturbance (trouble sleeping or sleeping too much)
- Change in appetite or weight
- Psychomotor retardation or agitation (i.e., slowing down of thought processes and/or physical activity)
- Low energy
- Poor concentration
- Thoughts of worthlessness or guilt
- Recurring thoughts about death or suicide

If you have five or more of these symptoms, you are probably depressed. Depression can also cause physical symptoms such as fatigue, headaches, abdominal pain, and muscle aches.

As mentioned earlier, physical symptoms will trigger more depression. Conversely, depression will worsen physical symptoms, regardless of which disease is present. For instance, depression is a major risk for death after a heart attack.[1] In another study done on diabetic patients, it was found that all cause mortality (i.e., death from any cause) increased by 36–38 percent over a two-year period in depressed patients.[2] So, when you have depression, not only do you suffer the symptoms, but your life expectancy shortens, as well. In addition, depression will diminish your ability to carry out God's mission for your life (i.e., the Great Commission, living out the Christian life, your purpose in life). This is why depression must be recognized and treated.

The treatment of depression can include medications and/or psychotherapy/counseling. In addition, *alcoholic beverages and street drugs should be avoided.* Alcohol in particular will worsen depression. Exercise will help depression—even mild exercise, such as going for a walk. Seeking out well-lit rooms, as well as the outdoors and fresh air, should be encouraged.

Antidepressant medications seem to have a negative social stigma attached to them. Many people wrongly believe that they are addictive or that they are only for crazy people or weak people, or that they are dangerous. In fact, they are not addictive, and the very large majority of people who take them would not be considered crazy or weak by anyone. Antidepressants are actually very safe medicines. The one caveat to this is in depressed teenagers with suicidal tendencies. The antidepressants might relax them enough so that they actually carry out their intent. When someone has depression, there are actual neurochemical transmitters in the brain (such as serotonin and norepinephrine) that are imbalanced. Antidepressants work by correcting these levels. This is similar to medications for diabetic patients that correct insulin levels.

Antidepressant medications do have side effects, but most people do not have a problem with them. If an intolerable side effect does arise, then the medicine can easily be stopped. Often, the medication side effect profile can be used to benefit the patient. For instance, in addition to helping depression, the medicine might help a patient with their bowels, sleep, or appetite. Antidepressants can often also help alleviate chronic pain.

Antidepressants usually take a few weeks to take effect. They work slowly and gradually, and often a family member or friend will notice improvement before the patient does. All antidepressant medicines work, but sometimes two or three different antidepressants have to be tried before the right one for the patient is found.

Overall, the advantages of antidepressants outweigh the disadvantages, making them a major asset in our arsenal of treatments. In the case of the dying patient, where time is of the essence, we should not hesitate to use antidepressants where appropriate.

Psychotherapy can be equally effective as antidepressant medication in treating depression. Counseling can come from a psychiatrist, a psychologist, a social worker, or a member of the clergy. Spiritual counseling should definitely be a part of the program. Counseling can be individual, one-on-one, or group therapy. Self-counseling can be accomplished by working through the book *The Feeling Good Handbook*,[3] by Dr. David Burns (which I highly recommend).

Anxiety is another form of mental suffering and often goes hand-in-hand with depression, but it can be present without depression, as well. All of the treatments discussed for depression (exercises, counseling, or *The Feeling Good Handbook*) can also be used to treat anxiety. Even in the absence of depression, antidepressant medicines can be a good treatment for anxiety.

Benzodiazepines (such as Valium and Xanax) are a class of medications that work well for anxiety. They can also help alleviate nausea and insomnia. Benzodiazepines are addictive medicines, but in terminally ill patients with a real need, this is usually a non-issue.

Other activities can also be calming and help relieve anxiety. This includes listening to relaxation tapes and calming music (such as classical or jazz) and doing artwork or crafts. Prayer and meditation should, of course, be used. One suggestion is to slowly, very slowly, read through the psalms or other Bible verses and contemplate their meaning.

Stephen is a patient of mine who uses short spiritual phrases or prayers to help relieve anxiety and to refocus on God. He uses this technique to calm himself in stressful situations. For instance, when he feels wronged, he might say the phrase: *"Father, forgive them, for they know not what they do."* In tough times, he might simply use the phrase: *"Jesus, I trust in You!"* These short prayers help him to refocus on God, and they remind him of the relatively trivial nature of the stressful situation when compared to the majesty of God.

Eastern Orthodox monks use a technique called hesychastic prayer to focus on God.[4] Hesychastic prayer is an attempt to abide by

1 Thessalonians 5:16–17, where Paul says: "Be joyful always; pray continually." They literally try to pray unceasingly by repeating the Jesus Prayer thousands of times. The Jesus Prayer is simply:

Lord Jesus Christ, Son of God, have mercy on me, a sinner.

The method they use is to silently repeat the prayer over and over again. They time the prayer with rhythmic breathing. The idea is to always have the name of Jesus on the lips. It keeps one focused on God and helps to relieve inner anxieties. The prayer can be shortened to just the name of Jesus, or another prayer can be used.

Irritability and Anger

Irritability and anger can be a part of depression and anxiety, or it can be a separate issue. When you find yourself irritable or angry, you need to ask yourself, "Why am I feeling this way, and what is making my reaction worse?" Let's look at a typical life example:

You are driving down the road and another car suddenly passes you and then recklessly cuts in front of you, causing you to brake. Now a couple of emotional responses to this event might occur:

1. You are relieved that there was no accident.

2. You become angry or worked up over the experience.

Notice that you would be happier later in the day if your response was "a" rather than "b." Either way, the incident that triggered the response was the same. If your response was "b" (you became angry or irritable), then you need to ask yourself, *What else is going on with me to cause the worse response?* Possibilities would include: underlying depression/anxiety, fatigue, lack of sleep, pain or other physical symptoms, hunger, dehydration, other situational stress, and alcohol or illegal street drug use.

This sort of self-examination can be hard to do. You really need to stop and work at it. However, you still have to recognize and treat the underlying cause to help with irritability and anger symptoms. In other words, you cannot always change the problems that come up in life, but you can change your response to them. You will help ease your suffering if your response is not anger or irritability.

Another example comes from my own life recently. I had just come home from work and was in the house not more than two minutes, when I snapped at the kids for not putting away the trash cans. I am usually pretty laid-back and would have either ignored the issue or calmly asked them to put the trash cans away. So snapping at the kids was not a good feeling. I proceeded to feel irritable for about ten minutes when it occurred to me that I needed to think about why I reacted the way I did. After further thought, I realized that I was tired and hungry since I had just put in a twelve-hour shift and had not stopped for lunch. Sitting down to dinner was a simple solution in that case. This is a perfect example of how physical symptoms worsen mental suffering, and treating the physical helps the mental issues as well.

Confusion

Another form of mental suffering to be covered in this chapter is confusion. (The remaining types of mental suffering, such as fear, are discussed in other chapters.) Confusion can come in one of two forms: dementia and delirium.

Delirium is confusion that arises from acute illness. Potential causes include infection, surgery, pain, liver failure, heart failure, kidney failure, trauma, alcohol intoxication or withdrawal, medications, fluid or electrolyte imbalances, respiratory failure, and seizure. People at greatest risk for delirium include the elderly, the malnourished, and those with underlying dementia, or a history of stroke.

Treatment of delirium is primarily centered around finding and treating the underlying cause. Antipsychotic medications can be given if the patient is very agitated. Physical restraints should be reserved only for cases when needed for physical safety.

Delirium is typically much harder on the family and friends of the patient. For the patient, suffering associated with delirium is really whatever the underlying disease state is. Typically, the patient will not even remember the delirium episode.

Dementia is a degenerative brain disorder that causes a chronic form of confusion. Alzheimer's disease is by far the most common type of dementia, but other types include multi-infarct dementia (arising from strokes), Lewy body disease, Parkinson's disease, and many others. Depression can cause a dementia-like picture and should be treated when appropriate.

In general, the distress from dementia will be much worse for the family/caregiver than the patient. The one major exception to that statement is when the patient's privileges need to be taken away due to safety. For instance, taking away a patient's driver's license can be very hard on them. A similar situation arises when the patient can no longer live alone or safely use appliances. The best answer here is probably to give the patient as much decision-making power as safely or practically possible. For instance, if a patient does not want to take a bath, then you tell them that they need to take a bath, but they can choose whether to do so in the morning or afternoon.

Gratitude and Motivation

As with physical suffering, the effects of the treatment of mental suffering can be greatly enhanced by expressions of gratitude. Particularly with mental suffering, it may be very hard to give thanks when everything seems to be going wrong.

For both physical and mental suffering, the exercise of spending a few minutes each morning and evening writing down things for which you can be grateful is very useful. This can include an act of kindness that someone did for you, the relief of a physical or mental symptom—no matter how small the improvement—a drink of cool water, the ability to write/talk/hear, a restful nap, a calming passage of the Bible, or even the ability to pray. This gratitude improves mental outlook, which helps ease physical symptoms, which diminishes mental suffering, and so on and so on.

There is always something for which we can be thankful. When we are, He will reward us by easing our suffering. In fact, we can even be grateful for the suffering itself in that it allows us to see the actions of God in our lives when that suffering is alleviated.

Gratitude is the key to amplifying the benefits of treatment for suffering. Gratitude needs to be used in conjunction with motivation, the driving force to getting through suffering.

You need to find a motivation, or purpose, for overcoming suffering.

The purpose needs to be above and beyond yourself. For instance, to say "I don't want to die," while understandable, is not a good motivation for overcoming suffering. It would be like fighting a battle with all shields and no offensive weapons. With this strategy, you are most likely to lose.

Instead, you should take a much more positive approach in choosing your motivation. A strong positive motivation would be, "I am living so that I can serve God's purpose by _____" (fill in the blank). The strongest of possible positive motivators is when you touch someone else's life in a positive way. (Refer back to the chapter that describes active and passive evangelism.)

A strong positive motivator can be something that brings personal pleasure, but the strongest positive motivator will also mix in something that touches someone else in a positive way. For instance, suppose you want to live so that you can see your grandchild get married. This would bring great pleasure to you. Well, you could add to that by planning to do the floral decorations for the wedding (assuming that's an area in which you have talent), or maybe write them a little manual on how to build a good marriage rooted in your own living example. Whatever it is, find something that makes you feel good inside for having done it. This will undoubtedly be based upon some of the Christian values discussed in the chapter on evangelism.

One great example of someone using positive motivation is that of Steve Jobs, who was a high-tech pioneer, one of the founders of Apple Computer. Jobs was diagnosed with pancreatic cancer in 2003 and eventually died of the disease in 2011. In those intervening years, his company introduced the iPhone, which gave the cell phone a touch screen and a Web browser. In 2010, Apple released the iPad tablet computer, an extremely popular consumer item.

Jobs wanted to make "a dent in the universe" by using technology to improve human life and unleash creativity. He found mortality to be a force against complacency. In other words, it spurred him on in a positive, motivating way. At a Stanford University commencement speech in 2005, he said, "Death is very likely the best invention of life. All pride, all fear of embarrassment or failure, these things just fall away in the face of death, leaving only what is truly important."[5]

I've had the opportunity to experience the power of strong positive motivation in my own life. This relates back to the time when I was in a propane fire and my fear of being a patient in the burn unit.

For this reason (the fear of the burn ward), I was actually tempted to not survive the propane fire. It occurred to me while in the fire to stay there and have a quick death rather than get out of the fire and suffer through burn wound recovery. Fortunately, the motivation to stay on and serve as father and husband to my family, as God intended, got me out of the flames and allowed me to endure the subsequent wounds. While I have not yet fully accomplished that goal, I have at least made some accomplishments and give thanks to God for that ability.

In addition to serving my family, I have now added a second positive motivating goal to my life. The goal is actually working on this book. I pray it will help alleviate someone else's concerns and struggles with death and the dying process. Whether or not anyone else is helped, it certainly has helped me with my own diagnosis of non-Hodgkin's lymphoma. By focusing my mind on the goal, my worries have faded to the background. My motivator has given me power and freedom over victimhood.

The apostle Paul gives us a great historical example of how to use an underlying motivator or purpose to withstand undue hardship and suffering. Paul spent the last twenty years of his life traveling the Roman and Greek world. Traveling two thousand years before modern conveniences was a hardship in and of itself. During this time he was also flogged, shipwrecked, spent time in and out of jails, and was eventually beheaded.

Paul gives us the answer to how he was able to withstand these twenty years of suffering without breaking or giving up. He tells us in the book of Acts 20:22–24:

And now, compelled by the Spirit, I am going to Jerusalem, not knowing what will happen to me there. I only know that in every city the Holy Spirit warns me that prison and hardships are facing me. However, I consider my life worth nothing to me, if only I may finish the race and complete the task the Lord Jesus has given me—the task of testifying to the gospel of God's grace.

There were probably many times on his journeys when he could have just quit and released himself from further suffering, but dedication to his mission enabled him to endure further hard times. The key: he was truly dedicated to his goal. We need to learn from this. Although we may not hope to accomplish what Paul accomplished, we can strive to have his type of dedication to our own personal goals.

In summary, suffering comes in many forms. But suffering can be endured, eased, and overcome. The foundation of our battle plan against suffering needs to be a strong, positive purpose for living. We then follow that up with gratitude for every bit of help we receive. We need to give gratitude to God for every accomplishment that we are able to achieve.

Remember that Jesus had motivation for enduring His suffering. His motivation was our salvation. We need to show our gratitude to Jesus by battling our own suffering in a strong, positive fashion, one that serves not only our own purpose, but especially His.

15

Humor: Lifting the Mood

Three friends were talking about what they would want people to say about them at their open-casket funeral.

The first guy says, "I'd like them to say, 'He was totally dedicated to his church.'"

The second guy says, "I'd like them to say, 'He was totally dedicated to his family.'"

The third guy says, "I'd like them to say, 'Wait, he's still moving.'"

—*Anonymous joke sent to me via the Internet*

Everybody looks at life situations in their own way. I was able to experience this phenomenon firsthand shortly after I was burned in the propane fire. Three of my children, Austin, Lauren, and Travis, had seen me catch fire in the backyard. After I got back from the hospital, we asked the kids to share their thoughts on the fire.

Lauren said she was worried that I was going to die. Austin was worried that the house was going to burn down and that we would be homeless. But I had to laugh at Travis's response. You see, Travis (the youngest, just eight years old at the time) was excited about all the money he would make selling tickets to the neighborhood kids so that they could see the burnt man. Being able to laugh at the situation helped lighten the mood and made me feel better.

There are both spiritual as well as physical reasons for humor. Whereas laughter at someone else's expense is detrimental, laughing with someone or, at times, self-deprecating humor can be beneficial. Done in the right way, God does want us to laugh.

The Bible is notable for its lack of jokes and humor. However, this really only seems logical for the following reasons:

1. The Bible was originally written in Hebrew and needed to be translated into many languages. Typically, a joke loses its humor in translation.

2. Humor is often based on the sudden, unexpected, or double meaning. This quite likely could lead to misinterpretation when translated.

3. There is so much serious information in the Bible that the sudden humor could be misinterpreted or take away from the basic point.

Despite the lack of humor in the Bible, it seems clear that God does want us to laugh. First, God created humor and laughter, and we know from Genesis that whatever God created was good. Second, God created us for His enjoyment. Surely humor was part of that enjoyment. Third, if God didn't enjoy laughter, He certainly wouldn't have made us capable of doing such goofy things. Fourth, God's chosen people were the Jews. It certainly makes sense that He might have chosen the Jews for their great sense of humor. After all, there is definitely a disproportionate representation of Jewish comedians. (Jews are about 2 percent of the U.S. population, but comprise 80 percent of the comedians.[1]) A short list of Jewish comics includes:

The Three Stooges, The Marx Brothers, Allen King, George Burns, Marty Feldman, Marty Allen, Woody Allen, Morey Amsterdam, Jeff Goldblum, Shecky Greene, Laraine Newman, Milton Berle, Joey Bishop, Pee-Wee Herman, Jerry Seinfeld, Adam Sandler, Louis Nye, Sandra Bernhard, Jack Black, Jack Benny, Bette Midler, Howard Stern, Rob Reiner, Harold Ramis, Joan Rivers, Don Rickles, Seth Rogen, Mel Brooks, Lenny Bruce, Red Buttons, Andy Kaufman, Danny Kaye, Robert Klein, Sid Caesar, Soupy Sales, Peter Sellers, Billy Crystal, Rodney Dangerfield, Jerry Lewis, Rob Schneider, David Schwimmer,

Howie Mandel, Victor Borge, Gilda Radner, Mel Blanc, Jackie Mason, Jon Stewart, David Brenner, Henny Youngman, Sacha Baron Cohen, Sarah Silverman, Andy Samberg, Michael Showalter, Ben Stiller, Gene Wilder, Adolf Hitler...

Wait a minute—Hitler wasn't Jewish. But then again, he wasn't funny either! You get my point.

The Jews were not persecuted over the centuries because their jokes were so bad. Rather, Jews have used humor over the years as a survival mechanism. Humor is an excellent defense mechanism for redirecting the pressure of life's struggles.

Now the most important point from a spiritual standpoint is what humor can do for us. Take a moment and think back to the last time you shared a really good laugh with someone. Didn't it draw you closer and increase the bond of friendship? Think again of various funny moments in your life. Are these not moments of happiness and joy? Take it a step further and realize that these are moments for which you want to give thanks to God. These are moments when you can feel closer to heaven.

Humor can not only lift your mood, but it has physical benefits, as well. One of the first people in modern times to look at the benefits of laughter was Dr. Norman Cousins.[2] He suffered from ankylosing spondylitis, which is a painful arthritic condition of the back. He started watching old comedy shows, such as the Marx Brothers movies. He found that ten minutes of laughter would give him two hours of pain-free sleep. Since then scientists have found that laughter causes the release of endorphins in the body. Endorphins are our natural pain relievers—i.e., our body's "morphine," if you will. For example, a study at UCLA revealed that watching funny shows increased children's tolerance for pain.[3]

A sense of humor may even promote longevity. Sven Svebok did a study of 53,000 Norwegians over a seven-year period. He found that those in the top quartile of people who found things funny to have a 35 percent improved survival rate over those in the bottom quartile. That benefit improved from 35 percent to 70 percent when just looking at cancer patients.[4]

Humor might increase life expectancy in the following ways:

1. Laughter reduces blood sugar in diabetic patients.[5]
2. To increase heart rate, one minute of laughter is equivalent to a ten-minute workout on a rowing machine.[6]
3. Laughter dilates blood vessels. A study by Jun Sugawara at the University of Texas at Austin found blood flow through the carotid arteries increased for twenty-four hours after watching a thirty-minute comedy.[7]
4. Dr. Michael Miller at the University of Maryland found that people with heart disease were 40 percent less likely to laugh than those without.[8]
5. Laughter reduces stress hormones—cortisol, epinephrine, and norepinephrine.[9]
6. Laughter increases levels of T cells and natural killer cells—these are cells that help fight infection.[10]

To top off all these data points, a study at Texas A&M University shows that laughter increases levels of hope. Hope lifts our mood and helps to make us optimists rather than pessimists. David H. Rosen, a psychologist at Texas A&M, stated that humor could lead a person to develop a greater sense of self-worth, maintain an increased ability to develop a "plan of attack" for a specific problem, and increase the person's perceived ability to overcome obstacles in dealing with that problem.[11]

So it's good to laugh. Laughter can be brought on in a variety of ways. We can watch funny TV shows or movies. We can read funny books or comics. Jokes can be told. We can think back on funny moments or events in our lives.

Interestingly, it looks like laughter benefits can be attained without humor. In other words, we can fake laughter, by just forcing ourselves to laugh. This may be done best by meeting groups of people and starting to laugh. A little bit of fake laughter will often bring on real laughter. A doctor in India meets with people to do deep breathing exercises combined with laughter and calls it "laughter yoga."[12] At the Cancer Treatment Centers of America, there is a laughter group in which participants pretend to put ice down each other's backs. All of these methods are good and help to lift mood and spirits.

Bob C. is a ninety-five-year-old patient of mine whom I have known for a long time. He survived a serious battle with colon cancer when he was in his eighties, and it is like nothing ever happened to him. He had a stroke earlier this year and is doing amazingly well with it. The really amazing part of this to me is that he didn't have a stroke fifteen years prior. You see, Bob has had very elevated blood pressure—in the 180/100—range for years. We've tried putting him on multiple blood pressure medications, which he didn't tolerate due to their side effects.

I am convinced that Bob's sense of humor is what has kept him going strong for so many years. I have never met anyone even remotely close to having Bob's sense of humor. I don't think I've ever seen Bob go for more than about a half of a sentence without smiling. That smile is almost always accompanied by a chortle, guffaw, or out-and-out belly laugh. He is laughing usually without even telling a joke. He laughed when he had colon cancer. He laughed when he had a stroke. He laughs whether or not there is anything funny to laugh about. No one can help but laugh whenever they are around him. Bob is truly a shining monument to the benefits of laughter, both for himself as well as for those around him.

I think back now on when my own diagnosis of non-Hodgkin's lymphoma was made after a routine colonoscopy in which a lump in the wall of the colon was biopsied. The initial pathology report indicated possible lymphoma but more testing needed to be done. My doctor said that it was so unusual that he thought it was just an anomaly, or an error in the data. In fact, he used the old euphemism and called it a red herring.

My wife, Caryl, responded to this by saying that I hadn't been swimming for months and that I don't even like fish, so how in the world did a red herring get up there? I had to laugh. Oh, did I mention that Caryl is related to Moe of the Three Stooges? No, she really is. I had to laugh some more. The laughter helped ease a tense moment. I am grateful for that laughter. Yes, with gratitude and humor, the trials of life don't seem so bad. *Attitude* makes a difference.

16

Heaven: A New Perspective

A continual looking forward to the eternal world is not a form of escapism or wishful thinking, but one of the things a Christian is meant to do. —*C. S. Lewis*

The purpose of this chapter on heaven is to stress its importance and great benefits. We need to take time and stress the concept of heaven as it is infrequently and maybe even rarely emphasized elsewhere. Try to think back to when you last had a conversation about heaven. Try to think back to how often you hear heaven mentioned in a church sermon. Now try to think back to how often heaven has ever been the main topic of a church sermon (not just mentioned). You would probably have to do a word search to find heaven mentioned in the mainstream media. Imagine any other destination we go to (let alone move to and live in) being so rarely discussed.

There are really two reasons we hear so little talk of heaven. The first reason is that at times we may have secret doubts about our faith. Remember the story of "the doubting Thomas." He was a man who had the opportunity to walk and talk with Jesus, yet he did not believe in His resurrection until he saw Him in the flesh. The second reason for a lack of discussion on heaven is that we do not have a lot of detailed information about it. No one has e-mailed us pictures of heaven from their camera-phone. We don't have any maps to tell us how to get there, nor do we have any guidebooks to tell us what we will do there.

We do not have a detailed description of heaven. The Bible mentions heaven, but it does not give a full picture. Even anecdotal descriptions from people who have had near-death experiences really only tell us that heaven is a glorious place. Unfortunately, we cannot expect a full account of a place from someone who has only been there for a few minutes. The real question here is: could someone who spent years in heaven be able to come and adequately describe it to us? Personally, I would have to say no.

Let's suppose that Moses came down from heaven to tell us about it. After thousands of years in heaven, would Moses be able to tell us all about it? Probably not. After all, Moses came down from Mount Sinai after meeting with God and could not tell the people His name. This is likely because human language is inadequate to describe the immensity and power of God. For this same reason, he would not be able to describe God's dwelling place.

What we are able to say about heaven is that it will be a totally joyous place. Consider that in heaven:

There will be no sadness, only happiness.

There will be no fighting, only peace.

There will be no tears of sadness, only tears of joy.

There will be no suffering, only glad tidings.

There will be no yearnings, only spiritual rewards.

There will be no regrets, only thankfulness.

There will be no wailing, only laughter.

There will be no loss of loved ones, only reunion.

There will be no hatred or anger, only love.

There will be no pain, only comfort.

There will be no pride, only satisfaction.

There will be no self-doubt, only confidence.

There will be no depression, only elation.

There will be no loss, only gain.

There will be no uncertainty, only knowledge.

There will be no jealousy, only friendship.

There will be no blame, only forgiveness.

There will be no boredom, only amazement.

There will be no shame, only glory.

There will be no hunger or thirst, only fullness of spirit.

There will be no end, only blissful eternity.

Yes, indeed, we do know these things about heaven. We know this because in John 14:1–3, Jesus says:

> Do not let your hearts be troubled. Trust in God, trust also in me. In my father's house are many rooms; if it were not so, I would have told you. I am going there to prepare a place for you. And if I go and prepare a place for you, I will come back and take you to be with me so that you may also be where I am.

And there you have it. Jesus has gone to prepare a place for us in His Father's house (heaven). And if Jesus prepared it, we can be sure that it will be…perfect.

No Sadness

Profound sadness will always be an issue surrounding death and the dying process. Fortunately, heaven is the antidote to that sadness. Though nothing on this earth could completely remove that sadness, the existence and contemplation of heaven can ease our mental burden. To see how this might work, we need to look at the situation in perspective—both from a heavenly as well as an earthly perspective. The key here is to keep an open mind and try to view our earthly existence as if we were already in heaven. An example from my own life can help illustrate this point.

When I was a young child, pre-kindergarten age, maybe three to four years old, my mother never left me. One day, she decided to go to a ladies' luncheon. They had a child day care in the same building. She put me in the day care and went off to her luncheon. Like I said, I had never been left behind before and I was devastated.

It was the worst hour of my life—at least up to that point. An hour at that age can seem like a lifetime. I was filled with both anger and sadness. Thoughts raced through my head: *How could she have done this to ME? What was she thinking? What is going to happen? Will I ever see her again? How could she have left me here all alone?* I thought this even though there were other kids there and the day-care lady was there with me. I broke down and cried.

The day-care lady tried to comfort me by giving me some blocks and a little plastic horse to play with, but there was no consoling me; I was too sad. *How can I stack blocks and have fun at a time like this? What am I supposed to do with a stupid little plastic horse?"*

Eventually, after forever had come and gone, the luncheon ended and I was reunited with my mom. Naturally, I was shocked to find out she went a whole hour without missing me. And she had a *good* time! Talk about adding insult to grievous injury. I was finally able to forgive my mom that day, but only after I made her promise to never let that happen again. Today I am grateful for that lesson of lessons, even though it took me years to grasp the true point of it.

Now, fast-forward a few years to when I was in high school—age sixteen. My parents decided to go on vacation and leave me home alone for a whole week! To top it off, they left me a credit card and the keys to the car—a 1974 Chevy Malibu! I couldn't believe they trusted me like that. I must have been a boring kid, or else they recognized that the movie *Ferris Bueller's Day Off* had yet to come out and give me any ideas.

Surviving the week away from my parents at age sixteen was certainly much easier than the hour spent away from my mom when I was three or four. That week did get a little hard at the end, though, especially since it was still in the pre-microwave era.

Now, let's fast-forward to today. My mom died from ovarian cancer over thirty years ago. I still think about her from time to time and get a little sad. Yes, I still miss her. I'd like to be able to tell her about all the good things that have happened since she passed away. I'd like to be able to tell her about blocks—yes, blocks and obstacles that I've overcome since she passed on. I'd like to be able to tell her I still haven't figured out what I was supposed to do with that little plastic horse.

The big question arises: Does my mom miss me? Or, in other words, is she sad to not still be with me? The answer is an astonishing, resounding no—and I don't think that's because she doesn't love me, as I'm sure she does. My mom does not miss me because she is in heaven! Remember, heaven is absolutely filled with joy. There is no room for even one iota of sadness. Heaven is perfect happiness. She now has a heavenly perspective and no longer sees things the way we do here on earth.

You see, heaven runs on God's time, which has the measure of eternity. Earth runs on man's time, which is measured in hours, days, weeks, months, and years. (It may help here to review the chapter in this book on time.) From my mom's heavenly perspective, the thirty-plus years that she's been gone is just a drop in the bucket. It's as if she were back enjoying her luncheon while knowing that I was just a few minutes away. She can't possibly miss me because the time that she has been gone is so minuscule in the big scheme of things. My mom is not sad because, from her heavenly perspective, it feels like she's not been gone long at all.

The really exciting part of heaven is that it gets even better. It gets better through the dimension of space—i.e., distance. Here we have to ask the question: Is my mom sad to be far away from me? The answer again is obviously a resounding no! Again, she can't possibly be sad in heaven. Heaven is perfect and joyous.

How can this work? Consider this: God is in heaven. Heaven is where God resides. God is everywhere. Therefore, heaven is everywhere. Moreover, my mom is in heaven with God. Once again, from her heavenly perspective, I am not far away at all. From her heavenly perspective, it's as if she were enjoying her luncheon and I'm just down the hall in the day-care room, in fact, even closer than that. What a deal!

As I reflect on my mom in heaven, I know that she is perfectly happy. She is enjoying heaven's glory, and at the same time, from her perspective, she is close to me in time and space. But wait, if she is close to me in time and space, then I must also be close to her in time and space. Yes, it's as if I'm still that little kid in the day care. Only this time, I know that she will not be gone long at all in the big scheme of things. Also, she is close, very close—in fact, she is only a breath away. Wonderfully, a breath can be measured in distance—a very short distance, such as inches, even millimeters. A breath can also be measured in time—is that breath her breath in the past, my breath in the future, or God's ever-present breath?

Yes, I have learned to look at life through a heavenly perspective—the *BIG picture*. When I do this, the sadness fades. If I had known to do this when I was three or four, then I would have just enjoyed my time playing in the day care. Today, life is much better. Instead of being the little kid in the day care, I now feel more like the teenager, but now, with a microwave.

I guess that's why they call it heaven…

Encore

(Yes, heaven deserves an encore!)

At this point, I suggest you take some time, maybe even a day or two (or maybe even the rest of your life), to contemplate the reality that is heaven. It may help to reread this chapter and again think of heaven. Let it sink in. Bask in its glories. Try to look at your own earthly life through a heavenly perspective, just as my mom in heaven looks at my life on earth through a heavenly perspective. Make it personal for your own situation. Get the big picture. Let it ease any mental anguish that may be troubling you.

Finally, consider that in heaven there are no losses, only gains. That means that heaven must be getting bigger. Meanwhile, back here on earth, astrophysicists have discovered that the universe is expanding. Yes, God's heavenly plan does fit in with our earthly experiences. Life is beautiful, and thanks to Jesus Christ, it never ends.

THAT is why they call it heaven!

17

Hospice: A Way of Caring

We should not pray for hardships to not happen, but rather we should pray for the grace to overcome those hardships. —*paraphrased from Saint Anthony*

Hospice care benefits both you and your loved ones as a potential hospice patient or family member. While volumes have been written on the subject, my intent is to just pull out key points of what I think you should know. Even if you are not in hospice, many of the care principles can still be utilized. A word of caution: Some of this chapter may be hard for the squeamish to read, so if you are so inclined, feel free to skip this chapter.

Hospice care is a philosophy of terminal patient care with the primary goal of comfort and support. It is an excellent option for those who qualify. One goal of hospice is to give patients a chance to die in the warmth and comfort of their own home, or a residential hospice facility, rather than in a cold, clinical hospital environment.

Table I on the next page contrasts and compares hospice care with traditional medical care.[1]

Table I

Comparisons of Hospice versus Traditional Care

Hospice View	**Traditional View**
1. Death—part of life cycle	1. Cure at all costs, avoid death
2. People oriented & patient centered	2. Techology-oriented in order to save life
3. Emphasis on patient/family	3. Emphasis on disease process
4. Emphasis on quality of life	4. Emphasis on quantity of life
5. Dying patient seen as an opportunity to relieve pain, etc.	5. Dying patient seen as defeat/medical failure
6. Dying patient surrounded with communication & support	6. Dying patient frequently isolated
7. Dying presents an opportunity to participate with reality	7. Dying frequently results in a conspiracy of silence.
8. Symptomatic treatment used	8. Curative therapies/life support
9. Major emphasis on pain avoidance—addiction is not main concern.	9. Pain treated with limited amounts of meds to avoid addiction
10. Emphasis on dying at home when hospitalization not needed	10. Emphasis on admitting the dying to acute care wards or nursing homes
11. Continuity of care	11. Fragmentation of care
12. Individuality	12. Depersonalization
13. Participation of patient and family in planning care	13. Care is one way frequently with caregivers planning it
14. Support of family at death with bereavement follow-up program	14. All contact w/family ends almost always at death

In a nutshell, I think of traditional medical care as fighting death by kicking and screaming with everything you have, whereas hospice care gives a peaceful, quiet dignity to the dying process. Unfortunately, when someone is fighting death, it can be tough for them to realize the point at which hospice is their best option. The answer, when in doubt, is to get their doctor's opinion. The following story of Caryl's friend Ruth illustrates the point.

Ruth was blessed with a large, loving family, an enormous collection of souvenir spoons from the many vacations she had shared with family and friends, and an ability to create magnificent quilts. Her home had a special room in which she had her fabrics neatly categorized, a cutting table, hand-quilting hoops, and many of her past quilt creations on display. As Ruth aged, she spent most of her days creating handmade treasures with her beloved calico cat, Calliemae, resting at her feet. Her biggest fear was dying in a hospital away from her prized family photographs, as well as her sewing room.

Ruth had also spent many years battling cancer. On several occasions, she and her oncologist had successfully fought it into remission. The last time it returned, her oncologist explained to her that all good treatment options had been exhausted. After knowing Ruth for so many years and realizing her passions, he suggested hospice care. By utilizing hospice, Ruth could return home to Calliemae, continue to quilt, and visit with family and friends while spending her final days being surrounded by the familiar things she loved most. For the first time, her doctor also discussed with Ruth about signing a POLST form requesting DNR (i.e., using comfort care measures only).

With her body betraying her, Ruth insisted on more chemotherapy. She also chose to have all heroic measures used to extend her life, including CPR, tube feeding, and mechanical ventilation (i.e., breathing machines) if needed.

Due to her advanced age and debility, she had her treatments at the hospital as an inpatient. Depression set in. Ruth missed Calliemae, her home, and her sewing room. Now her days were a maze of never-ending tests, scans, blood draws, and scheduled medication deliveries, all choreographed to the incessant blips of a heart monitor and hum of oxygen. While in the hospital, with her immunity weakened by the

treatments, Ruth caught a superbug, which is an infection that is difficult if not impossible to treat with antibiotics. This made life even more
unbearable.

Sadly, Ruth's final months were spent sharing a hospital room with
a variety of strangers parading in and out. She never achieved a full
night of complete rest. Ruth spent most of her time distressed because
she could not go home, take care of her cat, and sew.

Her final days were as she had dreaded, spent alone in a sterile
hospital. Ruth never enjoyed completing her final quilt. In retrospect, if
Ruth had elected to use the hospice option, she would have greatly
improved her quality of life. She would have been at home surrounded
by her memories, creating her quilts, and spending time with her family
and friends. When her time came, it would have been in her own
peaceful bedroom, under a beautiful handmade quilt, cuddling
Calliemae.

To qualify for *hospice care*, the patient has to be terminally ill with
six months or less to live. Keep in mind that this is the doctor's best guess
based on the extent of the disease and its expected progression. There is
no lab test to determine this, no crystal ball to look into (which is good
as I was not trained to read one).

The classic image of hospice is taking care of patients with
advanced, incurable cancer. These are patients whose disease has
progressed. Often, there have been multiple visits to the emergency
room or hospital. There can be poor nutritional status, such as an unintentional 10 percent body weight loss or low protein levels. The functional status has also declined to the point of requiring considerable
assistance and medical care.

In addition to cancer patients, hospice cares for patients with a variety
of terminal illnesses. A list of common causes has been suggested:[2]

1. *Heart failure* with symptoms at rest despite optimal treatment.

2. *Severe lung disease* requiring supplemental oxygen with shortness
   of breath at rest. It would often be accompanied by rapid heart
   rates at rest (over 100), unintentional 10 percent body weight
   loss, and heart failure causing edema (swelling of the legs).

3. *Severe dementia.* This would include patients who need help in all areas such as dressing, bathing, walking, bathroom use, and those who cannot talk meaningfully. They often have medical complications such as bed sores, infections, and trouble eating.

4. *Advanced HIV disease (AIDS)* with life-threatening complications.

5. *End-stage liver disease*, which can be accompanied by malnutrition, hepatic encephalopathy (i.e., mental confusion), kidney failure, swelling, infections, and bleeding.

6. *Renal failure* patients who are either wanting to discontinue dialysis or close to needing dialysis and not wanting to initiate it. Reasons patients might want to decline dialysis include other organ failure (such as lung, heart, liver), terminal cancer, AIDS, being elderly, being chronically ill or malnourished, and dementia. It should be noted that hemodialysis is a major ordeal for patients, which typically requires them to spend three days a week at a dialysis center, and which leaves them feeling completely debilitated afterward. Also, dying of renal failure is typically thought of as "a good way to go" by medical personnel, in that it is relatively painless and symptom-free.

7. *Severe acute or chronic stroke* patients. A patient who is in a persistent coma or vegetative state beyond three days after a stroke could be such a hospice candidate. This could also be a post-stroke patient who can't swallow and does not desire artificial nutrition due to deteriorated mental status and/or loss of other bodily functions and/or other major medical illnesses. A chronic stroke patient may be a hospice candidate due to dementia, poor functional status, and medical complications such as bed sores, recurrent infections, and malnutrition.

Unfortunately, studies have shown that physicians tend to be optimistic in predicting a patient's survival (thinking patients have longer to live than they really do). This means that hospice has probably been underutilized by many patients.[3]

While we expect that a hospice patient has six months or less to live, more often than not, patients who enter hospice survive only days or weeks. However, it's not rare for patients to live beyond the six months. Patients who live beyond six months are not "kicked out" of hospice. I have had patients "graduate" hospice in that they stabilized and were doing so well that they were discharged from hospice care. If these patients worsen again, then they may go back into hospice. Overall, in a study of 260,000 Medicare patients in hospice for terminal cancer, less than 8 percent lived beyond six months.[4]

There are over three thousand hospice agencies in the United States. To enter a hospice program, the patient's physician must recommend a patient based on an expected survival time of six months or less and the patient/family's understanding of the diagnosis, for which they are planning for comfort care rather than cure. The patient is required to have a "do not resuscitate" (i.e., no CPR) order from the doctor. For most hospices, the plan would be for in-home comfort care rather than transporting the patient to the hospital for treatment. There are hospices in some states that have created their own facility where the patient can live out their final days.

A hospice program is a multidisciplinary team approach to treatment. It looks to treat a patient physically, emotionally, socially, and spiritually. Typically, there is a primary caregiver, usually a family member. The caregiver will be supported by an RN, a social worker, a pharmacist, a hospice chaplain, a personal physician, a physician who is the hospice medical director, and volunteers and/or other hired caregivers.

The RN is available on call 24 hours a day, 365 days a year to help ensure that the patient's every need is taken care of. The RN makes sure that the patient has enough medications or medical equipment needed for symptom control. (I've been woken up in the middle of a weekend night due to a patient in need of more pain medicine, and the RN was there to make sure it happened.)

Hospice care is typically a big financial benefit for patients and families, in that all hospice expenses are usually taken care of to ease financial worries. The social worker is also available for counselling and helping with whatever community or social needs the patient may have.

The hospice chaplain is there to help with any spiritual needs. The chaplain can also help prepare for a funeral or memorial service if desired. The chaplain is not there to replace your regular clergy, but as a valuable secondary resource to assist in whatever way they can, often in ways your regular clergy does not.

A big part of the hospice benefit is in counseling the patient, in terms of both physical as well as emotional needs. Physical need counseling can include proper medication administration, training in patient transferring (i.e., moving from bed to chair), positioning, feeding, mouth care, cleaning, bathing, changing, wound care, and proper equipment usage.

The physical counseling may also include suggestions for the patient's environmental surroundings. For instance, although odors, scents, and perfumes can be pleasing or relaxing to most people, they can also cause increased nausea in the terminal patient. A well-lit, clean, attractive room and clothing can help lift spirits. The environment should be full of love and warmth, such as familiar and pleasing items and pictures.

Throughout this book, I have emphasized building spiritual strength as the key to getting through the death and dying process. Hospice patients tend to place more emphasis on emotional support, which is also an important piece to the puzzle.

Emotional counseling is a vital service provided by hospice. It is often based on the work of Dr. Elizabeth Kubler-Ross, who described the five stages of dying. In order, they are: denial, anger, bargaining, depression, and acceptance. An initial "shock" stage can be added.

Table II on the next page describes the patient's stage and an appropriate family response.[5]

Table II
Stages of Dying and Appropriate Family Response

Patient Behavior	State	Family Response
Denial		
In effect, the patient says, "It cannot be true." Patients often search frantically for a favorable diagnosis.		Understand why the patient is grasping at straws. Patience and willingness to talk are important.
Anger		
The patient says, "Yes, but why me?" Deep anger follows, and this patient may bitterly envy those who are well and complain incessantly about almost everything.		Consider that the patient is angry over the coming loss of everything: family, friends, home, work, play. Treat patient with understanding respect and not returning anger.
Bargaining		
The patient says, "Maybe I can bargain with God and get a time extension." Promises of good behavior are made in return for time and some freedom from physical pain.		If the patient's bargain is revealed, it should be listened to, not brushed off. This stage passes in a short time.
Depression		
The patient grieves and mourns approaching death.		Attempts to cheer up or reassure the patient mean very little. The patient needs to express sorrow fully and without hindrance.
Acceptance		
The patient is neither angry nor depressed, only quietly expectant.		News of the outside world means little, and few visitors are required. There will be little talk, and it is time merely for the presence of close family.

Dying and Appropriate Family Response

It is important to be available to listen and talk to dying patients. A list of some suggested communication skills follows.[6]

1. **Listen.**
   - Be a sounding board; allow people to explore their own feelings, and draw their own conclusions.
   - Do not interrupt, pontificate, show impatience, or try to analyze the reasons for the other person's feelings.
   - Recognize when a person needs privacy, accept his need to be alone, and provide a specific place where you can be reached.
   - When necessary, repeat the person's own words in the form of a question to help him express himself when he has difficulty.
   - Be an active listener, acknowledge statements, make frequent eye contact, use the person's name, lean forward, and exclude distractions.

2. **Reassure.**
   - Do not minimize; avoid telling the patient about the experiences of others or yourself that might overshadow the patient's experience.
   - Do affirm the significance of the patient's experience and situation.

3. **Empathize.**
   - Use your voice, gestures, and facial expression to demonstrate your involvement with the other person; show your caring.
   - Make the other person feel unique, singular, and important.
   - Use phrases that demonstrate you understand his or her feelings.
   - Touch his or her hand, or give a spontaneous hug. Not everyone wants to be touched, however. Touching, when accepted by the other, gives the recipient permission to let go and to vent emotions.

4. **Recognize the other person's autonomy.**
    - Help the other person to remain independent, find their own solutions, and accept the need to be interdependent or even dependent.
    - Help the person to receive help without losing their dignity.
    - Give the person a sense of self-sufficiency; ask pertinent questions that will point thinking toward alternatives.
    - Demonstrate confidence in the other person's own resources. People need to generate their own solutions, to be reminded that they have their own strength and autonomy to cope.

5. **Control your own emotions and fears.**
    - Concentrate on the other person.

6. **Acknowledge the legitimacy of the person's emotions.**
    - Give permission for them to be angry.
    - Recognize their right to be hurt, angry, or depressed.

7. **Strengthen their self-esteem.**
    - Say "You can!" *not* "You should."
    - Reassure them of their self-worth.
    - Tell them they are worthwhile, capable human beings.
    - Be a special friend, be gentle; demonstrate your capacity to listen, to understand, to be sensitive, and to care.
    - Allow your mind, your spirit, your sense of humor to be free.

8. **Demonstrate caring in a practical, special way.**
    - Chauffeur, cook, shop, or simply sit with them.
    - Do not wait to be asked; observe and do.

9. **Be available; be there.**

10. **Respect all confidences.**
    - Reassure them that you will not betray their trust.
    - Respect their feelings and privacy.

11. **Be yourself; act on your "gut" response.**
   - Act from your intuition.
   - You are a builder of bridges, not a fixer.

12. **Adapt various communication skills to fix your personal, unique caregiving skills.**

13. **Accept the patient's limitations: spiritual, emotional, psychological, and physical.**
   - Never be judgmental.
   - Meet the patient where he is, *not* where you think he should be.
   - Attempt to bring the patient up to the level of functioning that was the norm before the crisis.
   - Help the patient set realistic goals.

Notice that it is important to listen and let the patient gather their own thoughts rather than imposing your thoughts upon them.

A huge advantage of hospice programs is that they provide bereavement counseling for families of patients who have died. I've had several patients whose loved one has died, and they greatly appreciated the bereavement counseling and support they received from hospice. The family of a deceased patient can go through the same stages that the patient did: shock, denial, anger, bargaining, depression, and acceptance. Everyone is different in how they work through these stages, and they may go back and forth between stages. However, it's important for people to get to the acceptance stage, and hospice counseling can help.

Hospice is usually thought of as being a home-based program in that the patient is still living in their own home. However, there are circumstances when that is not necessarily the case. Sometimes a patient may be residing in an assisted-living facility or a skilled nursing facility when they enter a hospice program. Hospice can still attend to the patient in those facilities. However, in California at least, the assisted-living facility would need to have a hospice waiver in order to care for a patient in hospice. This law may vary from state to state.

Another aspect of hospice is *respite* care. Respite care is set up in order to prevent caregiver burnout. For instance, suppose a wife is caring for her husband in hospice, and this has been going on for a few months and she is getting tired. She could take a week off by placing her husband in respite care. This might be a nursing facility that takes over his care for the week, while the wife takes a week off to rejuvenate herself. This is desirable because, if she is getting burned out, then both husband and wife will suffer.

The other area in which a hospice-like program comes into play is in the acute hospital inpatient setting. Let's say, for example, that a patient comes into the hospital debilitated with a major medical illness or perhaps trauma. If the patient is clearly not doing well and has a poor prognosis and death is expected in the near future, then the patient may be placed on a *comfort care pathway*. The goal of the comfort care pathway is to keep the patient as comfortable as possible without attempting to cure them. Like in hospice, this occurs with patient and/or family consent.

The comfort care pathway is like hospice care, only it takes place in a hospital room. Typically, the hospital tries to arrange a private room if at all possible, to provide the patient and family with personal time together with privacy. A social worker and chaplain are also available, in addition to the usual hospital nursing team, to try to keep the patient as comfortable as possible.

Both hospice and the hospital comfort care pathway generally do an excellent job of symptom control, which allows the patient to die peacefully. Potential symptoms to be addressed include pain, shortness of breath, nausea, dry mouth, constipation, edema (swelling), fatigue, poor appetite and/or trouble swallowing, anxiety, depression, and delirium. The frequency of some of these symptoms in hospice cancer patients is listed below[7]:

pain: 57 percent
nausea: 25 percent
anxiety: 50 percent
decreased appetite: 73 percent
shortness of breath: 38 percent

decreased activity: 83 percent
depression: 46 percent
drowsiness: 74 percent
decreased sense of well-being: 65 percent

Fortunately there are medicines that work well for pain, anxiety, nausea, constipation, and shortness of breath (see chapters in this book on pain and suffering). If these symptoms are kept at bay, then the patient is usually comfortable at the time of death.

There is debate on whether the dying patient should be given intravenous fluids. No study has conclusively said yes or no. One study[8] showed that IV fluids helped with sedation and controlling myoclonus (muscle spasms), but it did not help with fatigue or hallucinations. Arguments against IV hydration are a lesser need for the bed pan, fewer lung secretions, less vomiting, less edema (water retention), and decreased consciousness, which leads to less pain, suffering, and thirst sensations. A survey of hospice nurses concluded that patients who declined feeding and fluids died a "good death."[9] Based on this, I feel a good policy is to certainly provide food and fluids to those patients who are able to swallow, but artificial means do not need to be encouraged.

A few symptoms at the end of life should be mentioned here in order to ward off an unexpected surprise for the family. One is to expect the patient to become more unresponsive. During this period, the patient may move their body for no particular purpose and/or make facial expressions. These are to be expected and do not mean that the patient is experiencing pain. If there is doubt about pain assessment, the hospice nurse is an excellent resource to consult. Shortness of breath can be treated with oxygen and breathing treatments, if appropriate. However, shortness of breath is often best treated with narcotics, such as morphine, and by giving medicines for anxiety, as well. Patients will often have irregular breathing patterns. Also, patients will often make gurgling or crackling sounds when they breathe (which is sometimes called a "death rattle"). This can be upsetting to the family, but not to the patient. Medicines may be given to dry up these secretions. Finally, the family should not expect the patient to wake up and communicate before dying. If you are not present at the bedside at the end, do not feel guilty.

The final point to remember about hospice care is that there are always opportunities for spiritual strengthening. This can occur from a variety of perspectives. Family, friends, and caregivers can strengthen themselves spiritually, first and foremost, by caring for the patient. Providing loving care gives them a chance to practice their Christian values. In addition, they can witness the patient's inner strength (that would be the patient's true faith in Jesus Christ) and strengthen their own spirit.

Volunteering for a hospice program is a great way for Christians to put their faith to work. Most hospice programs rely on volunteers to help in a variety of areas that can include patient and family visits, patient care, running errands, pet therapy, and clerical assistance.

The hospice patient can strengthen their faith and *focus* through a variety of ways:

1. Discussions with the hospice chaplain, their personal clergy, family, caregivers, friends, and visitors

2. Studying the Bible or other religious and spiritual material

3. Displaying their strength in Christ

4. Expressing gratitude for the care they are receiving. Remember, expressing true heartfelt gratitude lifts the patient's spirits, as well. The other side of the coin is that there is not much better, from the caregiver's standpoint, than receiving a word of thanks. *Gratitude helps maintain a positive attitude.*

On a personal note, both of my parents were blessed with excellent hospice care before they died. As a physician, I have had many patients who were cared for by hospice staff straight through to a peaceful end. I am grateful for that.

18

Suicide, Alcohol, and "Recreational" Drugs

No temptation has seized you except what is common to man. And God is faithful; he will not let you be tempted beyond what you can bear. But when you are tempted, he will also provide a way out so that you can stand up under it. —1 Corinthians 10:13

I had no intention of writing a chapter on suicide when I first started writing this book. My goal was, and still is, to focus on a positive approach to death and the dying process. Suicide was not part of that initial equation. However, it dawned on me that I have had family members who have committed suicide. Unfortunately I have also had two patients commit suicide. Maybe if I had been able to foresee these events, then I could have said or done something to prevent their very premature deaths. I am therefore dedicating this chapter to them, so that maybe something good can come from their passing.

First and foremost, let me say that suicide is wrong, and it must be prevented. Let me also state that I believe I understand why people want to commit suicide. Let's look at these ideas and how we can use some of the principles discussed in this book to keep us from going down the path to suicide.

We know suicide is wrong because the Bible tells us so. Exodus 20:13 states "you must not murder." Suicide is murder of oneself. Leviticus 19:18 states to "love your neighbor as yourself." Suicide is not the answer if you are to love yourself.

151

Now, we know that at our death our soul will be saved for eternity because of our faith in Jesus Christ, the Savior. The question is, will our soul be saved if we purposefully hasten our death through suicide? Are we showing our faith in Jesus Christ as Savior if we commit suicide (knowing that He doesn't want us to do that)? We know that God is just and kind, so we can count on Him to make the situation right. However, it is not wise to test God in this way (in fact, it is not wise to test God at all). The problem with testing God is that we can be sure that He will know the correct answer. The rub is that we don't know what the correct answer to the test is. There is no reason to guess on a test, when we can be sure of the answer. You just need to make Jesus the solid answer.

There are a few reasons why someone would want to terminate their life through suicide. These include:

1. Sadness and depression—i.e., "Life is so miserable, what is the use in living?"
2. Self-hatred
3. Shame/embarrassment
4. Sudden, overwhelming loss, such as the loss of a loved one
5. Pain and physical suffering
6. Fear, such as fear of a worsening condition
7. Trying to "right" a wrong that you committed

Whatever the motive behind suicide, it is obviously severe and utterly devastating to the patient. The solutions, therefore, must be very powerful, which means using a Christian-based philosophy. A strong enough faith in Jesus can and will eventually forever conquer whatever it is that's troubling you. Keeping this in mind, let's tackle suicidal motives in a little more detail.

Depression is probably by far the most common cause of suicide. Depression can be so severe that the patient has no motivation to seek help or be compliant in taking medication. For these patients, family and friends must push them to get help. A patient who continues to resist may need psychiatric inpatient hospitalization. A patient can and should be held against their wishes, if they are deemed to be a risk to themselves or others. In California, this is called being placed on a "5150 Involuntary Psychiatric Hold," which holds a patient for seventy-two hours while he/she is evaluated by a medical professional. Other states have similar laws. Someone who sees a patient as a suicide risk needs to call the police, even if the patient is uncooperative.

Fortunately, the large majority of cases of depression can be alleviated through therapy, counseling, and/or the large number of antidepressant medications available to us today. Oftentimes, a patient may need to try several medications until they find what works for them. The key is to be persistent. Do not give up. Do not give up. Do not give up!

Unfortunately, there are patients whose depression seems resistant to all of our best efforts. If you are one of these patients, continue to seek help. Remember that time is on your side. I have seen patients whom I thought were permanently depressed, and years later that depression lifted, either because of improved life situations or through the healing work of time alone. During this time, remember to find a purpose—something positive to do.

All medical efforts at treating depression should be combined with a spiritual approach. Strengthen your faith. Talk to friends, clergy, and church members. Remember to find something to be grateful for—there must be something, however small or seemingly insignificant. It could be something as small as a glass of water or the shirt on your back. Use gratitude and your faith to build on the positive things in your life. If you can persevere in your faith, you will one day be rewarded, which will most likely be while you are still here on earth but eventually in heaven.

Self-hatred often goes hand-in-hand with depression as a motive for suicide. The depression needs to be treated as just mentioned. The self-hatred needs to be conquered by changing your thought processes. Again, *The Feeling Good Handbook* by Dr. David Burns is a great resource. Basically, you need to learn to build yourself up, rather than tear yourself down, by focusing on the positive. Find a positive, doable goal to work toward and cherish even small accomplishments as you work toward that goal.

The foundation for overcoming self-hatred must again be your faith in Jesus. Remember that God loves you. If you are good enough for God, then you should be good enough for yourself!

The suicidal motives of shame/embarrassment and sudden overwhelming loss will be addressed together here because I believe the solution is the same for both. First, some examples:

1. **Shame/embarrassment**. Last year there was a sad story in the news of a young man who was recorded doing a sexual act and it was posted on the Internet. Apparently, the shame and embarrassment were overwhelming, and he soon went out and committed suicide.

2. **Sudden, overwhelming loss**. When the stock market crashed, ushering in the Great Depression, some stock traders, who apparently lost much or all of their money, were so overwhelmed that they committed suicide.

In both of these examples, the devastating blow was so strong that they could not handle it, so they "escaped" via suicide.

I believe that these are examples of why people need to have a strong foundation of faith in their lives. We need to *build this strong faith foundation before* bad things happen to us. In the case of long-term illness, we have time to build faith along the way. When sudden losses occur, they can be so overwhelming that we react with a suicide attempt before there's any time to build up our faith. Faith needs to be present before events occur. Building faith early in life when things are good is like an acrobat putting up a safety net before attempting a high wire act.

When incredibly bad things happen to people of strong faith, they can rely on Jesus to get them through. This is what will keep you from committing suicide. Once you realize that you will not commit suicide (because you don't want to let God down), then you have time to heal the wounds. In the case of shame/embarrassment, people have a way of forgiving and forgetting just about anything you do (unless it's a great atrocity, which I'll address below).

Time, counseling, and faith will heal wounds of embarrassment or grief from sudden loss. But if you do not have strong faith and a desire to please God, you may not survive the initial horrible blow.

Other motives for suicide are to relieve pain and physical suffering (this includes physician-assisted suicide) and fear of worsening conditions. In both of these cases, the patient is seeking a preemptive death in order to avoid future suffering. Much, if not all of this book, is designed to relieve these problems so that suicide is not necessary. Again, faith in Jesus, God, and heaven is the key to pulling you through.

The final motive for suicide is in trying to "right" a wrong that you committed. For instance, there have been cases of a person committing suicide after they purposefully or even accidentally killed another person. In this case, one needs to remember that we have a forgiving God, if one is truly repentant. Although one can never make up for such an act, some healing can be accomplished through good works. These good works might include helping others or perhaps helping society in general work to prevent similar incidents in the future. Even if a person is in prison, they can help by being a model prisoner and helping other prisoners build their own faith.

Drug and Alcohol Abuse

The title of this chapter included alcohol and "recreational" drugs along with suicide. They are similar when the intent of the alcohol or drug use is to totally escape from the realities of this world. Suicide is a permanent total escape from the reality of this world. However, people who commit suicide forget that they are not escaping God's world, which is all encompassing and eternal, and exists beyond this mortal world.

The intent of alcohol or drug use is not like suicide, where total escape is intended. For instance, people may have a glass of wine because of a pleasing taste or because of its known benefit to the heart, when used in moderation. However, heavy use when intended to totally "escape" the realities of this world is like a "mini, yet reversible" suicide. When taken to the extreme, such usage may even cause a premature death. As mentioned earlier in this book, God has a planned purpose for our lives; seeking or even tempting a premature death is not God's plan. Therefore, alcohol and drug abuse is detrimental to building a strong faith. Building and having a strong faith is key to easing fears, anxiety, and the suffering of the death and dying process.

We also need to examine suicide and alcohol and drug abuse from a dignity standpoint, just as Catherine of Siena did in her letter to a prostitute. Catherine of Siena was a fourteenth-century Dominican sister who devoted her life to active charity, caring for the sick, and urging the pope to reform the church. A prolific letter writer, she once informed a prostitute that we get our dignity from Christ's sacrifice.[1] Indeed, your basic dignity comes from the fact that Jesus laid His life down for you. God considers your life to be worth a lot, and you should recognize and uphold the dignity that He bestowed on you, rather than throw it all away via suicide, alcohol, or drugs.

Life belongs to God, who created it. He is the only One who has a right to give or take it. We are "playing God" when we take that right away from Him.

Remembering to *focus on your faith* and *viewing situations from an eternal perspective* eases mental suffering and the need for escapism.

Keep in mind that depression is extremely common. Almost one in five Americans will experience major depression at some point in their lives. In my medical practice, I have seen hundreds of patients with depression. Many, if not most, of these patients have had suicidal thoughts at some point.

A recurring theme I hear from many of these patients is that their Christian faith is what kept them from acting on their suicidal ideation. Yes, Jesus does save lives. Do not let anyone tell you differently, for I have seen the living proof.

19

Emotional Pain: Regrets

Crying is all right in its own way while it lasts. But you have to stop sooner or later, and then you still have to decide what to do.
—C. S. Lewis

I lost a friend recently. Pastor Glen Cole was a truly good man, one who had been a leading voice for Christianity in the Sacramento region. His work included founding one of the largest churches in the area, the Capital Christian Center, as well as growing another church, the Trinity Life Center, to over a thousand members.

Pastor Cole died in the parking lot of the Trinity Life Center. He had driven his car into the parking lot, parked his car, unbuckled his seat belt, and proceeded to go on into God's house—heaven, that is. A member of Trinity's staff found him in his car, but it was too late.

I read about his death the next day in the morning paper. Glen Cole's death hit me especially hard; you see, I had been his doctor. At age seventy-eight, he had been the picture of good health. In fact, he had even played golf the day before he died. I had to ask myself whether there was something I could have done to prevent his death. I proceeded to review his medical record.

Glen had a history of high blood pressure and high cholesterol, but he was on medication to control both of those conditions, and his numbers were excellent. I remembered him passing a stress test of his heart a few years back, with flying colors. There are no guidelines for healthy patients to have stress tests every year. It looked like I had done everything right, but maybe I could have done more. What if I had been given the foresight to have him do another stress test last year? What if, what if, what if... I wanted to kick myself.

I suppose all physicians go through similar thoughts when they lose a patient. It's part of human nature; we all think back on times in our lives when we wish we had done something different, or avoided suffering some misfortune. So many times I have heard people make statements like:

"I should've done..."

"If I could do it over again, I would've done..."

"I regret that..."

"Things would've been different if..."

"I could've been somebody if..."

"I wasted my life on/for..."

"I used to be...and now..."

"Why did this have to happen to me instead of..."

"Why couldn't I have been lucky like..."

"Why did I have to lose..."

"I don't want to lose..."

Life is filled with emotions. The good emotions create delightful times in our lives, but how do we learn from and prevail over the dark times?

Along the same lines, how do we reconcile the notion of a life not well lived? Surely we have all done things that we are not proud of. Some have even performed deeds that deserve prison sentences. We are supposed to do good works that draw other people toward Christ, and yet some of our actions are so un-Christlike that others must surely question our moral code. How do we live with these thoughts?

To solve these disturbing problems, we need to first remind ourselves of a few stories from the life of Jesus:

In John 8:3–11 we read:

The teachers of the law and the Pharisees brought in a woman caught in the act of adultery. They made her stand before the group and said to

Jesus, "Teacher, this woman was caught in the act of adultery. In the Law, Moses commanded us to stone such women. Now what do you say?" They were using this question as a trap, in order to have a basis for accusing Him.

But Jesus bent down and started to write on the ground with His finger. When they kept on questioning Him, He straightened up and said to them, "If any of you is without sin, let him be the first to throw a stone at her." Again He stooped down and wrote on the ground.

At this, those who heard began to go away one at a time, the older ones first, until only Jesus was left, with the woman still standing there. Jesus straightened up and asked her, "Woman, where are they? Has no one condemned you?"

"No one, sir," she said.

"Then neither do I condemn you," Jesus declared. "Go now and leave your life of sin."

Notice that in those days adultery was comparable to the worst of crimes, worthy of capital punishment. Jesus pardoned even one of the most terrible sins, with the command given to no longer sin. The crucial concept, therefore, is to truly repent of your past actions, and henceforth lead a genuine Christian life. Bear in mind that (thanks to the Lord's saving grace) your time in heaven is eternal. This means you have plenty of time to show your love and gratitude to the Lord for His forgiveness. And if Jesus forgives you, then surely you should find it in your heart to forgive yourself, providing that your remorse is sincere. As C. S. Lewis put it: "I think that if God forgives us, we must forgive ourselves. Otherwise, it is almost like setting ourselves up as a higher tribunal than Him."

The other story is found in Matthew 14:22–32, when we learn of Jesus walking on water:

Immediately Jesus made the disciples get into the boat and go on ahead of Him to the other side, while He dismissed the crowd. After He had dismissed them, He went up on a mountainside by Himself to pray. When evening came, He was there alone, but the boat was already a considerable distance from land, buffeted by the waves because the wind was against it.

During the fourth watch of the night Jesus went out to them, walking on the lake. When the disciples saw Him walking on the lake, they were terrified. "It's a ghost," they said, and cried out in fear.

But Jesus immediately said to them: "Take courage! It is I. Don't be afraid."

"Lord, if it's you," Peter replied, "tell me to come out to you on the water."

"Come," He said.

Then Peter got down out of the boat, walked on the water and came toward Jesus. But when he saw the wind, he was afraid and, beginning to sink, cried out, "Lord save me!"

Immediately Jesus reached out His hand and caught him. "You of little faith," He said, "why did you doubt?"

And when they climbed into the boat, the wind died down.

Keeping these stories in mind, we also need to remind ourselves of what exactly we have as Christians in order to work out our emotional difficulties. If you are a Christian, then you believe and follow Christ's teachings, and you've accepted Him into your life as your Savior. *If He is in your life, then He is in you.* Somewhere, deep in your soul, is a bright spark of light named Jesus. You need to use that brilliant light to overcome and drive away all of the emotional darkness.

Just as Jesus pulled Peter up out of the depths, He can pull you up out of your emotional darkness. The key is to have ultimate faith in Jesus, and rely on the knowledge that He is the solution to all your inner turmoil and strife. When you have the promise of never-ending happiness in heaven, all else pales in significance. With faith in Jesus, you can walk above the depths of despair.

One more analogy further helps to illustrate the point:

Suppose you are watching a dramatic movie, uncertain of the outcome. It may make you frightened, worried, or sad. Now let's say you fast-forward to the end and see that everything turns out well.

Suddenly, any sadness or anxieties that the movie provoked are washed away. In similar fashion, you need to realize that your life will turn out well with Christ.

Like Peter, *focus on Christ* and walk out your faith!

20

A Patient's Approach

Affliction is often that thing which prepares an ordinary person for some sort of an extraordinary destiny. —*C. S. Lewis*

When I started writing this book three years ago, my goal was to ease people's fears and suffering regarding death and the dying process. A big concern of mine at the time was self-doubt. How could I phrase the discussion to convince people of my thoughts, beliefs, and knowledge on the subject? My fear was of a dying patient coming to me and asking: How can you tell me what I should be thinking about death when you haven't walked in my shoes?

I prayed to God for an answer to this problem. God, in His infinite wisdom, not only gave me an answer to the problem, but He taught me a lesson at the same time. The answer to the problem was slam-dunk brilliant. I was given a diagnosis of terminal cancer. Now I could write from the patient's perspective and know exactly what they were feeling. No dying patient could now say that I hadn't "walked in their shoes."

And so my prayer was answered, though not in the way that I expected or hoped for. The great lesson I learned from this is that when you pray to God, you should be very specific about what you ask for. Next time I know to just ask for the words to use, and I can skip the part about getting the disease too.

Be that as it may, I believe I am one of the most relaxed terminal cancer patients around. This is not because I have a very slow-growing cancer. Nor is it because I have a death wish (I do not). No, I am relaxed because of a very positive philosophical approach to death that is geared toward allaying fears and easing both physical and mental suffering. This chapter summarizes that positive approach from the dying patient's perspective.

The first crucial step to take is to demystify death in your mind. Taking the mystery out of the subject decreases fears and anxieties. A couple of examples may help to make the point:

When my kids were starting high school, they were given an orientation day, in which older students gave them tours of the campus, showed them where to go, and made suggestions of what to do and how to act. This made for a smooth transition from junior high to high school.

I conduct exercise treadmill tests on patients to evaluate for possible coronary artery disease (i.e., to see if they are at risk for a heart attack). Patients who have walked on a treadmill before generally have no problem doing the test. However, patients who have never been on a treadmill before tend to have trouble doing the test. In fact, some of them get so nervous that it's almost as if they have forgotten how to walk at all! So we see that when people get very nervous, anxious, and scared, they do not handle the most basic tasks very well—sometimes even something as simple as walking. If these people had practiced on a treadmill or had even seen a treadmill test in advance, they would have probably done better.

There is a specific thought process on handling death and dying so that it is no longer such a mystery. This will make it less frightening and allow for clearer thoughts. Also, decreased anxiety usually makes physical symptoms more tolerable, as well.

The first step in approaching death is to separate in your mind the physical and practical aspects from the mental/emotional/spiritual aspect. The physical is simply how to deal with the physical symptoms. The practical aspect is in addressing financial issues as well as the logistics of care.

Many of the practical aspects of care can and should be dealt with quickly and at the outset of care. You should complete paperwork appointing a durable power of attorney for health care as well as a will or living trust. Do this as soon as possible and get that behind you, so that you can concentrate on other matters. If these forms have already been done in the past, pull them out and review them to make sure they still fit your wishes. Make sure your appointed power of attorney for both health care and financial issues knows your wishes.

Next, get your financial papers in order and make sure your power of attorney knows about them so that they can step right in and take over in case you become incapacitated. This includes insurance papers (health, life, homeowner, auto, long-term care, etc.), savings accounts, stocks, bonds, investments, real estate, home deeds, car titles, any other investments, VA, social security, or disability benefits, etc.

Part of this planning should take into consideration possible needs for long-term care. Many people are so used to being self-sufficient for so long that they neglect or are in denial that they may need someone else to care for them. Do not let this be you. Make some plans for long-term care. This could include long-term care insurance. It might be plans for family or friends and caregivers to help. This process could include screening or hiring caretakers and evaluating assisted-living or skilled nursing facilities. Consider what you would want and how it might be financed, and ideally have a backup plan. Make your plans as soon as feasible to ease potential burdens on loved ones. Doing these things allows you to concentrate on your physical and mental health.

Make plans or at least put together some suggestions for a funeral or memorial service. Formulate a proposal that is meaningful and doable. Some think a service is not needed, or they don't want anyone to get together and grieve. You can't short-circuit the grieving process; remember that the service will provide important closure for your family and friends.

Early in the process, you should settle on a doctor (or doctors) and a plan of care. Your doctor will set the plan of care based on your disease in addition to input from you. You should be comfortable and confident in your doctor.

A second opinion can be a good idea, especially if you are not comfortable or confident in your doctor. Most doctors are happy to have you get a second opinion if you need reassurance that your plan of care is the right one for you. In fact, most doctors will initiate your getting a second opinion if they have any doubts about the diagnosis or plan of care. Therefore, do not be afraid to ask your doctor for a second opinion, if you'd be more comfortable having one. However, I encourage you to not seek third, fourth, fifth, etc., opinions. Multiple opinions tend to confuse and complicate the issue without adding any real benefit. Seeking care from multiple sources consumes precious time that could be spent doing enjoyable activities with family and friends, pursuing your goal or purpose in life, or concentrating on your mental and spiritual health.

When I was diagnosed with non-Hodgkin's lymphoma, my wife and I were inundated with well-meaning people suggesting treatments and multiple doctors that I should go see. My life would have been a little different if I had jumped at all of these suggestions, which included: traveling around the country seeing multiple specialists, doing colon cleanses, pureeing and juicing all my food, spending hours and days searching the Internet and the world for a miracle cure, not drinking tap water, becoming a vegan, shopping for a variety of herbs, and having weekly coffee enemas (I'm not sure if they wanted that coffee to be hot or cold!).

Following all these suggestions would not only have taken away from my quality of life (e.g., I enjoy a good steak on occasion), but it would also have taken time away from my exercise regimen, watching my kids' sports games, and my mental and spiritual health.

Yes, the medical field is an interesting arena where almost everyone has an opinion on what should be done. Here I am, a respected (I think), board-certified internal medicine physician, and I am having people with no medical training suggesting treatments to me. I could not imagine giving tips of the trade to my auto mechanic, telling the police how to catch the criminal, or suggesting accounting practices to the banker. Be that as it may, I am honored that people care enough to offer suggestions. However, I try not to let their ideas distract me.

Similarly, I encourage you not to let multiple opinions distract you from enjoyable activities or spiritual thoughts. By all means, get the second opinion if you desire but do not search for multiple opinions or spend hours or even days searching the Internet. Also, remember that you may already have a second opinion. For instance, your internist or family physician may be comfortable caring for congestive heart failure, and you may also have a cardiologist who serves as a second opinion. If you were hospitalized, you quite likely had a second opinion there from the hospitalist or specialist doctor who saw you in the hospital.

You could have had a second opinion and not known it. For instance, doctors frequently talk to each other when the patient is not around to get another opinion (often called a "curbside consult"). In my case, I know my oncologist discussed my case at the tumor board where a group of physicians offer advice to each other on patient care. This makes me relax with confidence in the care I receive and focus on the rest of my life outside of treatment. It's like letting the airline pilot fly the plane while you take a nap or read a book. Just remember to keep regular follow-up appointments with your doctor and report any new or worsening symptoms.

Easing fears and anxiety are equally important to the process. Remember that there is a mind-body interaction. Any stress, fear, or anxiety that you have will worsen whatever physical symptom you may have. Worsening physical symptoms can in turn worsen fear and anxiety, and it all becomes a vicious cycle. In addition, both these mental and physical symptoms will keep you from concentrating on a more important agenda—quality time for enjoyment with family and friends, working on your goals or purpose in life, and spiritual pursuits.

In the chapter on fear, I discussed that the moment of death does not hurt. This is a key concept to remember. The fear of the moment of death is a primary fear that people have, and we need to put that idea to rest. Next, people fear the potential pain and suffering prior to death. Remember that you quite likely have already gone through pain or suffering symptoms, just as bad if not worse, at some point in your life. Also, you definitely have had ancestors who have gone through these symptoms without the benefit of any modern medicine or technology to alleviate the symptoms. Keep this in mind because confidence and attitude mean everything. Time and time again, doctors see patients with similar problems, and those with positive attitudes and motivations do so much better than those without.

Just taking on a positive attitude will go a long way toward minimizing any fear or anxiety. Additional methods can be employed, including exercise, a simple stroll in the park, pet therapy, counseling, relaxing music, prayer and meditation, hobbies and crafts, and other distractions such as games, movies, comedies, and conversations. If a little anxiety remains, that is okay; use it as a motivator to keep you going. However, if you have done all of the above and your fear or anxiety is still so bad that it keeps you from focusing, then I suggest you see your doctor for a trial of medicine. Your fear and anxiety should be controlled well enough so that you can concentrate on the more important items.

After getting a medical plan of care started, and easing overwhelming fear and anxiety, it is time to really concentrate on your mental, emotional, and spiritual health. Mental, emotional, and spiritual health are really all a continuum of the same process. Ideally, it is something that you have worked on your whole life prior to any illness coming into the picture. However, after being diagnosed with a major illness, it is particularly important for this to become a primary focus. I talk about getting a medical care plan in place and reducing major fears and anxieties first, as these distractions can be paralyzing and keep you from what should be your primary focus.

Of paramount and primary importance in building spiritual health is being confident in the concept that you have a soul, above and beyond your flesh and bones. You cannot have *spiritual* health without a *spirit*. The early chapters in this book were written to try to convince you of that fact. However, ultimately you must take the leap of faith and believe. From there, everything else good will follow. If you don't think that you have a soul, then it's hard to believe in a higher power, or God. You must trust that you have a soul, or else there will be nothing for Jesus to save. Before believing Jesus can save you, you must accept that you are your soul. At some point you must just believe.

An example of how this might work came not long ago on a father-daughter adventure that I had with my daughter, Lauren. She decided that we should go zip-lining in the giant redwoods. I have to tell you, first, that I do not like heights. Zip-lining involves being connected to and sliding down a metal cable that is strung between two trees. Basically, you have to jump out of a two-hundred-foot-tall tree and dangle in the air while you glide to another tree. Before jumping, you can try to see if the cable, trees, and equipment are strong and good. However, even the best of equipment will eventually break, and even big, strong trees will eventually fall over. You can never be absolutely sure that everything will hold you up until you take that daring jump and find out. Then the rewards of gliding peacefully in a beautiful forest can be had. In the same way, you must jump aboard in the belief of your soul, and then the full rewards of your faith can be reaped.

Be firm in your belief in your own soul and use that to build on. In similar fashion, a building has footings set securely in the ground at the corners, and under the support walls, to make sure the entire structure stays in place. Make your belief in your soul one of the corner foundations of your own personal spiritual house. The other three corners are the Holy Trinity. Therefore, the foundation of your spiritual home should look something like this:

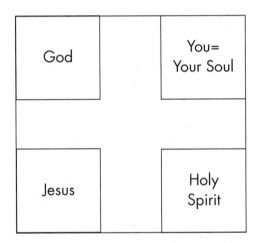

You need to build on all of these foundations for spiritual growth. Do not doubt yourself or your faith. If you doubt, your personal house of spiritual faith will crumble, allowing depression, fear, and anxiety to intensify. As a result, physical suffering will worsen due to the mind-body interaction.

Start with the knowledge of your own being, which is your soul, and then build on your faith in God. Build your faith in God in multiple ways. This can be done through Bible study and other religious readings, attending church, going to faith group meetings, praying, meditating on God, experiencing religious music and art, and talking with other believers.

Continue to strengthen, build, and focus on your faith in God. At the same time, strengthen your faith in Jesus as the Savior of your soul. As your faith builds, it will approach true knowledge, while fear, anxiety, and depression will fade away. Because of your faith in Jesus, your soul has overcome death. Everything else discussed in this book pales in comparison. Because of Jesus, your soul will wind up in heaven, regardless of whether you are able to take advantage of other topics discussed in this book. All the other topics only serve to ease that transition.

The other cornerstone foundation of your spiritual home is the Holy Spirit. The Holy Spirit provides gifts from God, which we can use not only to enjoy for our own purpose, but especially to serve God.

One of our gifts is giving gratitude, which serves to lift our own mood. Remember to give gratitude at least daily for that which we have or are given. This can include, but is not limited to: family, friends, caregivers, pets, medicine and other medical care and equipment, food, shelter, the church, the Bible, books, hobbies, clothes, entertainment, modern technology, etc.

Give gratitude for your medical conditions, and it will help you maintain a positive attitude. For instance, I have non-Hodgkin's lymphoma, which is a terminal cancer, and it seems bad at first glance. I am grateful, however, that I have non-Hodgkin's lymphoma rather than other diseases that could be worse. No matter how bad things may be, your situation can always be worse; be grateful that you don't have a worse problem. Always find a way to give gratitude. Whenever you feel down, work at finding something positive about the situation.

I had a patient, whom we'll call J. He suffered from end-stage lung disease that left him very weak. However, J. had a great positive attitude. Every time I saw him, he gave thanks for the fact that he had an oxygen tank that let him do a few things. In fact, he hooked up the oxygen so that he could work out by riding a stationary bike. J. eventually died, but he lived about five years longer than he would have, due to his great attitude.

Remember the power of laughter and find humor wherever you can.

Remember to find a strong, positive purpose to your life that incorporates evangelism, either active or passive. Again, passive evangelism means living out the Christian lifestyle values that make others want to either strengthen their own Christian beliefs or become interested in wanting to seek out Christ for the first time because your example inspired them. Focus your life on achieving your life's purpose. This will not only serve the Lord, but it will also help improve your longevity. Gratitude, laughter, and focusing on your life's purpose will also help alleviate any pain or suffering symptoms that you may have.

Remember to pray. Always pray. Pray at least once a day. Pray for healing. Pray for alleviation of symptoms. Feel free to let God know your emotions—be they anger, fear, sadness, or gladness, but always remember to express gratitude in your prayers. Pray for strength and focus in achieving your life's purpose.

There are two frequent and pervasive thoughts or concerns that I hear from dying patients. The first is a concern over being a burden to family and caregivers. The second is sadness over leaving family, friends, and loved ones.

When considering whether or not you are a burden to others, refer back to the chapter on code status (Chapter 13). That chapter talked about whether or not you are still able to evangelize for Christ—either actively or passively. If you are still able to evangelize, then I strongly encourage you not to feel like you are a burden. In fact, if you are still well enough to be reading this book, then you are *not* a burden.

The reason that you should not feel like you're a burden, despite all that your family and caregivers are doing for you, is that you can still do even more for them. One very powerful thing that you can do for your caregiver is express gratitude. Caryl and I had an experience that high-lights this concept.

The last few years, Caryl has been working on our church's Christmas sharing project. This involves gathering and giving gifts (such as toys and clothes) and food to underprivileged families in our area. One year, I went out with her to deliver the goods. We drove down a gravel road and came upon a small home out in the middle of a field. A young boy was waiting for us out front, knowing that it was the day for us to make deliveries. He called his father and siblings to come out and meet us at our car. We handed out the wrapped gifts and bags of food. One of the gifts had a small Hot Wheels car taped on the outside. The boy beamed in delight. He then looked in one of the bags and pumped his arm in the air and cheered. As we got back in the car, I turned to Caryl and asked her what was in the bag. The answer was a frozen turkey.

That boy's expression of gratitude over a small toy car and a frozen turkey was the best Christmas present I ever received. We were the ones delivering the goods to a poor family, yet we felt truly rewarded, thanks to the boy's reaction. *That* is what I mean by the power of gratitude. Give gratitude and free yourself from being a burden.

The second pervasive thought that I see is sadness in the dying patient over leaving this world. If you ever had to move from your beloved longtime home to a new and unfamiliar location, then you know something about this type of sadness that people have. This sadness is certainly understandable and even expected. However, this sadness can become an overwhelming, paralyzing mental suffering.

One way to break free from your sadness is to take advantage of your spiritual home. Remember that your spiritual home is built upon the solid four-corner foundation of your soul plus the Holy Trinity. The problem we run into is that we get so caught up in the earthly world, we forget that our spiritual home belongs with God.

What really brought this point across to me is one word from the Bible. It is my favorite word in the Bible, and it is the word *our*. Jesus gives us this word in the Lord's Prayer when He says, "*Our* Father who art in heaven." Yes, He said "*Our* Father," not "*your* Father" or "*My* Father," but "**Our** Father." This means we (mankind) are included in God's family. We are God's children, and He is our Father, through spiritual adoption. What a terrific, awe-inspiring gift.

As a result, our spiritual home belongs with our Father, God, who is in heaven. This means that when our bodies die, and we go to heaven, we are not going to an unfamiliar place, but rather we are coming home. All this time we have felt that we belong on earth, and then we leave and go to heaven, when actually the opposite is true: we belong in our home, in heaven, with God (our Father) and Jesus (our Brother), and we have just been visiting this rather strange, imperfect world here on earth. A very brief synopsis of the Bible can be summarized as follows:

1. We (mankind) left home when Adam and Eve left the Garden of Eden.

2. God gave us free will when He told Noah He wouldn't meddle in earthly affairs anymore.

3. Because of free will, we can choose our own way. Our actions have consequences. If we were perfectly protected, we would not truly have free will. Bad things can happen to good people. It is easy to get lost in the confusion.

4. God sent Jesus to give us the road map to come home. The way home includes dying and leaving this imperfect earthly home and building our spiritual home for our soul, which requires God our Father, Jesus, and the Holy Spirit as our foundation.

5. During our sojourn here on earth, we should live out our Christian values and try to help others by sharing the road map home, and Jesus is that road map.

Use these facts to help ease your sadness. Most of all, remember that heaven is perfect (very perfect). This means that all your concerns, anxieties, fears, and sadness will be gone. Happiness will remain. You will not need to worry about those of us still here on earth. Your faith and hope will turn into knowledge and pure joy. God the Father, Jesus, and the Holy Sprit will take care of us. Finally, remember that the three keys to your thought process need to be:

1. **Attitude**. This means a positive attitude, which includes a strong positive motivator and gratitude. Give gratitude for small things, as well as gifts from the *Holy Spirit*.

2. **Perspective**. Remember the perspective of time and heaven. Remember that you have an everlasting soul, thanks to the saving grace of *Christ*.

3. **Focus**. Remember to focus on *God*, especially when times get tough.

Use these three thought processes to *mirror and reflect* the Holy Trinity. In this fashion, your spiritual home will be rock solid. Keep in mind that you are not alone in your spiritual home. The Holy Trinity, as well as your brothers and sisters in Christ, are there to surround you with love. Thanks be to God, the Father, the Son, and the Holy Spirit!

21

A Family/Friend/Caregiver's Approach

Faith is to believe what you do not see; the reward of this faith is to
see what you believe. —*Saint Augustine*

Obviously, being a patient who is dying is a very tough position to
be in. However, being the family or friend of that patient is frequently
an even harder position to be in. Seeing a loved one in decline, and then
losing that loved one, may be the hardest thing that we ever have to
experience, mentally and emotionally. It can not only be mentally
exhausting, but also physically exhausting. Caregiving is not easy work.
Sleep disturbance is common. Fatigue sets in with lack of sleep. In addition, fatigue can make our emotions raw. Far too often, we neglect our
own physical and mental health while concentrating on a dying loved
one. In this chapter we'll go over some tips to have a more balanced
approach to death and help ease the mental and physical suffering of all
concerned.

The first and foremost rule for caregivers is to take care of yourself
first and then concentrate on your loved one. Far too many times, I have
seen caregivers totally neglect their own health in dedication to the
patient. For instance, I have seen caregivers totally ignore their own
diabetes, including not taking their medicines, ignoring their diet, and
not exercising. Mental health is also neglected when people become
secluded and don't allow any time for their own enjoyable activities.

If you are a full-time caregiver, you *must* make time for yourself.
Find time to get away. Take a break. This may mean asking a family
member, friend, neighbor, church member to come in, or even hiring

someone to care for the patient for a few hours while you get away. Make sure you tend to your own health, such as getting medicines and not neglecting your own doctor's appointments. Try to exercise thirty minutes a day. I frequently hear caregivers say they don't have time for exercise, or the patient can't be left alone. In reality, the percentage of patients who can't be left alone for half an hour is a very small number. The scenario should go something like this:

> Make sure the patient has had some food and drink. Help the patient to the restroom and get clothes, blankets, a book, TV, etc. if needed. Make sure their medicines are taken as needed. Then say to the patient, "I need to go for a walk (exercise) and will be back in half an hour."

If the patient truly cannot be left alone for thirty minutes, then find a way to exercise right there, indoors (such as using a stationary bike, an exercise video, calisthenics, etc.).

If the caregiving has been long-term (e.g., months), then plan for an extended break. Find someone to take over for at least several days while you get away and refresh yourself. This might mean respite care (discussed in the hospice chapter).

Remember that if you do not take care of yourself first, then you are not fully serving God's purpose. In fact, He even commanded one day a week of rest. Also, don't you think that the person you are caring for also cares about you? If you were the patient, you would not want your caregiver's health to decline while taking care of you. The patient has enough burden—don't add guilt to their load by neglecting yourself. Finally, if you neglect your own health, you will become more tired, irritable, depressed, and a less effective caregiver. This frequently happens without you even realizing it. You need balance in your life—*don't neglect yourself.*

The second rule for caregivers/family/friends is that actions speak louder than words. This is especially true since we frequently find ourselves at a loss for the right words to say. The actions or deeds can depend on the level of closeness to the patient. If the relationship is close, then the actions can include feeding, dressing, bathing, changing, giving medicines and massages, and wound care if appropriate. Also, assistance with financial estate planning may be needed. It is important to be sure that the patient has a power of attorney for both their health care as well as financial matters. If you are not the primary caregiver, then you can offer to give the primary caregiver a break. Other deeds can include cleaning, house chores, yard work, meal preparation, shopping, driving to doctor's appointments, giving "warming" gifts such as flowers, balloons, or thoughtful cards/letters or phone calls. Be creative. Maybe the patient would like you to read them a book, listen to some music with them, or play a game.

Organizing and/or participating in community help programs is a wonderful way to aid the patient as well as family and caregivers. For instance, our community has rallied support for various patients and their families on a number of occasions. These activities have been organized by the church as well as by the neighborhood as a whole. This help included meal trains—where people sign up to bring a meal to patients and their families on different days. We've had community blood and bone marrow donor drives. We've had volunteers organizing sign ups to drive patients to appointments or their kids to activities. There have been breast cancer and cancer society fundraising walks to show support for patients. There have also been direct fundraisers for patients and their families who are in financial need such as: bake sales, car washes, auctions, and direct donation fundraisers. All of these deeds are terrific, as they really put Christian values into action. The rewards are great on a number of levels and provide:

1. Direct care to the patient.

2. Practical support for the family and caregivers.

3. Emotional support for both the patient and their family.

4. The opportunity for all involved to express gratitude, which, as we've seen, make people feel better.

5. Strengthens bonds, including patient-family/caregiver bonds, patient-friend bonds, and bonds between family, friends, and neighbors.

6. Helps to unify both the church as well as the community as a whole, in working toward a common goal.

7. Expresses Christian values and draws people to the church who may not otherwise have had contact.

8. Empowers people through good works. These are people who otherwise would feel powerless in a tough situation.

9. Puts a positive attitude into a negative situation.

Again, offer gratitude for the ability to take action.

The third rule for friends and family of the dying patient is to give the *present of presence.* The gift of your presence alone will help heal raw emotional wounds. This goes also for friends and family of close survivors of a deceased loved one. People of the Jewish faith do this well in a process termed "sitting shiva." Basically, friends and family gather together for a week of mourning after a death. Just the gathering and presence of people help support the survivors.

The shiva process was evident in the book of Job when Job's friends came and sat with him for a week after Job had lost everything. They did not say anything; just their presence was enough to let Job know he wasn't alone. In fact, Job's friends did well with their presence but not their words. As you may recall, their words were that Job must have done something wrong to deserve his suffering (not exactly the right words to cheer him up). Remember that you do not have to find the right words—*your presence alone* will serve the purpose of providing emotional support.

The fourth rule for family and friends of the dying patient is to *provide spiritual support.* Help to strengthen their faith wherever you can. As faith strengthens, it approaches knowledge. With the knowledge of saving grace through Jesus Christ, we can overcome any hurdle or obstacle in our way.

A key concept to remember in dealing with the spirituality of another person is that you cannot force beliefs on people. People like their freedom, which includes the ability to act and believe as they see fit. It is human nature to want to reject that which is forced upon us. In fact, I believe that this is why God gave us free will. Faith is a matter of personal choice and personal belief. You can give someone information, but it is their choice to believe.

Remember, when dealing with a dying patient, that there are times when it is appropriate, and times when it is not appropriate, to discuss spirituality. When feeling particularly poorly, the patient may not want to talk at all. It is common for the patient to become angry at God, depressed, frustrated with the situation, and not in the mood to work on faith building. If the patient wants to vent anger and frustration, then allow him/her to do so without arguing. At these times, it is best to back off and pray silently for their spiritual healing. Spiritual health works to heal emotions and lessens physical symptoms.

Spirituality and faith building is best done when the patient is ready for it. At times, it will be obvious that spiritual discussions are inappropriate. At other times, the best way to tell if the patient is open to faith building is to ask them. When caring for the non-Christian, keep in mind that they may react negatively to efforts to convert them. Spiritual conversations need to be approached with sensitivity and respect for the dying person's thoughts, convictions, and choices—not out of anxiety.

Faith building can be achieved through a variety of means, including prayer, attending church, reading and discussing the Bible and other religious material, listening to spiritual music, enjoying nature, and quiet contemplation. Sometimes, you may be able to give a patient new information or a new perspective on their faith, but most often, the greatest benefit will be to strengthen faith through reminders (see Chapter 10 on memory).

We've talked about supporting the patient physically, mentally, emotionally, and spiritually. At some point in the process, you need to think about supporting the patient by "letting go." Letting go means letting the patient make the transition from our earthly experience to the heavenly realm. If your loved one has been chronically ill and debilitated, you may need to let go before they die.

In the chapters on evangelism and code status, we discussed that we need to live out and disseminate Christian values, either through active or passive evangelism. When our loved one has become too debilitated (i.e., there is extreme loss of mental and/or physical function) to live out either active or passive evangelism, then it is time for us to let go of aggressive life-sustaining measures and just provide comfort care. Obviously, this can be a very hard decision to make, and it is wise to pray for and seek guidance. Advantages of letting go can include:

1. It brings an end to the patient's suffering. Remember that heaven is perfect and will always be far superior to even the best of lives lived here on earth.

2. It displays our Christian values, showing that we have faith in Jesus Christ to bring us an everlasting, perfect life. We do not need to cling to an earthly existence. The great benefits of Christianity become obvious here.

3. It displays our Christian values through the wise use of resources. When I am so debilitated that I can no longer serve God's purpose by spreading Christian values through active or passive evangelism, then resources to prolong my life here on earth can better be used to spread Christian values in other ways—such as preventing disease, feeding the poor, supporting church missions, etc. Remember that Jesus preached the wise use of resources in the parable of the master and the three servants. Each servant who put his resources to good use was rewarded. The servant who did not use his resources wisely was punished.

4. The concept of letting go hammers home the point that life is not all about us. Life is about our relationship with God and Jesus Christ. When we cling to the patient's life here on earth rather than letting go, we are really saying one of two things: 1) Our relationship with the patient is more important than the patient's relationship to God through Jesus, or 2) The patient's relationship to life here on earth is more important than the patient's relationship to God through Jesus.

5. When the patient is so debilitated that he or she can no longer serve God's purpose here on earth, then it is time to let go. Letting go means giving priority or precedence to more important spiritual matters, over less important earthly matters.

6. Letting go does not mean there is no sadness or that you will not miss the patient. It is, however, an emotional release. You have given control of the situation over to the saving grace of Jesus. It is acceptance. It is coming to terms with the situation. It is to the benefit of your emotional health.

7. Letting go needs to happen at some point. It allows for normal grief, acceptance, and recovery. In the case of chronic, debilitating disease in the patient, letting go may happen before the patient dies. In other cases, such as sudden unexpected death, it happens after the patient dies.

Letting go is never easy. It is particularly difficult when the devastating blows keep us from focusing on the spiritual. It is also very hard when we have doubts about our faith. A case in point is that of my sister-in-law, Tanya. Tanya's twenty-year-old son, Kyle, died tragically in a motorcycle accident. Months later, Tanya was visiting us. She was obviously still quite heartbroken over Kyle's death. I gave her a copy of the chapter on heaven in hopes that it would help heal some wounds. Her response after reading about heaven was: "It would help if only I knew for sure it was true." When it came down to the critical moment (i.e., death of a loved one), she had doubts about her faith. There were doubts about the existence of God, Jesus, and heaven. These are doubts that I suspect most everyone has had at one time or another. Tanya was just honest enough to admit to having them.

So how could I prove, absolutely, the existence of God to Tanya? This is a question that man has been asking for centuries. Conversely, atheists have been trying to prove there is no God. The amazing thing is that both sides keep trying to prove that either there is a God or there isn't a God. Both sides have been spinning their wheels needlessly, because God purposely designed it so that we cannot prove His existence.

In fact, we can actually prove that we cannot prove His existence. The reasoning here is as follows:

God gave man free will when He told Noah that He would no longer interfere. Because of this free will, we cannot prove His existence. God wants us to choose to believe in Him and follow Him and Jesus' teachings. However, we can also choose to not believe in God and not follow Jesus' teachings. If we could prove that there is definitely an almighty, all-powerful, all-knowing God, then we would not have this free will to choose. That is because if we knew for certain that there was an almighty, all-powerful, all-knowing God, then everyone would obviously have to follow and do what He says. There would be no free will.

A similar situation can be seen in looking at the mathematical equation 2+2=4. This has been proven to us. We all believe it. We really have no choice to not believe it, once it's been proven to us.

Likewise, if God had been undisputably proven to mankind, we really would have no choice but to believe and follow Him. Humanity would be stripped of its free will. Our free will is what enables us to experience a loving Father-loving child relationship with God. If God was "proven," we would be destined to servitude. There would only be a master-slave relationship with Him. Our existence would be no more than chess pieces on a board of His creation. There would be resentment over losing our freedom. However, through the free will of faith, we show our love for God. God showed love for us by giving up power over us through His gift of free will; we need to return that love through our faith in Him. This, in fact, strengthens our loving bond with the Father.

This is mirrored in our family relationships, and anyone who has been a parent of a teenager knows what I am talking about. We make rules for our kids to keep them safe when they are young. However, as our kids grow up, they start to resent these rules, and we must eventually give up all the rules and give them the freedom to do as they please, when they become adults. Hopefully, because of their love for us, they will freely choose to continue to please us.

In similar fashion, in the early days of man's history, God gave His people, the Israelites, lots of rules to follow. As mankind aged, God gave up the need for all the rules, and instead we were given the loving freedom to continue to choose to follow Him through our Lord Jesus Christ. What a perfect family life model!

The free will of faith allows for a much more beautiful, loving relationship between us and God. The consequence of having this more beautiful relationship is that we must rely on faith in Jesus rather than proof of God. We need to build a rock solid faith in Jesus in order to relieve the anguish of letting go when the time comes.

Regret is a common problem that many of us have after a loved one dies. We might wish we had done something differently while they were still alive. Sometimes our thoughts become filled with would-have's, should-have's, and could-have's. This can lead to mental anguish, and we wind up literally punishing ourselves with our own thoughts and regrets.

Letting go means freeing ourselves from these regrets. When we truly let go, we've given the situation over to God. We allow God to take over care of our loved one, and there can be no more regrets once it's in God's hands, as we know He will make everything right. Letting go is a beautiful acceptance of God blessing our loved one with the saving grace of Jesus Christ.

Letting go does not mean giving up the memory of our loved one. In fact, the memory should be cherished and even used to strengthen Christian values in the community. In other words, your loved one's memory is the motivation behind a positive purpose to your life. Several examples of how this can play out follow:

In 1993, twelve-year-old Polly Klaas was kidnapped and murdered. This motivated her friends and family in a strong positive way. The result was creation of the Polly Klaas Foundation, which works to keep children safe in their own communities.

Candice Lightner lost her daughter in a tragic motor vehicle accident involving a drunk driver. This motivated her in a strong positive way. The result was MADD (Mothers Against Drunk Driving), which has worked hard to reduce drunk driving. The result has possibly saved thousands of lives.

Each year, thousands of people participate in the American Cancer Society's Relay for Life in memory of their loved ones. The result has been millions of dollars in cancer research.

A teenage girl in our neighborhood, Christina Rodness, died of cancer. Her sister was motivated in a strong positive way. The result was that she started up a support group for other kids who have lost a sibling.

John Walsh lost his son, Adam, to a tragic kidnapping and murder. This motivated John Walsh in a strong positive way. The result was the TV show *America's Most Wanted,* which has potentially saved thousands of innocent people from becoming crime victims. It also created the Adam Walsh Child Protection and Safety Act, which initiated a national sex offender registry.

Race car driver Danica Patrick had a grandmother who suffered from COPD, which is a deadly lung disease. Patrick became a spokesperson for DRIVE4COPD, a car race that raises money to support screening people for COPD.

Each day in the newspaper we can read obituaries where the family asks for donations to go to hospice groups, the American Heart Association, the American Diabetic Association, the Lung Association, and other groups in order to use their loved ones' memory to help others. People also volunteer for their charity of choice to help.

So, there are numerous ways we can live out and further Christian values in order to "make our loved ones proud of us." In doing so, we promote our own mental health as well as serving the Lord's purpose, and we've turned a negative into a positive.

When a loved one dies, one goes through stages of grief, which may include: shock and feeling numb, denial, anger, depression, and finally acceptance. This is natural. Remember to keep a positive and constructive attitude, focus on the spiritual, and have an eternal perspective.

22

Suicide and the Death of a Non-Christian

There are a dozen views about everything until you know the answer. Then there is never more than one. —C. S. Lewis, in *That Hideous Strength*

So far in this book we have addressed the death of Christian patients. However, two big concerns are, how do we deal with the death of a non-Christian, and do suicidal victims go to heaven? Christians are naturally concerned, as they want to see their loved ones in heaven. They are disturbed by the thought that their loved ones will not go to heaven, which makes them sad. Again, we should not lose sight of the fact that God loves us and is merciful.

So let's take up the case of the suicide victim. Let us assume that they believed in Christ but were just too depressed to carry on in this life anymore. The example that I'll use is that of my own paternal grandmother.

I never really knew my grandmother since she died when I was a young child. I assume she was a Christian as my dad was raised in a Christian church. She committed suicide after my grandfather died. Clearly, she was suffering from major depression. Major depression is a disease where there is a neurochemical imbalance. It was not just sadness at the loss of her husband. People without depression certainly go through very sad events in their life, but they do not kill themselves unless they are seriously depressed. Not only did she suffer from an illness, but her two sons and her grandchildren suffered a loss, as well.

Now the question is, did my grandmother make it to heaven? The answer is yes, I believe she did. We know this because she believed in Christ, and John 3:16 states that "whoever believes in him shall not perish, but have eternal life." She was a "whoever." Her suicide violated the commandment to not kill and was not pleasing to God. However, God surely understands diseases, and God is forgiving. God keeps His Word, and according to John 3:16, eternal life was given.

Now let's turn to the question of what happens in the case of the death of a non-Christian, whether it is by suicide or any other cause. Christians become sad at the thought of being in heaven without some of their family, friends, and loved ones being there with them.

Once again, God loves us and has planned well for our ultimate happiness. First, let's look at children. In Matthew 19:14, Jesus said, "Let the little children come to me, and do not hinder them, for the kingdom of God belongs to such as these." Children have not really had a chance to accept/know Christianity, and yet Jesus tells us that they belong to the kingdom of God, which is heaven.

Now, let us turn to the case of people who have heard the Word and yet refuse to believe. Perhaps they refuse to believe because they were brought up in another religion, given false teachings, or they find the biblical story to be too fantastic to believe. Indeed, the concept of an almighty God who created everything, parted the Red Sea, and sent Jesus to save the world is a fantastic and amazing story! We can see how people who are too wrapped up in the secular world have trouble seeing the forest through the trees. Also, when terrible things happen to good people, we can see how it is so overwhelming that they lose their focus and perspective on God.

So I think we can understand how good people get confused and falsely reject Christianity. Some people say that non-Christians should be forgiven and also be allowed to enter the kingdom of heaven. Others point to the Bible and say anyone who fails to accept Christ here on earth will be forbidden from heaven. This leaves their Christian family and friends in a state of mental anguish. How are we to solve this conundrum?

The answer once again is to turn to the Lord and rely on *ultimate faith*. Ultimate faith, as in extraordinary faith or supreme faith, is above and beyond just saying we believe. Ultimate faith in God is required to hold us up when we are sinking. Ultimate faith in God is required to correct any injustices that we perceive. Even if we think God is the One being unfair, we must put all our hope and faith in Him to know that He will rectify the situation. This giving of our worries to Him is ultimate faith. Ultimate faith means you have truly given all of your mental sorrow over to Him. When you have *fully* relied on the Lord in this way, your mental distress will be gone. Above all, never forget that God is love.

Dr. Charles Seielstad, of Trinity Life Church, relates the story of a woman he knows whom I'll call Jackie. She was naturally upset about her father, who was critically ill in the hospital. She was especially fearful that he would die without accepting Christ. Her father fell into a coma, and when he awoke, she tried to convince him to believe. Her father became angry, cursed at her, and told her he didn't want to hear anything about her religion. Three times he fell into a coma and came out of it cursing her religion and falling back into a coma. Jackie tried to talk with him again the fourth time he came out of a coma. But this time he stopped her and said, "It's okay, honey—Jesus came and talked to me while I was asleep, and I've accepted Him, and I'm ready to go home with Him." And then he passed.

Never lose faith in the Lord's ability to save. *That* is ultimate faith.

23

Emotional Pain: Surviving the Loss

After a few days, while I was absent, the fever returned, and he died. "Grief darkened my heart" (Lamentations 5:17). Everything on which I set my gaze was death. My home town became a torture to me; my father's house a strange world of unhappiness; all that I had shared with him was without him transformed into a cruel torment. My eyes looked for him everywhere, and he was not there. I hated everything because they did not have him, nor could they now tell me "Look, he is on the way," as used to be the case when he was alive and absent from me. I had become to myself a vast problem, and I questioned my soul, "why are you so sad, and why are you very distressed?" But my soul did not know what reply to give.[1] —from *Confessions*, by Saint Augustine

Emptiness. Loneliness. Devastation. Loss. Bewilderment. Sorrow. Misery. Perhaps Saint Augustine described his emotion of grief best upon learning of the death of his friend when he wrote, "My eyes looked for him everywhere, and he was not there." Notably, this story from his life experiences came before his conversion to Christianity.

We, as Christians, will experience grief when we lose a friend or family member; grief is the normal response. Christian thoughts and actions, however, can mitigate the sadness.

The first action to take is *giving and receiving support.* The coming together of friends and loved ones heals emotional wounds. Friends and family can reminisce on old stories or express their feelings. It is not even necessary to talk at all. If you don't know what to say, then just your presence can be supportive. This is especially true for supporting the survivor who lived with the deceased loved one. Physical support can include helping with funeral plans, chores, and meal preparation. Spiritual support from your minister, priest, or church group should be sought.

The key period for providing support is in the first week or two after the loved one has died, but periodic contact over at least the following year is important, as well. A normal grief response can include depressed mood, sadness, trouble sleeping, loss of appetite, difficulty in concentrating, and loss of interest and pleasure in activities. However, if these symptoms are still present after three months, then the help of a counselor or physician should be obtained.

The initial reaction to a death is typically shock and grief, although sometimes it can be relief in the case where long suffering has come to an end. Guilt over feeling relief can also be common. Oftentimes the emotions can be overwhelming and pull us into mental darkness. When we find our mood slipping is when we need to take full advantage of the three key concepts stressed in this book: **attitude, focus, and perspective**.

Remember that there are two components to *attitude*, which are a positive attitude and gratitude. In gratitude, give thanks to God for the time you had together with your deceased friend or loved one here on earth. Not only should you give praise to God for the time you had together, but you should also give thanks and praise because you had the opportunity to know the deceased in the first place. After all, how fortunate was that? Truly sincere gratitude has the capability to elevate your mood.

Work at maintaining a positive attitude with respect to all three parts of time: past, present, and future. In terms of the past, take pleasure in remembering happy and joyful times that you shared together. Try to get a sense of fulfillment from any accomplishment that the deceased achieved here on earth. It is important to think back, but dwelling too much on the past is not fruitful. In the initial period (one to two weeks) after a death, maybe 80 to 90 percent of one's thoughts will be on the past. Over the next two months, that number should become closer to 10 to 20 percent. In other words, after two months one should be performing usual daily activities such as work, exercise, hobbies, and getting out with friends. Journaling, eating well, avoiding alcohol, exercising, and getting proper sleep are also beneficial to the healing of emotional wounds.

Much of one's time should therefore be spent staying positive and in the present. One question to ask yourself is, **How would the deceased want you to be living your life?** For most of us, that answer would be in happiness and in doing positive actions, such as taking care of family and friends, and performing good works.

Looking to the future, we should plan to honor the deceased's memory. Remember that we mentally do better if we have a purpose or a strong positive motivator to our lives. Examples could include charity work or just planning to live your life in a way that would make the deceased proud of you. For instance, if your parents died and you were raised in a Christian household, then seek a sense of accomplishment by living out Christian principles with actions rather than just words. Take solace in whatever good deeds you perform.

Focusing on the Lord is key to staying out of the depths of despair. When we lose someone, there is a tendency to dwell on the loss. It can be so overwhelming that we forget about God in the process. Concentrating on the loss, rather than returning thoughts to God, causes our mood to spiral downward. It may even cause us to question our faith: "How can I think about God when God let this happen?"

If you find yourself trapped in sadness and despair or feeling lost and lonesome, you need to find a way to refocus on God and what He can do for you. Reminders may be needed to turn your focus on God. Again, reminders can come from family and friends, your church, the Bible and other religious texts, art, jewelry, music, and posted sayings or quotes.

The loss may lead to the placement of blame, depending on the circumstances of death. We may place blame on ourselves if we think there was something we could have done to save the deceased's life, or if there was something we wished we had said or done for the deceased. We may also criticize or condemn another person if we think they are at fault. Examples would include a drunk driver causing the death, or perhaps we think there was something else the doctor should have done to save the life. The blame might also fall upon God for letting our loved one die instead of answering our prayers by stepping in to prevent the death. Continued criticizing and condemning thoughts lead to anger and irritability.

The solution to blame is forgiveness. The really great thing about forgiveness is that we are the ones who are rewarded psychologically. We get rid of blame when we forgive, whereas continuing to blame pulls our focus away from God and toward darker thoughts. Forgiveness frees our mind to focus on God as well as to seek a positive attitude and perspective. Without forgiveness, our emotions get trapped in anger and bitterness.

If you find yourself angry, you need to find someone to forgive. Determine who you are angry at and forgive that person. You may need to forgive yourself, the deceased, another person, or even God, if He is the One with whom you are angry. It's okay to feel anger, but at some point you need to find a way to forgive because not only is it to your benefit, but Jesus tells us to forgive. Forgiveness is the process of giving yourself permission to stop blaming and therefore be able to let go of your anger. After you have forgiven, thank God for the ability to free yourself from those feelings. Next, turn your focus to God and the light that He offers on the situation.

Going hand-in-hand with the need to forgive is the need to accept. After the death of a loved one, we often find ourselves tormented by the question "why?" It keeps replaying like a broken record: "Why did this happen?" and "Why now?" The response usually does not come. The solution is to accept that while here on earth, we may never know the answer to why. After accepting our limitations, we need to pray for comfort and refocus on God and the perspective that He provides.

Perspective turns a pessimistic picture into upbeat thoughts. Perspective helps tremendously when we approach a problem from a different angle. When someone dies, it is common to be disappointed in God for not preventing the death. In fact, many people will say that there must not be a God or else this wouldn't have happened: "If God is good, and God exists, then He wouldn't have let my loved one die."

The answer to this riddle is to put yourself in God's shoes and view the problem from His vantage point (which is far superior to ours). From God's perspective, He did prevent the death of your loved one;

He did it by sacrificing His only Son, Jesus, for the eternal salvation of all, including you and your loved one. This is a much greater act of kindness than a one-time divine intervention to prevent a tragic death here on earth. Keep in mind that death of the body is inevitable. If we want God to intervene to save a life, He already did it at the right place and at the right time. We need to remain forever grateful for that; we do that by turning from our self-centered perspective and look at it from His self-sacrificing perspective.

The second huge advantage of examining your loved one's death from God's perspective is that of time. Temporarily, here on earth, you are separated from the deceased. You'll one day be reunited in heaven for all of eternity. The period of time that you are apart is minuscule when compared to the eternity that exists in heaven. Once again, the reward of being together forever in heaven more than makes up for any period of separation. I encourage you to reread Chapter 16, on heaven, to help cement this concept.

"It's not easy being a widow." These were the first words out of the mouth of one of my patients the other day. She had just recently lost her husband. She's right, it certainly isn't easy; and this holds true no matter whom you lose. Fortunately, she has a very supportive group of family and friends so she is not alone in her loss. She can also take comfort in knowing all the good her husband did in his earthly lifetime.

By God's providence, the blow of death for any of us can be softened by remembering to **stay focused on Him**, keeping a **heavenly perspective**, and maintaining a **positive attitude**.

Epilogue

For the present is the point at which time touches eternity.
—*C. S. Lewis*

Remember. Remember to keep focused on the Lord and heaven. Doing so will help you maintain a positive attitude in the face of adversity. When times get dark, consider rereading portions of this book to strengthen you and serve as a reminder. Hopefully, it will help you stay focused on God and keep things in perspective. We all forget.

I started this book by discussing how Christians as a whole seem to be the worst at coping with death, when they should clearly stand out as a pillar of strength because of their faith.

I pray that some of the strategies discussed in this book will shine a positive light on you. I pray that the Lord Jesus helps you through times of physical pain and suffering. I pray that the Lord Jesus helps you through times of mental anguish. I pray that your hopes turn into known certainties. I pray that your time of troubles be a small drop in the bucket compared to the everlasting glories of God's eternal kingdom. I pray that your doctors and caregivers be wise and your friendships be strong. I pray that you have the strength to turn hardships into good works to serve the Lord. I pray that you can shine like a beacon of light on the rest of the world so that they may know the goodness of Jesus. I pray that your inner anxieties be transformed into the energy of excitement for the Lord. I pray that the Holy Spirit turns any doubts or regrets into inner peace for you. I pray that any depression that you may have be washed away by love. Our heavenly Father loves you because you have value and worth. I pray that you may know that Jesus is proud of you, because when all has been said and done—you've turned to Him.

Remember to keep focused on God and heaven.

Remember. Always.

Amen.

The Prayer of Saint Francis

Lord, make me an instrument of Your peace.
Where there is hatred, let me sow love.
Where there is injury, pardon.
Where there is doubt, faith.
Where there is despair, hope.
Where there is darkness, light.
Where there is sadness, joy.
O Divine Master,
grant that I may not so much seek to be consoled, as to console;
to be understood, as to understand;
to be loved, as to love.
For it is in giving that we receive.
It is in pardoning that we are pardoned,
and it is in dying that we are born to eternal life.
Amen.

Appendix

Questions to Ponder

I encourage you to reflect on what you read in each chapter. Here are some questions to ponder:

Introduction

Consider either yourself, or someone you know, who has really struggled with the death of a friend or loved one. What would have mitigated the process?

How would you initiate a discussion about death and dying with a friend or loved one?

Have you developed any spiritual relationships with another person, and if so, how did it strengthen the relationship?

Chapter 1: Getting the News

Receiving bad news is always difficult. What do you use for emotional support in tough times? How can you maintain inner strength?

Chapter 2: Hope: Jesus Is the Model

Hope, and ultimately knowledge of an expected positive outcome, allows us to persevere in the toughest of times. People give up when they are hopeless. Does your faith give you hope or knowledge? How can you draw on your faith in order to maintain a positive attitude in the face of adversity?

How does looking at your life from Jesus' perspective (i.e., with knowledge of salvation) change your perspective? Your attitude?

Chapter 3: Conquering Fear

Reflect back on a time in your life when you experienced awful fear. How could you have used your current knowledge and faith to alleviate that fear?

Chapter 4: Let's Look at History

Consider the early Christian martyrs. How certain would you have to be in the existence of your soul to risk your earthly life for it? How certain are you that you have a soul? Do you spend more time focusing on the health of your soul or the health of your body?

Chapter 5: Near-Death Experiences

Review the six takeaway points at the end of this chapter. Have you, or someone you know, ever had a near-death or other deeply moving spiritual experience? How does that change your perspective on life?

Chapter 6: Immortality of Your Soul?

Consider the fact that Jesus is immortal. If you've accepted Jesus into your soul, how much power over death do you hold? How does that transform your perspective on death?

Chapter 7: "Doc, I've Outlived My Money"

This chapter emphasizes maintaining a positive attitude and focusing on God to ease financial worries.

What are you grateful for?

Consider a time when you let money concerns take precedence over important aspects of your life. How could you better balance practical issues while maintaining emotional well-being?

Chapter 8: Dealing with Physical Pain

This chapter discussed many different mental techniques, as well as modern technologies, that can be used together to alleviate pain. Now consider Jesus' crucifixion. Even at the end, He was still teaching (quoting Psalm 22). What sustained Him through His pain?

Chapter 9: Time Is on Your Side

Attitude, perspective, and focusing on God makes all the difference in times of suffering. Consider Jesus praying in the Garden of Gethsemane prior to His crucifixion. How did He use His ultimate knowledge of finite time on the cross and eternal resurrection to His advantage? How can you model this concept to assist you through difficult times?

Chapter 10: Memory: The Chapter That I Nearly Forgot

Reflect on a difficult time in your life in which you at least temporarily neglected to focus on God. Create a plan to help you keep Him in mind.

Chapter 11: Starting Treatment

If you are a Christian, consider that you've received Jesus into your life. He resides in your soul. Given that, when you are in a difficult situation, ask yourself, "How would Jesus respond?" How can you use this strategy to your advantage?

Chapter 12: Evangelism: A Chance for Empowerment

When the missionary E. Stanley Jones met with Gandhi, he asked him, "Mr. Gandhi, though you quote the words of Christ often, why is it that you appear to so adamantly reject becoming His follower?" Gandhi replied, "Oh, I don't reject Christ. I love Christ. It's just that so many of you Christians are so unlike Christ. If Christians would really live according to the teachings of Christ, as found in the Bible, all of India would be Christian today."1

How can you use this statement to bring new or greater motivation and meaning to your life? What specifically can you do?

Chapter 13: Code Status and End-of-Life Decisions

What is the difference between living and existing?

If you have not completed advanced health-care directive paperwork, then do so now. Make a plan. Be sure to discuss your wishes with your appointed agent(s).

Chapter 14: Overcoming Suffering

Consider attitude, focus, and perspective.

No matter how bad things are for you, have you considered that someone has had it worse?

What small acts of kindness have you felt true gratitude for?

The apostles endured many hardships and were eventually killed for professing Jesus to be the Messiah. They could have given up and freed themselves from suffering, but yet they persisted. List five reasons for gratitude and at least two positive motivators that they could have used to allow them to carry on.

Chapter 15: Humor: Lifting the Mood

Student: "Rabbi, why did God make man before woman?"

Rabbi: "Because He didn't want any advice on how to make man!"[2]

Do you think this joke made God smile?

Health benefits of laughter were discussed in this chapter. Humor can also ease the tension of a stressful situation. Think of some times in your life when humor lifted your mood. What can you do to bring more humor into your life?

Chapter 16: Heaven: A New Perspective

Look at your life situation and reflect on the chapter on heaven. Are you the little kid in the day care? The teenager? Imagine yourself years down the road residing happily in heaven forever with your friends and loved ones. Which of your current problems do you think will seem trivial when you examine them from a heavenly perspective?

Chapter 17: Hospice: A Way for Caring

Think of small things in life that give you pleasure. How many can you name?

Whom do you care about? What are you doing about it?

Which biblical characters would have made the best hospice caregivers? Try to name several.

Chapter 18: Suicide, Alcohol, and "Recreational" Drugs

Matthew 4:1–11 describes the temptation of Jesus:

Then Jesus was led by the Spirit into the desert to be tempted by the devil. After fasting forty days and forty nights, he was hungry. The tempter came to him and said, "If you are the Son of God, tell these stones to become bread."

Jesus answered, "It is written: 'Man does not live on bread alone, but on every word that comes from the mouth of God.'"

Then the devil took him to the holy city and had him stand on the highest point of the temple. "If you are the Son of God," he said, "throw yourself down. For it is written: "He will command his angels concerning you, and they will lift you up in their hands, so that you will not strike your foot against a stone.""

Jesus answered him, "It is also written: 'Do not put the Lord your God to the test.'"

Again the devil took him to a very high mountain and showed him all the kingdoms of the world and their splendor. "All this I will give You," he said, "if you will bow down and worship me."

Jesus said to him, "Away from me, Satan! For it is written: 'Worship the Lord your God, and serve him only.'"

Then the devil left him. And angels came and attended him.

Keeping in mind that Jesus was fully human, how did Jesus resist these temptations?

Chapter 19: Emotional Pain: Regrets

Perspective is of key importance. Consider something you have done that you wish you had done differently. Your good friend is trying to console you. Now, look at it honestly from your friend's reference point. What would you tell yourself?

Chapter 20: A Patient's Approach

You have gone through many transitions in your life...a change of schools, a change of living conditions, marital status, illnesses, accomplishments, etc. Some of the changes have been good, some of them maybe not so good. Given a strong faith, you can know that your circumstances will be vastly improved when you transition into heaven. What is your plan to maximize a positive experience in your time left here on earth?

Chapter 21: A Family/Friend/Caregiver's Approach

How did the apostles respond to the death of their friend, Jesus:
1. Immediately after His death?

2. Once they realized He was resurrected?

Chapter 22: Suicide and the Death of a Non-Christian
What are the advantages of being a Christian in a secular-based world? Name several.

Chapter 23: Emotional Pain: Surviving the Loss
Identify some times in your life when a change of attitude, focus, and perspective would have improved your response to the situation.

Notes

CHAPTER 1: GETTING THE NEWS

1. Blaise Pascal. *Pensees.* London, Penguin, 1966, Pensee 326, 128.

CHAPTER 2: HOPE: JESUS IS THE MODEL

1. Saint Augustine. *Commentaries on the Psalms.* 72, 34.

CHAPTER 4: LET'S LOOK AT HISTORY

1. Pascal. *Pensees,* Pensee 108, 57.

2. Joe Rosenbloom III. "Waco: More than Simple Blunders?" PBS. Web. 16 Mar. 2012. http://www.pbs.org/wgbh/pages/frontline/waco/blunders.html

   Justin Sturken, and Mary Dore. "Remembering the Waco Siege." Abcnews.go.com. ABC News, 28 Feb. 2007. Web. 16 Mar. 2012. http://abcnews.go.com/us/story?id=2908955&page=1.

CHAPTER 5: NEAR-DEATH EXPERIENCES

1. Saint Augustine. *Soliloquies.* New York. Cosmopolitan Science and Art Service, Inc. 1943. Book Two, Chapter 14, 125.

2. Raymond A. Moody. *Life After Life: The Investigation of a Phenomenon-Survival of a Bodily Death.* New York, HarperCollins, 1975.

3. W. Van Lommel, R. Van Wees, V. Meyers, and I. Elfferich, "Near-death experiences in survivors of cardiac arrest: a prospective study in the Netherlands." *Lancet* 2001; 758: 2039–2045.

4. About the continuity of our consciousness by Pim Van Lommel IN: Brain Death and Disorders of Consciousness. C. Machado and D. A. Shewmon, eds. New York, Boston, Dordrecht, London, Moscow: Kluwer Academic/ Plenum Publishers, Advances in Experimental medicine and Biology *Adv Exp Med Biol.* 2004; 550:115–132.

5. K. Ring and S. Cooper. *Mindsight: Near Death and Out-of-Body Experiences in the Blind.* Palo Alto: William James Center for Consciousness Studies, 1999.

6. N. Kerr and G. W. Domhoff. (2004). "Do the blind literally 'see' in their dreams? A critique of recent claims that they do." *Dreaming,* 14, 230–233

   C. Hurowitz, S. Dunn, G. W. Domhoff, and H. Fiss. (1999). "The dreams of women: A replication and extension of previous findings." *Dreaming,* 9, 183–193.

7. Penny Sartori. *The Near Death Experiences of Hospitalized Intensive Care Patients; A Five Year Clinical Study.* The Edwin Mellen Press, 2008.

8. Michael Sabom. *Light and Death: One Doctor's Fascinating Account of Near-Death Experiences.* Grand Rapids, MI: Zondervan, 1998;

   BBC Documentary. *The Day I Died,* directed by Kate Broome, 2002.

9. Don Piper and Cecil Murphy. *90 Minutes in Heaven*. Grand Rapids, Mi., Revell, 2004.

10. G. Gallup and W. Proctor. (1982). *Adventures in immortality: a look beyond the threshold of death,* New York, McGraw Hill, 198–200

    M. Perera, G. Padmasekara, and J. Belanti. (2005), "Prevalence of Near Death Experiences in Australia." *Journal of Near-Death Studies,* 24(2), 109–116

    H. Knoblauch, I. Schmeid, and B. Schnettler. (2001). "Different Kinds of Near-Death Experiences: a report on a survey of Near-Death experiences in Germany." *Journal of Near-Death Studies,* 20, 15–29.

11. Van Lommel, 2039–2045 "About the continuity of our consciousness," 550:115-132.

    S. Parnia, D. G. Waller, R. Yeares, and P. Fenwick. (2001). "A qualitative and quantitative study of the incidence, features, and aetiology of near death experiences in cardiac arrest survivors." *Resuscitation.* Feb; 48(2): 149–56. PubMed abstract.

12. Jeff Markin. *Back from the Dead, Reborn Into the Light,* by Sheryl Fountain, *The 700 Club,* CBN. 15 Sept., 2010.

CHAPTER 6: IMMORTALITY OF YOUR SOUL?

1. Saint Augustine. *Soliloquies,* 75–77.

2. Ibid., 127.

CHAPTER 7: "DOC, I'VE OUTLIVED MY MONEY"

1. Saint Augustine. *Sermons,* 80, 1.

2. Calculation done prior to author being diagnosed with lymphoma.

3. Long-Term Care, Medicare.gov. www.medicare.gov/longtermcare/static/home.asp.

4. Philip Koslow. *El Cid.* New York. Chelsea House Publishers, 1993

    Thomas F. X. Noble. *Great Authors of the Western Literary Tradition, 2nd Edition.* The Teaching Company, 2004. Lecture 27: El Cid.

5. William R. Cook and Ronald B. Herzman. "Francis of Assisi." The Teaching Company, 2000. Lecture 4: From Worldly Knight to Knight of Christ

    Regis J. Armstrong, Wayne Hellman, and William Short, eds., *Francis of Assisi: Early Documents. Vol. I: The Saint.* New York: New York City Press, 1999

    Regis J. Armstrong. *Francis of Assisi: Early Documents. Vol. II: The Founder.* New York: New York City Press, 2000

    Regis J. Armstrong. *Francis of Assisi: Early Documents. Vol. III: The Prophet.* New York: New York City Press, 2001.

CHAPTER 8: DEALING WITH PHYSICAL PAIN

1. Saint Augustine. *Commentaries on the Psalms*, 82, 5.

2. *Life Is Beautiful*. Miramax Films, 1997.

3. *Monty Python and the Holy Grail*. Sony Pictures, 1974.

4. "The Holy Rosary." *EWTN*. Global Catholic Television Network. Web. 16 Mar. 2012. www.ewtn.com/devotionals/prayers/rosary.

5. Armstrong, *Francis of Assisi*; William R. Cook and Ronald B. Herzman. "Francis of Assisi," The Teaching Company, 2000. Lecture 12: A Message for Our Time.

6. E. Alessandra Strada and Russell K. Portenoy. "Psychological, Rehabilitative, and Integrative Therapies for Cancer Pain," *UpToDate*, 19.2; J. Achterberg. *Imagery in healing: shamanism and modern medicine*. Boston: Shambala, 1985.

CHAPTER 10: MEMORY: THE CHAPTER THAT I NEARLY FORGOT

1. Pascal. *Pensees*, Pensee 651, 240.

2. Saint Augustine. *City of God*. London, Penguin, 1972, 375–376.

CHAPTER 12: EVANGELISM: A CHANCE FOR EMPOWERMENT

1. Pascal. *Pensees*, Pensee 322, 127.

2. Rick Warren. *The Purpose Driven Life*. Grand Rapids, Michigan. Zondervan, 2002.

3. Viktor Frankl. *Man's Search for Meaning*. Boston, Beacon, 1959.

4. Jorge Moll and Jordan Grafman. "Human fronto-mesolimbic networks guide decisions about charitable donation," Proceedings of the National Academy of Science 2006:103(42), 15623–15628

   Shankar Vedahtan. "If It Feels Good to Be Good, It Might Be Only Natural," *Washington Post*, May 2007.

CHAPTER 13: CODE STATUS AND END-OF-LIFE DECISIONS

1. Robert Fogel. "Forecasting the Cost of U.S. Healthcare." *The Journal of the American Enterprise Institute*, Sept. 3, 2009.

CHAPTER 14: OVERCOMING SUFFERING

1. D. L. Musselman, D. L. Evans, and C. B. Nemeroff. "The Relationship of Depression to Cardiovascular Disease: epidemiology, biology and treatment." *Arch Gen Psychiatry* 1998; 55: 580.

2. W. Katon, M. Y. Fan, J. Unutzer, et. al. "Depression and Diabetes: A Potentially Lethal Combination." *J. Gen. Intern. Med.* 2008; 23:1571.

3. David D. Burns M.D. *The Feeling Good Handbook*. New York. William Morrow and Company, Inc., 1989.

4. Luke Timothy Johnson. "Mystical Tradition: Judaism, Christianity, and Islam." The Teaching Company, 2008. Lecture 17: Eastern Monks and the Hesychastic Tradition

A. Pentovsky, ed. "The Pilgrims Tale," in *The Classics of Western Spirituality*. New York: Paulist Press, 1999.

5. "Garage entrepreneur became the face of Apple's innovation." *The Sacramento Bee*, Oct. 6, 2011, sec. A: 1, 14.

CHAPTER 15: HUMOR: LIFTING THE MOOD

1. Aleza Goldsmith. "Prolific professor takes serious look at Jewish funny men in new book." *Jweekly.com*, Dec. 21, 2001.

2. Norman Cousins. *Anatomy of an Illness (As Perceived by the Patient)*. Boston: Bantam, 1981.

3. "Study at UCLA showed watching funny shows increase children's tolerance for pain." *Science Daily*. Oct. 26, 2007.

4. Sven Svebak, Solfrid Romunstad, and Jostein Holmen. "A 7-year prospective study of sense of humor and mortality in an adult county population: the Hunt-2 study." *International Journal of Psychiatry in Medicine* 2010; 40(2):125–46.

5. "Fight Diabetes with Sweet Laughter." *Psychology Today*. May 28, 2003.

6. R. Morgan Griffin. "Give Your Body a Boost—With Laughter." *WebMD*. Oct. 30, 2011.

7. Jun Sugawara, Takashi Tarumi, and Hirofumi Tanaka. "Effect of Mirthful Laughter on Vascular Function." *The American Journal of Cardiology* 106.6 (2010): 856–59.

8. M. Miller, C. Mangano, Y. Park, and R. Goel. "Impact of Cinematic Viewing on Endothelial Function." *Heart* 92.2 (2006): 261–2.

9. Lee S. Berk, Stanley A. Tan, William F. Fry, Barbara J. Napier, Jerry W. Lee, Richard W. Hubbard, John E. Lewis, and William C. Eby. "Neuroendocrine and Stress Hormone Changes during Mirthful Laughter." *The American Journal of the Medical Sciences* 298.6 (1989): 390–6.

10. Jan Ziegler. "Immune System May Benefit from the Ability to Laugh." *Journal of the National Cancer Institute* 87.5 (1995): 342–3.

11. "Humor Can Increase Hope, Research Shows." *Science Daily*, Feb. 11, 2005.

12. "Humor Therapy." *American Cancer Society*. 1 Nov. 2008. Web. 16 Mar. 2012. http://www.cancer.org/Treatment/TreatmentsandSideEffects/ComplementaryandAlternativeMedicine/MindBodyandSpirit/humor-therapy

Raffi Khatchadourian. "The Laughing Guru." *The New Yorker*. 30 Aug. 2010. Web. 16 Mar. 2012. http://www.newyorker.com/reporting/2010/08/30/100830fa_fact_khatchadourian.

CHAPTER 17: HOSPICE: A WAY FOR CARING

1. *Caregiver's Manual, Hospice of Howard County*, Columbia, Maryland, 1990, Section I, page 4.

2. J. Lynn. "Perspectives on Care at the Close of Life. Serving patients who may die soon and their families: the role of hospice and other services." *JAMA* 2001; 285–95.

3. N. A. Christakis and E. B. Lamont. "Extent and determinants of error in doctors' prognosis of terminally ill patients: a prospective cohort study." *BMJ* 2000; 320:469

   P. Glare, K. Virik, M. Jones, et. al. "A systematic review of physicians' survival predictions in terminally ill cancer patients." *BMJ* 2003; 327:195

   E. Chow, T. Harth, G. Hruby, et. al. "How accurate are physicians' clinical predictions of survival and the available prognostic tools in estimating survival times in terminally ill cancer patients? A systematic review." *Clinical Oncology* (R Coll Radiol) 2001; 13:209.

4. E. P. McCarthy, R. B. Burns, Q. Ngo-Metzger, et. al. "Hospice use among Medicare managed care and fee-for-service patients dying with cancer." *JAMA* 2003; 289:2238.

5. *Caregiver's Manual, Hospice of Howard County,* Columbia, Maryland, 1990, Section IV, 10.

6. Ibid., 7-9.

7. "Overview of Symptom Control in the Terminally Ill Cancer Patient." *UpToDate* 18.3, 2011.

8. E. Bruera, R. Sala, M. A. Rico, et. al. "Effects of parenteral hydration in terminally ill cancer patients: a preliminary study." *J Clin Oncol* 2005; 23:2366.

9. L. Ganzini, E. R. Goy, L. L. Miller, et. al. "Nurses' experiences with hospice patients who refuse food and fluids to hasten death." *N Engl J Med* 2003; 349:359.

CHAPTER 18: SUICIDE, ALCOHOL, AND "RECREATIONAL" DRUGS

1. William R. Cook. *The Lives of Great Christians*, The Teaching Company, 2007, Lecture Thirteen: Catherine of Siena

   "The Letters of Catherine of Siena," translated by Suzanne Noffke. Tempe: Arizona Center for Medieval and Renaissance Studies, 2000.

CHAPTER 23: EMOTIONAL PAIN: SURVIVING THE LOSS

1. Saint Augustine, *Confessions*. Trans. Henry Chadwick. New York: Oxford University Press. 1991. Book IV, page 57–58.

APPENDIX A: QUESTIONS TO PONDER

1. James Edward Stroud, *The Knights Templar and the Protestant Reform, The Case for a Modern-Day Monk.* Xulon Press, 2011, 162.

2. Henry D. Spalding, *Joys of Jewish Humor.* New York: Gramercy Books, 1985, 107.

Glossary

5150 Involuntary Psychiatric Hold: A section of the California Welfare and Institutions Code that allows an officer or clinician to involuntarily confine a person if they are deemed to have a mental disorder that causes danger to themselves or others or if he/she is gravely disabled.

Acupressure: The treatment of conditions by using manual pressure on the skin.

Acupuncture: The treatment of conditions by the placement of needles into the skin.

Acetaminophen: A common analgesic. It is the generic form of Tylenol.

Actuarial: Relating to the statistical calculation of life expectancy.

Addiction: Physiological or psychological dependence on a drug.

AIDS (acquired immune deficiency syndrome): A disease of the immune system caused by the HIV virus.

Alleviate: To make pain or other symptoms less severe.

Alternative Medicine: Medical care that falls outside of conventional (scientific based) medicine.

Alzheimer's Disease: A common progressive form of dementia that affects memory, judgment, and behavior.

Ameliorate: To make a condition better.

Amputation: A surgical procedure to cut off a body part.

Analgesic: A type of medication that reduces pain without causing loss of consciousness.

Anaphylaxis: An unusual/exaggerated allergic reaction to a substance. It can lead to shock and respiratory failure (inability to breathe).

Anesthesia: The loss of sensation to pain. It may be just part of the body or it can be general anesthesia that causes the patient to be unconscious.

Ankylosing Spondylitis: A joint disease of the spine that causes pain and immobility.

Antianxiety Medicine: Medication that relieves anxiety.

Anticholinergic Medicine: Medication that blocks the parasympathetic nervous system. These can be used to relax muscles and dry secretions.

Antidepressant Medicine: Medication that reduces depression. They generally work by increasing chemical levels in the brain to improve nerve function.

Antihistamine: Medication that blocks histamine response. Commonly used for allergies and to relieve itching.

Antithesis: The exact opposite of something.

Armamentarium: Any or all equipment/tools and knowledge that are used to combat a disease, illness, or symptoms. This can include helpful devices, medication, surgical procedures, various therapies, prayer, etc.

Arrhythmia: Any variation from the normal rhythm of the heartbeat.

Artificial Respiration: Respiration (breathing) of a patient that is not natural or generated from the person's own body. This can be mouth-to-mouth respiration, but more commonly is performed by a machine.

Arteries: Blood vessels that carry blood from the heart to the rest of the body.

Arthritis: Any of a number of diseases that causes inflammation of the joints.

Atrial Fibrillation: An irregular heart rhythm that originates in the atrium (or upper) chamber of the heart. It is common, and it can cause the heart to beat fast or slow.

Atrophy: A wasting away or shrinkage of body tissue.

Atypical B-cell: An unusual or irregular specific type of white blood cell that can be found in lymphoma cancers.

Autonomy: Functioning independently, or self-sufficient.

Bed Sores: A breakdown or deterioration of skin from prolonged pressure. Typically from lying in bed from a weakened state. Also known as decubitus ulcers.

Benign: Not malignant. A favorable recovery is expected.

Benzodiazepine: A class of medications that are minor tranquilizers. They are used for anxiety, muscle relaxation, sleep, and sedative effects.

Bereavement Counseling: Therapeutic counseling of a person who is experiencing grief over the loss of a loved one.

Biopsy: The removal for examination of tissue from a living body to establish a diagnosis.

Brainstem Aneurysm: The dilatation and weakening of the wall of an artery at the base of the brain. It can cause a massive and often lethal stroke.

Bronchodilator: A medication that opens airways, making it easier to breathe.

Bubble Pack: An individual sorting and wrapping of a patient's daily medication done by the pharmacist in order to help a patient keep track of taking their pills regularly.

Cadaver: A dead body that is generally preserved for scientific study.

Calisthenics: A system of light gymnastics or exercises for promoting strength.

Cardiac Arrest: Sudden cessation of heart function.

Cardiologist: A physician skilled in the diagnosis and treatment of heart disease.

Cardiovascular: Pertaining to the heart and blood vessels.

Carotid Artery: The principal artery in the neck leading to the brain.

Caryl: My wonderful wife.

Chemo: Common abbreviation for chemotherapy.

Chemotherapy: The treatment of disease with chemical agents (medications). Typically refers to treatment of cancers.

Chest Compression: The act of pushing on a patient's chest when their heart has stopped in order to keep blood flowing. This is done during CPR.

CHF (congestive heart failure): The accumulation of blood in the body due to poor heart function. It typically causes shortness of breath, generalized weakness, and swelling.

Chiropractic (manipulations): A system of therapeutics that attempts to restore normal nerve function by manipulation of the body.

Cholesterol: A fatlike chemical substance that circulates in the bloodstream and contributes to blockage of arteries.

Chronic Lung Disease: Refers to a number of long term lung diseases that impairs a person's ability to breathe.

Circulation: The movement of blood through the heart and blood vessels.

Cirrhosis: Liver disease that leads to a loss of normal structure and function of the liver. There are a number of possible causes.

Code Status: A patient's stated wishes regarding CPR and life support. It directs the physician on how aggressive to be in trying to preserve a patient's life.

Cognitive Ability: The ability of a person to perceive, think, and remember.

Colonoscopy: The procedure wherein the inside of the colon is examined with a fiberoptic endoscope (i.e., a flexible tube that allows the doctor to see the inside of the colon).

Colon Polyp: A growth of tissue inside the colon. It can potentially lead to cancer.

Coma: A state of unconsciousness from which the patient can't be aroused.

Comfort Care: Pertaining to the care of a patient with the goal of providing comfort only and not attempting to cure.

Comfort Care Pathway: A set guideline of care provided in the hospital or nursing home for the intended purpose of keeping the terminal patient comfortable.

Congestive Heart Failure: The accumulation of blood in the body due to poor heart function. It typically causes shortness of breath, generalized weakness, and swelling.

COPD (chronic obstructive pulmonary disease): A classification of lung diseases that impair a person's ability to breathe. It includes chronic bronchitis and emphysema.

Coronary Bypass Surgery: Surgery that enables blood supply to be restored to heart muscle. It is necessitated by blocked heart arteries with the goal of preventing heart attacks.

Coronary Disease: Disease involving arteries that supply the heart muscle.

CPR (cardiopulmonary resuscitation): A process or series of steps performed in an attempt to preserve life when the heart or lungs stop or fail. It can involve any or all of the following: chest compressions, artificial respiration, medications, and electric shocks to try and restart the heart.

Crash Cart: A mobile cart that contains medication and equipment used during CPR.

CT Scan: An X-ray imaging of the body or body part that uses a computer to generate it.

Curbside Consult: An informal communication between doctors in order to obtain another doctor's assistance or opinion.

Cyanotic: A bluish discoloration due to poor circulation or oxygen content in the blood.

Death Rattle: The sound of a dying patient's breathing when mucous or secretions accumulate in the throat. It is a gurgling type of sound that is typically more disconcerting to family members than for the patient.

Debridement: The removal of foreign material and dead or infected tissue from the underlying healthy tissue.

Delirium: A mental disturbance marked by confusion, incoherence, and can include delusions, hallucinations, and agitation. It typically results from an acute or short-term illness.

Dementia: A loss of intellectual function that can include memory, judgment, and behavior. It can result from a number of different disease processes.

Denial: A psychological defense mechanism in which the existence of an intolerable personal problem or reality is unconsciously denied.

Depersonalization: A psychological alteration in the perception of the self so that the usual sense of one's own reality is temporarily lost or changed.

Depression: A psychiatric syndrome that can include dejected mood, sadness, psychomotor retardation (slowing of thought and activity), sleep disturbance, weight loss or gain, loss of pleasure, hopelessness, and suicidal thoughts.

Dermal Reaction: The reaction of the skin to an insult (e.g., trauma, drug, chemical, infection). This can include a rash, peeling, swelling, discoloration, etc.

Diabetes Mellitus: A metabolic disorder where the ability to process sugar and carbohydrates is lost.

Dialysis: A life-sustaining medical process that removes unwanted chemical substances from the body. It is typically used when the kidneys fail.

Disc: Structures consisting of cartilage between vertebral bodies (i.e., bones of the neck and back).

Diuretics: Medications that promote excretion of urine. Commonly used for treating swelling or high blood pressure.

DNA (deoxyribonucleic acid): The chemical substance that makes up genes.

DNR (Do Not Resuscitate): The code status designation for a patient that tells medical personnel not to perform CPR in an emergent situation.

Dopamine Antagonist: Medication that blocks the effects of the chemical, dopamine, on the brain and body. Commonly used to treat nausea and psychiatric disorders.

Durable Power of Attorney for Health Care: A legal document where you appoint a trusted person to be your spokesperson for making health-care decisions in the event that you become incapacitated and unable to do so.

Dysfunction: Impairment or abnormality of the functioning of an organ, or body system.

Edema: The presence of abnormally large amounts of fluid in the tissue spaces of the body.

EEG (electroencephalogram): A recording of the electric currents developed in the brain by means of placing electrodes on the scalp. It is used to determine if a patient is having seizures, abnormal brain activity, or lack of brain activity.

Ejection Fraction: The percent of blood in the heart that is pumped out to the body each time the heart contracts. Normal numbers are about 50 to 60 percent.

Encephalopathy: Any degenerative disease of the brain.

Endorphins: A group of naturally occurring substances in the brain that raise the pain threshold (i.e., alleviate pain).

Endoscopy: A visual inspection of any cavity, or opening of the body, using an endoscope, which is typically a flexible, fiberoptic instrument.

End-Stage Liver Disease: A common cause of death that arises from liver disease, such as alcoholic cirrhosis, viral hepatitis, and other disorders.

End-Stage Renal Disease: The end stage of chronic, progressive kidney disease that will result in death or the need for dialysis. Common causes are diabetes and high blood pressure.

Erythropoietin: A hormone secreted by the kidneys that stimulates the bone marrow to produce red blood cells. It can be given to some patients to treat anemia.

Ethical Review Board: A committee that reviews medical studies and patient care to ensure ethical care is being delivered.

Executor: A person entrusted with protecting a deceased person's property until all debts and taxes have been paid, and seeing that what's left is transferred to the people entitled to it.

Gastroenterologist: A doctor who specializes in care of the digestive tract.

Gastroenterology: The study of the esophagus, stomach, intestines, and their diseases.

General Anesthesia: A state of unconsciousness resulting from the administration of medications in order to perform surgical procedures.

Glabella: The area between the eyebrows.

Glaucoma: A group of diseases that cause increased pressure in the eye, and can result in loss of vision.

Hallucination: A sensory perception in the absence of a source. For example, seeing or hearing things that aren't really there.

Heart Attack: An acute episode of heart disease marked by death or damage to the heart muscle where the blood supply to the heart is insufficient. Typically from blockage of a coronary artery.

Heart Failure: A group of symptoms and signs resulting from a disturbance in heart output. Typically, the amount of blood the heart is pumping is inadequate to match the body's needs.

Heart Rate: A measure of heart activity in terms of beats per minute.

Heart Rhythm: The pattern of recurrence of the heartbeat. It can be regular or irregular as well as fast, slow, and normal.

Hemodialysis: The medical procedure where blood is filtered and certain substances are removed.

Hip Fracture: A break in the bone(s) of the hip joint. It can be a devastating trauma, especially for elderly people.

HIV (human immunodeficiency virus): The virus that causes AIDS.

Hospice: A program designed to provide physical and emotional care for the terminally ill.

Hydrocephalus: A condition where there can be an accumulation of too much cerebrospinal fluid in the skull. It can cause mental deterioration, convulsions, and loss of muscle control.

Hypertension: High blood pressure. It can lead to heart attacks, strokes, and kidney failure.

ICU (Intensive Care Unit): A hospital unit in which there is concentrated special equipment and skilled personnel for the care of seriously ill patients requiring immediate and continuous attention.

Ideation: The capacity for or act of forming ideas, or thoughts.

Immunocompromised: Having a decreased immune response, or decreased ability to fight infection. This can be due to irradiation, malnutrition, and certain drugs, infections, and diseases (e.g., some cancers, AIDS, etc.).

Incontinence: Losing control of bowel or bladder.

Infusion: The therapeutic introduction of fluid other than blood into a vein.

Injection: The act of forcing a liquid into a body part, such as under the skin, or into a muscle or vein.

Insomnia: Inability to sleep, or abnormal wakefulness.

Insulin: A hormone produced in the pancreas to control blood sugar levels. It is often required to be given to diabetic patients to control blood sugar.

Internal Medicine: The branch of medicine that includes the diagnosis and medical, as opposed to surgical, treatment of diseases of adults.

Internist: A physician who specializes in internal medicine. This is not the same as an "intern," who is a first-year physician in training.

Intracranial Pressure: The pressure inside the skull; also, it is the pressure around the brain. Increased pressure can lead to decreased mental function and even death.

Intractable Pain: Pain that is resistant to cure, relief, or control.

Intravenous (IV): Within a vein. For instance, medicine and fluids can be given per IV.

Intubate: The insertion of a tube into a body canal. Most commonly refers to a tube going through the mouth leading into the lungs. For instance, this is done during CPR to provide oxygen for the patient.

Kegel Exercise: Exercises where the pelvic muscles are repeatedly tightened and relaxed. These can help with urine incontinence.

Lewy Body Disease: A common type of dementia characterized with loss of thought processes, hallucinations, and movement disorder, such as decreased ability to walk.

Living Trust: A legal arrangement where one person, called the trustee, holds title to property for another person, the beneficiary. You can be the trustee for your own living trust. It can reduce estate taxes and set up property management.

Living Will: A legal written statement where you detail the care that you want or don't want if you become incapacitated.

Long-Term Care Insurance: A type of insurance that covers care in the event of incapacitation. It may cover in home care, assisted living, adult day care, and nursing home care.

Lumpectomy: A surgical procedure to remove a lump from the body. For instance, it would take a lump, or mass, out of the breast without removing the entire breast.

Malignant: Tending to become progressively worse, potentially resulting in death. A malignant tumor would be a cancer, whereas a benign tumor would not be a cancer.

Massage: Therapeutic friction, stroking, and kneading of the body.

Mayo Clinic: A well-known medical practice and research group that specializes in treating difficult patients.

Medicaid: The United States health program for people with low income and resources.

MediCal: The name of the Medicaid program in California.

Medical Residency: The hospital-based training program that a graduated and licensed physician attends after medical school to learn a specialty.

Medicare: The United States health insurance program that covers Americans over sixty-five and younger persons with disabilities.

Melanoma: A type of skin cancer, generally the most aggressive type.

Meningioma: A type of slow-growing brain tumor.

Metastasize: To form a new cancerous growth in a distant part of the body. It's a transfer, or spreading of cancer. Usually a cancer that metastasizes is not curable.

Monoclonal Antibody: One of a number of antibodies that are made from a single cell. An antibody is a molecule made by the body's immune system that fights off disease. Pharmaceutical companies make monoclonal antibodies targeted to fight certain diseases.

Mortality: Relating to being mortal, or certain to die eventually.

MRI (magnetic resonance imaging): A type of imaging (i.e., picture taking) of the inside of the body that utilizes a magnetic field. Often thought of as a fancy X-ray.

MS (multiple sclerosis): A disease that affects the nervous system. It can cause weakness, poor coordination, paralysis, and vision and speech problems. It can be progressive as well as periodically get better and worse.

Multidisciplinary: Using many fields of study or skill sets.

Multi-infarct Dementia: A type of dementia resulting from strokes.

Multiple Personalities: A psychiatric disorder in which an individual has two or more distinct personalities. This is not schizophrenia, and much less common than schizophrenia.

Muscle Relaxer: One of a class of medicine that relaxes muscles.

Narcotic: A group of drugs that dulls the senses, relieves pain, and induces sleep. Usually refers to opiate-based drugs, such as morphine.

Natural Killer Cell: A type of cell that fights disease by targeting and destroying foreign cells. Part of the body's immune system.

Near-Death Experience: Sensory or emotional experiences that happen when a person is at or on the verge of death.

Neurochemical Transmitter: A chemical, or molecule, that is used to deliver messages from one nerve to another.

NHL: See non-Hodgkin's lymphoma

Nocebo: A harmless substance that when taken by a patient is associated with harmful effects due to negative expectations.

No Code Blue: A patient designation telling medical staff not to do CPR on a patient in an emergent condition. Also refers to DNR (Do Not Resuscitate) status.

Non-Hodgkin's Lymphoma (NHL): A type of lymphoma, or cancer of the lymph tissue. Lymphomas can be classified as Hodgkin's disease, or non-Hodgkin's.

Nonsteroidal Anti-inflammatory: A group of anti-inflammatory drugs that are used to relieve pain and reduce inflammation. Common examples are aspirin, ibuprofen, and naproxen.

Norepinephrine: A neurohormone, or chemical, that transmits messages to nerves. It is a stress hormone that increases heart rate, blood pressure, alertness, and arousal.

Obesity: An increase in body weight beyond normal requirements due to excessive accumulation of fat.

Oncologist: A physician that specializes in oncology (i.e., cancer).

Operating Room: The room, or part of the hospital, where surgery is performed.

Operating Table: The table that the patient is placed on for surgery to be performed.

Opioid: Any synthetic narcotic that has opiate-like effects, but is not made from opium.

Osteoarthritis: Degenerative arthritis of aging.

Osteopathic (manipulations): A system of therapeutic intervention based on the theory that diseases are largely a result of loss of structural integrity that can be restored by manipulation of the body parts.

Osteoporosis: Demineralization, or thinning, of the bone. It predisposes the patient to fractures.

Ovarian Cancer: Cancer of the ovary, the female sex organ.

Pain Pump: A medical device that is surgically implanted in the body to deliver pain medication to a targeted area of the body.

Palliative: Alleviating a symptom without eliminating the cause.

Paralyzed: Loss of motor function. Unable to move a body part, such as from trauma, disease, or stroke.

Parlance: The style of speech used in a particular context or profession.

Parenteral Nutrition: Nourishment given by means other than the gut. For instance, nutrition given intravenously (IV).

Parkinson's Disease: A slowly progressing neurological disease that can cause slowness of movement, tremor, lack of facial expression, difficulty walking, and dementia.

Path Lab: Abbreviation for pathology lab. This is where laboratory methods are used to diagnose diseases.

Pathology: The branch of medicine that studies the structural and functional changes in tissues.

PET scan: Abbreviation for Positron Emission Tomography. It uses a radioactive substance to image (i.e., take a picture of) the inside of the body.

Phantom Limb Pain: Pain that is sensed at a site of an amputated limb as if it were still there.

Physician Assisted Suicide: The action where a physician helps a patient voluntarily to end their own life.

Placebo: An inactive substance given to a patient with the intention of deceiving them to think it is an actual treatment. It can have a positive, helpful effect, which is called the placebo effect.

Power of Attorney: A written authorization to act on another's behalf for private affairs, business, or some legal matter. A *durable* power of attorney will stay in effect even if a person becomes incapacitated.

Premedication: Preliminary medicine given prior to other medicine or surgical procedure. It is given to assist with desired effects or to minimize complications.

Prospective Study: An analytical study following a group of people over time following a condition or treatment.

Psychiatric Disorder: A mental illness.

Psychomotor Agitation: Unintentional movements of the body due to mental tension/anxiety.

Psychomotor Retardation: Slowing down of thought and reduced body movements due to a mental disorder.

Psychotherapy: Treatment designed to produce a response by mental effects. It can include suggestion, persuasion, reassurance, support, and psychoanalysis (i.e., examining a patient's past emotional experiences).

Psychotic (break): A major mental disorder where there is a loss of contact with reality, such as delusions and hallucinations.

Radiation Oncology: The branch of medicine involving the use of radiation to treat cancer.

Renal Failure: Decreased kidney function. When severe, or end-stage, it will require dialysis or kidney transplant in order to survive.

Respiratory Failure: Failure of the lungs to function properly. Commonly refers to a severe state where CPR or mechanical ventilation is required (i.e., a machine is needed to assist breathing for the patient).

Respite Care: Short-term, temporary care of a patient in order to give the family member or usual caregiver a break. This can be done by a temporary in-home caregiver, or the short-term placement of the patient in a care facility.

Rheumatologist: A physician who specializes in rheumatology (i.e., disorders of the muscle, connective tissue, and joints).

Schizophrenia: Any of a group of severe emotional disorders characterized by misinterpretation and retreat from reality, such as delusions, hallucinations, and bizarre behavior.

Secondary Gain: An advantage obtained resulting from an illness, such as attention, disability benefits, or avoidance of unpleasant activities.

Seizure: An attack of epilepsy, which is the disturbance of electrical activity of the brain. Symptoms can include loss of consciousness, abnormal body movements, and sensory disturbance such as hallucinations or dream states.

Serotonin: A neurochemical transmitter. This is a chemical substance that delivers messages in the nervous system.

Serotonin Antagonist: A drug that inhibits the actions of serotonin. It may be used to treat nausea and also some psychiatric disorders.

Soul: The essence, or spiritual principle, of oneself. The consciousness, thought, feeling, and will of a person, which is distinct from the physical body.

Spinal Column: Pertaining to the spine, or vertebral column.

Spinal Cord Compression: Compression of the spinal cord, which is the main bundle of nerves that run from the brain to the base of the spine. Compression could be from a tumor or ruptured disc for instance. Symptoms can include pain and paralysis.

Steroids: Refers to a class of hormones in the body as well as medicines. The medicines can have a variety of functions, but commonly refer to medicines that decrease inflammation, such as cortisone or prednisone.

Stevens-Johnson Syndrome: A severe form of skin reaction that can even be fatal. It can result from a drug reaction.

Stress Hormones: Hormones released in the body during times of stress including cortisol, growth hormone, and norepinephrine. These can lead to high blood pressure and increased susceptibility to infection.

Stroke: A loss of blood supply to a portion of the brain. It can cause loss of movement, speech, vision, mental function, and even death.

Sudden Cardiac Death: A sudden stoppage of the heart muscle, causing death.

Surgical Oncology: A branch of medicine involving the surgical treatment of cancer.

Systemic Lupus Erythematosus: An autoimmune connective tissue disorder. It can cause arthritis, rash, anemia, susceptibility to infection, and problems with various body organs.

T-Cell: A type of white blood cell, involved in the immune system.

Terminal: Leading ultimately to death.

Tendon: Connective tissue that attaches muscle to bone.

Thoracentesis: A surgical procedure involving a puncture of the chest wall in order to obtain fluid from around the lung.

Titrate: Slowly changing the dose or amount of a medication or substance until the desired effect is achieved.

Topical (medication): Medication that is applied to the skin.

Transplant: To transfer an organ or tissue from one body to another.

Tubal Ligation: A surgical procedure to prevent pregnancy in a woman.

Tumor Board: A meeting or committee of various physicians from different specialties to discuss treatment of cancer patients.

Unibrow: The appearance of one long eyebrow, due to growth of hair between the two eyebrows.

Uvula: The fleshy tissue that hangs down in the back of the mouth.

Vascular: Pertaining to the blood vessels.

Vascular Disease: Disease of the blood vessels. There are many vascular diseases, but the most common is atherosclerosis due to blockage of blood vessels. It can lead to heart attack, stroke, and loss of limb.

Vegetative State: The absence of responsiveness and awareness due to diminished brain function. The person in a vegetative state can have reflexes and involuntary movements but no awareness of self. Prognosis for a person in a prolonged vegetative state is very poor.

Ventilated: Being supplied with air. Commonly refers to mechanical ventilation, where a machine is breathing for the patient.

Will: The declaration of a person's wishes regarding the disposal of his or her property after their death.

Statement for the Live, Love, and Let Go Project

The Live, Love, and Let Go Project was created to help Christians utilize the maximum benefits of their faith in all aspects of death. The goal is to allow us to see humor, courage, and light in even the darkest of times.

If you found comfort or gained insight from this book, please keep it and refer back to it in hard times. Please help spread the word by letting others know about *Live, Love, and Let Go.*

Christians' ability to deal with death and dying is perhaps our greatest opportunity to spread the good Word of the Gospels. Please visit us at www.LiveLoveAndLetGo.com for other valuable information and to share stories of how this book touched your life.

About the Author

Dr. James Abshire worked his way through school flipping hamburgers, tossing pizzas, and selling vacuum cleaners door-to-door. He received his B.S. in Chemistry and B.S. in Chemical Engineering from Purdue University and was a senior chemical engineer in the petrochemical industry prior to receiving his M.D. from Southwestern Medical School. He completed his residency at U. C. Davis and works as a Board Certified Internist in Sacramento, California. He lives with his wife and four children in the Sacramento area.

Dr. Abshire began writing this book in 2008 after years of seeing patients encounter life's stressors and in particular, the crucial problem of dealing with death. He felt the need to give people an important positive, tactical approach to death that could not be accomplished in an office visit to the doctor.

In 2010, Dr. Abshire gained new insight for his book when he was given his own terminal diagnosis of lymphoma. His perspective gives valuable insight to overcoming the physical and mental struggles that come with life's ultimate challenge.

Dr. Abshire has pledged all royalties from this book to charity. You may contact him at www.LiveLoveAndLetGo.com.

CPSIA information can be obtained
at www.ICGtesting.com
Printed in the USA
FSHW01n1953230518
48628FS